THE COMPLETE
BOOK OF
WORLD HISTORY

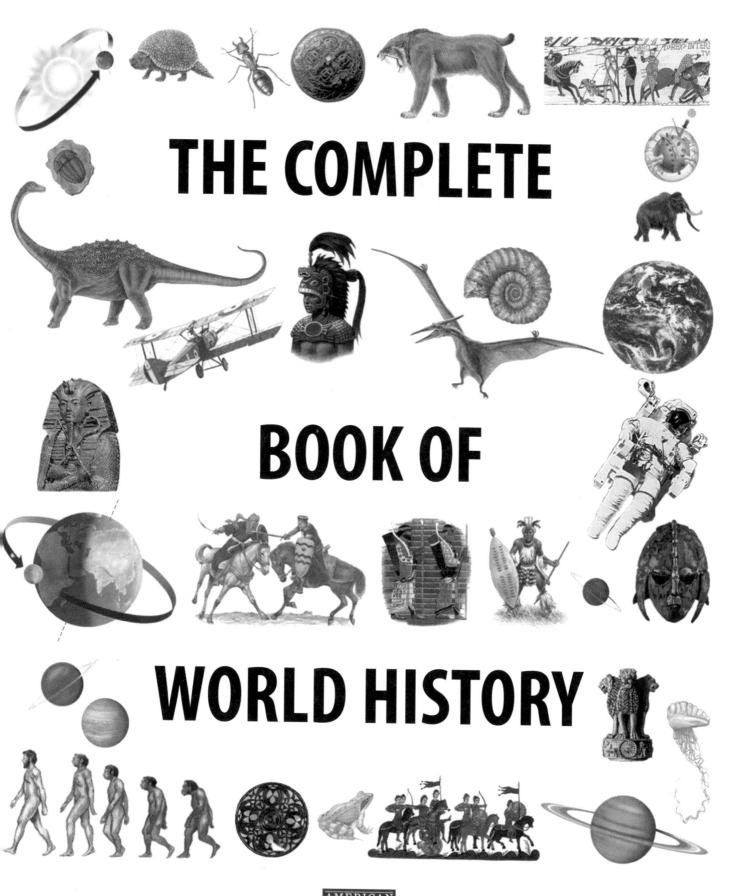

THE COMPLETE
BOOK OF
WORLD HISTORY

AMERICAN
EDUCATION
PUBLISHING™

Columbus, Ohio

This edition published in 2002 by American Education Publishing™,
an imprint of School Specialty Children's Publishing
8720 Orion Place
Columbus, OH 43240-2111

Copyright © 2001 Octopus Publishing Group Ltd.

Octopus Publishing Group Ltd.,
2-4 Heron Quays, London, England, E14 4JP

ISBN 1-56189-089-8
UPC 7-19531-90014-6

Printed by SNP Leefung, China

4 5 6 7 8 9 OCTO 09 08 07 06 05

Miles Kelly Publishing Limited

Editorial Director: Paula Borton
Art Director: Clare Sleven
Project Management: Neil de Cort
Editorial Assistant: Simon Nevill
Project Editor: Jane Walker
Designer: Jill Mumford
Artwork Commissioning: Kirsty Allen, Suzanne Grant
and Natasha Smith
Picture Research: Janice Bracken and Lesley Cartlidge
Kate Miles, Liberty Newton
Indexing: Lynn Bresler

The Publishers would like to thank the following
artists who have contributed to this book:
Vanessa Card
Mike Foster/ Maltings Partnership
Chris Forsey
Roger Gorringe/ Illustration Ltd.
Richard Hook
Janos Marffy
Chris Odgers
Terry Riley Studio
Rob Sheffield
Ross Watton/ SGA
Mike White/ Temple Rogers

PHOTOGRAPHIC CREDITS

44 (B/R) Robert Harding Picture Library; 57 (T/R) Bernard and Catherine Desjeux/CORBIS; 59 (T/R) Graham King;
62 (B/R) Diego Lezanna/CORBIS; 72 (B/R) Adam Woolfitt/CORBIS; 101 (C/L) Werner Forman/CORBIS;
107 (T/R) British Museum, London/ The Bridgeman Art Library; 117 (B/R) Robert Harding Picture Library;
125 (T/R) Wolfgang Kaehler/CORBIS; (T/L) Bettmann/CORBIS; 127 (T/R) Bettmann/CORBIS, (T/L) Archivo
Iconografico, S.A./CORBIS; 139 (B/L) Historical Picture Archive/ CORBIS; 140, (C) Archivo Iconografico, S.A./
CORBIS; 142 (B/L) Archivo Iconografico, S.A./CORBIS; 151 (C/L) Bettmann/CORBIS; 155 (T/L) CORBIS;
158 (C) Bettmann/CORBIS; 162 (C) Archivo Iconografico, S.A./CORBIS; 169 (T/R) Archivo Iconografico, S.A./CORBIS;
174, (B/R) Burstein Collection/CORBIS; 181 (B/C) Leonard de Selva/CORBIS; 182 (C) Hulton-Deutsch
Collection/CORBIS; 185 (B/R) Bettmann/CORBIS; 188 (B/R) CORBIS; 190 (C) Bettmann/CORBIS; 194 (C) Hulton-
Deutsch Collection/CORBIS; 200 (C) Archivo Iconografico, S.A./CORBIS; 203 (T/R) Museum of the City of New
York/CORBIS; 211 (T/R) CORBIS; 217 (T/L) Minnesota Historical Society/CORBIS; 219 (T/R) Bettmann/CORBIS;
220 (C) Hulton-Deutsch Collection/CORBIS; 222 (B/R) CORBIS; 223 (T/R) Bettmann/CORBIS; 228 (B/L) Leonard de
Selva/CORBIS; 230 (C) Hulton-Deutsch Collection/CORBIS; 232 (B) Bettmann/CORBIS; 235 (T/R) Sean Sexton
Collection/CORBIS; 236 (B) CORBIS; 239 (T/R) Archivo Iconografico, S.A./CORBIS; 240 (C) CORBIS;
248 (B/R) Hulton-Deutsch Collection/CORBIS; 254 (B/L) Bettmann/CORBIS; 255 (T/R) Tim Page/CORBIS;
258 (C) Bettmann/CORBIS; 259 (T/R) National Archives and Records Administration; 260 (B/R) Bettmann/CORBIS;
261 (B/R) reproduced courtesy of Nokia; 263 (T/R) AFP/CORBIS; 265 (T/L) reproduced courtesy of Greenpeace;
267 (B/L) Arne Hodalic/CORBIS, (T/R) reproduced courtesy of NASA. All other images from the Miles Kelly Archive.

QUOTATION ACKNOWLEDGEMENTS

Pages 39 (translated by Frederick Morgan), 77 (translated by Dell R. Hales), 81 (translated by Frank O'Connor),
95 (translated by Dennis Tedlock), 113 (translated by Frank O'Connor), published in *World Poetry* by W. W. Norton and
Company; page 54, *The Iliad*, translated by Martin Hammond, published by Penguin Classics; pages 83 and 57, *The Aeneid*,
translated by W.F. Jackson Knight, published by Penguin; page 65, *The Histories*, translated by Aubrey De Sélincourt, published
by Penguin; page 69, *The History of the Peleponnesian War*, translated by Rex Warner, published by Penguin; pages 93, 105, 127,
129, 143, 159, 173, 177, 183, 187, 195, 201, 213, 217, 221, 227, 235, 241 and 253 published in the *Oxford Dictionary of
Quotations* by the Oxford University Press; page 99, extract from *Murasaki Shikibu, her Diary and Poetic Memoirs*, translated by Richard
Bowring, published by Princeton University Press; page 107, extract from *Ecclesiastical History of the English Nation*, published in
Internet Medieval Sourcebook, Fordham University Centre for Medieval Studies; page 110, extract from *Whole Works*,
published by Jubilee Edition; pages 141, 155, 163, 167, quoted in *Millennium*, edited by Anthony Coleman, published by
Bantam Press; pages 149, 191 and 259 quoted in *World Book Encyclopedia*, published by World Book, Inc.; pages 179, 231, 245
and 263 quoted in *The Norton Anthology of Poetry*, published by W. W. Norton and Co.

Contents

The quickest way to find out about a period of history that interests you is to look at the table of contents on page 6. If you do not see a heading that is the same as the subject you are searching for, look in the index (pages 280–288). It will help you to find the information you want.

How to Use This Book

In addition to chapters on subjects such as ancient Egypt or the Russian Revolution, there are also special feature chapters which look at developments during a certain period and feature examples from more than one country.

These feature chapters cover topics such as society and government, religions, war and weapons, and trade and towns. From them, you can discover how people did things and how human lives changed over time. You will also learn how life through history was in some ways not so different from our own way of life today.

Each double page in the book contains a timeline with key dates for the period. To find the birth and death dates of a famous person, or when a certain ruler was in power, look on the timeline on the page in question or turn to the reference section which starts on page 268. It contains information about people and places through history.

Dates

Every ancient civilization had its own calendar. Today there are several religious calendars in use, for example the Jewish and the Islamic calendars. For practical convenience, most of the world uses the Christian calendar, which begins with the birth of Jesus Christ. Much of the history in this book took place before that date.

In most books, the letters BC and AD are used with dates. The letters BC after a date indicate the number of years before the birth of Jesus Christ (which for this purpose is taken to be the non-existent year 0). The letters AD (which stand for the Latin *Anno Domini*, meaning "in the year of Our Lord") are used with dates after Christ's birth. The letters BC and AD are used throughout this book.

This is a quick-reference guide to the time span covered by the double page.

The timeline provides you with the important dates from the period.

This panel will appear on some pages. It will give you the views and comments of someone's writing from that period.

War has been a part of life for as long as humans have existed. Prehistoric people fought for territory and food, using rocks and sticks as weapons. Later, they used stone-tipped spears and bows and arrows.

BC

2,000 BC 400,000 BC 100,000 BC 4,000 BC 20,000 BC 10,000 BC

War and Weapons

The discovery of bronze in about 3500 BC brought the first revolution in weaponry. Bronze swords and spear points were sharper than stone and bone weapons. Iron was even stronger still. Peoples of the Near East, such as the Hittites, were the first to master iron-making.

A sculpture shows an Egyptian king pictured defeating an enemy.	3100 BC
Sumerians make bronze war axes and spear points.	2500 BC
Body armour used by Egyptians and Mesopotamians.	2000 BC
Chariots in use in Egypt and Near East. Sickle-shaped swords of bronze.	1500 BC
First iron swords. End of Trojan War.	1200 BC
Assyrian armies include infantry, cavalry and chariots.	800 BC
Chainmail made from iron links replaces bronze armour.	500 BC
Sparta has the first full-time army in the Greek world.	400s BC

Armies and armour

Each of the ancient Near East superpowers rounded up civilians to serve in armies for the conquest of other countries, and for defence against enemies. To protect themselves, soldiers began wearing armour on their bodies. By the time of the Trojan War, about 1200 BC, armour was made from metal plates fastened with leather thongs. Soldiers

▷*Assyrian troops used wheeled siege towers with iron-tipped rams to batter down the walls of enemy towns.*

△ *Egyptian soldiers fought with spears, axes, clubs, javelins (throwing spears) swords and bows and arrows. Trumpeters blew signal calls to direct the troops.*

Hittite charioteers

The Hittites, a fierce people from Anatolia (modern Turkey), were the first to use chariots in war. Hittite archers fired their arrows from these chariots, giving them a great advantage over the enemy.

wore metal helmets to protect the head, and carried shields (usually round or rectangular). Some warriors scorned armour – the Greeks and Celts sometimes fought practically naked.

The first organized armies

Kings had small bodyguards of trained soldiers, including chariot-drivers, but they still relied on untrained peasants as foot soldiers. The Assyrians organized the first 'professional' army, and were greatly feared because of its ferocity. An Assyrian army included cavalry (soldiers on horses) and infantry (soldiers on foot).

Assyrian soldiers wore chainmail armour, and fought with iron swords and spears. Archers rode into battle on chariots, then sheltered behind basketwork shields to fire and reload. Slingers hurled stones, often farther than a javelin.

Infantry and cavalry

In China, soldiers traditionally fought on foot, and in huge armies (as many as 100,000 men). Facing marauders on horseback, the Chinese had to become horse-soldiers too. The Chinese composite bow of wood and bone had a longer range than a simple bow. Chinese archers also used crossbows.

△ *Axe heads were made from bronze (shown here) and iron. A popular weapon, particularly among Chinese troops, was a halberd, a long spear with an axelike head.*

There was the clash of shields, of spears and the fury of men cased in bronze... then there were mingled the groaning and the crowing of men killed and killing.

from THE ILIAD, HOMER (8TH CENTURY BC)

Nothing is known about Homer for certain. Tradition states he lived near Greece and wrote two great poems about the Trojan wars: The Iliad and The Odyssey.

The *Complete Book of World History* is designed to be easy to use while you enjoy its information-packed pages. The book is arranged in sections, each covering a period of time with a particular theme.

Introduction

△ *Newton's new telescope used a reflecting mirror instead of glass lenses to magnify images.*

Within each section are a number of two-page chapters. Each of these chapters deals with a specific aspect of history. This could be an important region or period, or a famous person or culture. It could also give you some extra information on a subject, like the first towns, or the development of weapons.

The opening section is called *The First* Humans and deals with the origins of humankind from its beginnings in Africa. There are also sections on *The First Civilizations*, *Empires East*

▽ *The old mosque at Mecca. The Islamic prophet Muhammad used to pray outside in his courtyard, and his followers still pray outside today.*

△ *Arab trading ships were famous for their long voyages. They traveled across the Indian Ocean to Indonesia, and then even further afield to China.*

and West and the *Early Middle Ages,* which cover the periods up to the invasion of William the Conqueror in 1066. These are followed by the *Late Middle Ages.* There are then sections on more recent history, starting with the *Renaissance* beginning in the 1400s, then *Empires and Expansion, Power and Rights, Revolution and the World Wars.* The final section, *Global Politics,* covers from 1945 to the present day and shows that history is made every day. Events that we live through will one day be studied in history books. History is alive and growing all the time.

▷ *This mask was used by soldiers in World War I to protect them from attacks with poison gas.*

◁ *After many years of repression, the Russian workers revolted against the tsar, the Russian king. Here you can see them as they attack the tsar's palace in Leningrad in 1917.*

△ This iron helmet was part of a series of treasures and artifacts unearthed at a burial site called Sutton Hoo.

▽ William the Conqueror invaded England in AD 1066. He was the first of the Norman kings.

We live in a world of rapid changes, and to many people anything that happened more than ten years ago is history! Of course it is, and some historians spend their time studying the events of the recent past.

What is History?

Many historians consider the beginning of the "modern world" to be in the 1400s – with the Renaissance in Europe. This was a time of new ideas and exploration, but it was also a time when people rediscovered the ancient past. The ancient world helped to shape the new world.

A long line of civilizations

Human history stretches back far beyond the invention of writing, about 5,000 years ago, reaching back even before the first farmers planted crops. For most of this time, Europe and America played little part in changing the world. Africa and Asia produced the first towns, the first farms, new wealth and new ideas.

Our modern technological civilization is the latest in a long series of civilizations. It is more widespread than any other, but still young – it has been around for fewer than 500 years. The civilizations you can read about in this book were smaller than our own, but some were much, much older. The civilization of ancient Egypt lasted 3,000 years. Chinese civilization was more or less unbroken for just as long, up until the 20th century.

Modern world, ancient traditions

The modern world has grown out of these ancient civilizations. Ancient peoples gave us the wheel, pottery, writing, mathematics, music, painting, and sculpture. They measured the Earth and studied the stars. The temples of the Maya in Central America are in ruins today, but local people still speak Mayan languages and follow ancient traditions. The Pyramids, the Parthenon, and the Great Wall of China still make visitors stand and stare in awe. The empires of the past have left their mark on the present.

Of course, history does not begin and end in neat sections. It is a flow of events and people, merging and overlapping with each other. One civilization influences another. People borrow from their neighbors. Wars of conquest reshape people's lives and customs. One empire falls, and another rises in its place.

△ Pearl Harbor. This attack during World War II by a Japanese strike force took place on 7 December 1941. It destroyed most of the U.S. Pacific Fleet.

Links to the past

Western art and philosophy, and our ideas of government, owe much to the Greeks and Romans, who in turn took many ideas from the civilizations of Persia, Babylon, and Egypt. The ancient world gave us the great religions of Hinduism, Buddhism, Judaism, Christianity, and Islam. The modern world in which we live has developed from these ancient civilizations. The knowledge gained has been passed on through the ages, until the great minds of the more recent past, like Newton, Darwin and Einstein were able to take them and develop them into laws and theories that have started to explain the universe, and life itself.

△ Astronomy flourished as a science in the ancient Islamic world. The Arab astronomers were among the first to name some of the brightest stars.

▷ Trajan's column. This is a part of a giant monument that the Roman emperor Trajan built to record his deeds. It also shows the day-to-day tasks of the Roman army.

The word "archaeology" comes from two Greek words and means "the study of old things." It is now a science, which uses techniques that make it possible for us to find out about people who lived long ago, long before history was written.

Archaeology

△ *The Nok people of Africa made terracotta sculptures of people, animals and heads.*

Many archaeological discoveries are made by digging in the ground at sites where ancient people lived. A city is often built in layers. The shops and offices of today stand on the ruins of temples and markets from the past. So a building site in a city may reveal unexpected finds. A low tide may uncover a ring of sacred wooden posts, built thousands of years ago and later covered by the sea and shifting sand.

▽ *Medieval monks spent some of their time copying out illuminated (decorated) books, mostly of religious texts.*

Planning and recording

Archaeologists work methodically and carefully. Photographs taken from the air may reveal outlines of a road or building that are invisible on the ground. A device called a magnetometer can detect pottery kilns or iron-working hearths. Metal detectors occasionally turn up buried treasures, such as hoards of old coins, jewelry, or weapons.

When archaeologists start to explore a site, they mark it out in a grid pattern to make an accurate plan, on which the location of each find is recorded. Wood and cloth rot, but traces of them may survive even after hundreds, or thousands, of years. Pottery, glass, and metal last longer. Each piece found is cleaned and numbered.

A rubbish pit can tell experts what people ate, because animal bones, shells and seeds are often preserved in it. Graves may contain "grave goods" buried with the dead person, such as weapons, jewelery, and pottery. A skeleton can reveal medical evidence of how a person died and how healthy he or she was in life.

How old?

During the 19th century a Danish archaeologist, Christian Jurgensen Thomsen, suggested that there were three "ages" of ancient history. He called them the Stone Age (the oldest), the Bronze Age, and the Iron

△ Frankish (French) soldiers heading for battle under the command of King Charlemagne in the late AD 700s.

▽ The Battle of the Somme during World War I resulted in the deaths of over a million soldiers on both sides.

Age – after the kinds of tools people used in each period. We still use these names, but it is important to remember that the ages happened at different times in different places.

Two useful scientific methods of dating objects are radiocarbon dating (used for wood, charcoal, and bones) and thermoluminescence (used for burned stones and pottery).

Famous finds

Archaeological work was first carried out seriously in the 1800s, when some of the most famous finds were made. The Rosetta Stone, found in 1822 by the French in Egypt, contains the same words in three forms of ancient writing: hieroglyphics, a simpler form of Egyptian script, and Greek. Scholars could read the Greek and the simple Egyptian writing, so they were able to decode the hieroglyphics and read the many ancient inscriptions that had previously baffled them.

The German archaeologist Heinrich Schliemann discovered the site of Troy in the 1870s. Probably the most sensational find of the 20th century came in 1922, when British archaeologist Howard Carter dug into the undisturbed tomb of the pharaoh Tutankhamun.

More important 20th-century discoveries about the ancient world came when Sir Leonard Woolley found the graves of the kings of Sumer at Ur, and when Sir Arthur Evans found the ruins of the Minoan palace of Knossos on the island of Crete. There have been many other fascinating finds: the uncovering of the Roman town of Pompeii buried by a volcanic eruption in AD 79, the excavation in 1939 of the 7th-century Sutton Hoo ship in England, and the discovery of the tomb of the Chinese emperor Shih Huang-di, with its army of terracotta soldiers, in 1974. Each new discovery tells us more about the ancient world. As archaeology develops further, new finds will continue to be made.

History comes from a Greek word meaning "what is known by asking." The job of a historian is to ask questions and make sense of the answers.

Historians

△ The ancient priest kings were thought to link the people and their god.

▽ Nelson Mandela was born in 1918. By 1944 he had become an important figure in the fight against apartheid, the racist policy of separating black and white people in South Africa. He was imprisoned in 1964 for political offenses, but was released in 1990.

The Greeks were among the first people to write history based on first-hand "reporting" of the facts. Herodotus (who died in 425 BC) wrote about the wars between the Greeks and the Persians. He traveled and talked to people who had taken part in the wars. Another Greek historian was Thucydides, who wrote a history of the Peloponnesian War between Athens and Sparta. He took part in the fighting and met war leaders.

Stories and legends

Historians work from a viewpoint. The first people to write their own history were the Chinese. We know the name of one early Chinese historian, Sima Qian, who wrote a history of China in about 100 BC. The Egyptians and other peoples recorded the names of their kings, as well as victories in battles.

Early historians were keen to show their own side in a good light. People felt it was important to write down the stories and legends about the past, and show how their state had come into existence. The Roman historian Livy collected scraps of information from various sources, listened to stories passed down by word of mouth, and turned them into the first full history of the Romans (up to the year 9 BC). Another Roman writer, Tacitus, wrote of the period from AD 14 to 96. He wrote about the Roman wars with the Celts in Germany and Britain. Since the Celts left no written histories of their own, we have only his description of what they were like, and of what happened. Sometimes people who made history also wrote it. Julius Caesar, the Roman general, wrote his own book about his campaigns in Gaul.

Ordinary lives

Before the AD 1900s, historians were mostly interested in governments and famous people. Today, historians are just as interested in the lives of ordinary men and women – how they lived, what they ate, the clothes they wore, the work they did, and so on. Some historians are interested in how economic changes affect people. Others study military history

▷ A World War I dog-fight. The first true fighter battle took place during World War I on October 5, 1914, when a French V89 shot down a German Aviatik aircraft with its machine gun.

△ During the Reformation, the Bible became available for all to read, thanks to the new printing technology and the fact that it was translated 'into the vernacular'– the language of each country.

△ Elizabeth's signature on the death warrant of Mary Stuart, Mary Queen of Scots.

(wars and weapons), the history of the arts or the development of religion.

What kind of source?

Like a detective, the historian relies on evidence. It may include writings such as books, law documents, letters, wills, and even household bills. Many different kinds of sources may contain clues.

Historians have primary and secondary sources. Primary sources are documents or objects made in the period being studied, for example a stone marked with Egyptian hieroglyphs or a mummy. Secondary sources are materials prepared later by people who saw the primary sources. A Roman traveler's account of his visit to Egypt is a secondary source, so is a drawing made in the 1700s of a tomb or monument which was later damaged or altered. To study the ancient world, where written records often do not exist, historians rely on evidence found by archaeologists.

△ A Mayan priest.

The beginning of human history can be traced back long before the first human beings appeared – to the earliest forms of life on Earth about 3 billion years ago. Of the enormous variety of animals that evolved over millions of years, among the most advanced were tree-living mammals called primates. These included the first apes.

The First Humans

About 10 million years ago, some apes left the trees to walk on the open plains. They had large brains and used their fingers to pick up food. About 4 million years ago, the humanlike ape *Australopithecus* (southern ape) lived in Africa. It probably used sticks or stones as tools, in the same way that chimpanzees do.

The first humans

The first human species was *Homo habilis* (handy man), who lived in East Africa 2 million years ago. By 1.5 million years ago, the more advanced *Homo erectus*

(upright man) had appeared, and by 500,000 years ago, *Homo erectus* had learned to make fire. The first humans lived in family groups. They communicated in some form of language and worked together gathering plants and hunting animals for food.

Modern humans

About 400,000 years ago, a new species, more like us and known to scientists as *Homo sapiens* (wise man), had become the dominant human species. These humans made tools from stone and other materials. This "stone age" lasted until about 10,000 years ago, although isolated groups of people continued using stone tools until the present day.

In a series of migrations, humans spread to every continent. They crossed over land bridges, which were uncovered as seawater turned to ice during the Ice Age. People moved in groups from Africa across Europe and Asia, and into America and Australasia. Their social organization and developing technology helped them survive the harsh climate of the Ice Age.

Hunters become farmers

About 10,000 years ago, people became farmers for the first time. They planted crops and kept goats, cattle, and sheep. The earliest centers of the farming revolution were in the Near East and Asia. Here, people first settled in towns and developed a new way of life – the beginnings of civilization.

The first modern human was *Homo sapiens* (meaning "wise man"), who appeared between 400,000 and 300,000 years ago. His body looked like ours, but he had a large brain and small jaws. His limbs were longer and straighter than those of earlier people.

The First People

The ape-humans had used tools that were simply pebbles picked up from the ground. *Homo sapiens* were much more skillful, choosing stones with care. They chipped or flaked off bits to make shaped tools including hand axes, choppers, knives, and scrapers. These people also made use of other materials, such as animal bones and horns. The new humans spread from Africa into new territories. Several early forms of *Homo sapiens* seem to have lived in Africa, the Near East, and Asia. By about 35,000 years ago, they had reached Europe and Australia.

Early modern human (Homo sapiens) appears.	c. 350,000 BC
Neanderthal people appear.	c. 120,000 BC
Modern human (Homo sapiens sapiens) appears.	c. 100,000 BC
Modern humans spread to Europe and later to Australia.	c. 40,000 BC
Cro-Magnons appear in Europe.	c. 33,000 BC
Neanderthals either die out or are interbred into modern human populations.	c. 30,000 BC
Hunters roam Europe. Cave paintings are made.	c. 13,000 BC
Latest date for people to reach America from Asia.	c. 11,000 BC

Neanderthals

In Europe, there was another human species, known as Neanderthal man, who for a time lived alongside modern humans. Scientists think Neanderthals were an "offshoot" of *Homo sapiens*, who adapted to life in the cold climates of the last Ice Age.

Neanderthal people lived in Europe from about 100,000 to 35,000 years ago. They took shelter in caves,

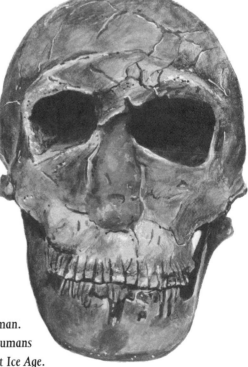

▷ The large skull of a Neanderthal man. These people lived alongside modern humans during the last Ice Age.

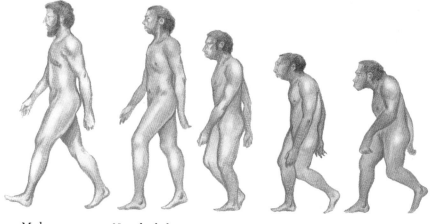

▷ Early peoples gradually looked less like humanoid apes and more like human beings. Bodies became more suited to walking upright, and legs became longer than arms.

| Modern man | Neanderthal man | Upright man | Handy man | Southern ape |

△ Stone Age people hunted with bows, spears, and flint axes. On the American grasslands, groups of hunters drove large grazing animals, such as mastodons and giant bison, to extinction.

made fire, and hunted animals, using stone tools and wooden spears. Although they had large brains, the heavily built Neanderthals were slower moving and less adaptable than the newcomers who started moving into Europe about 40,000 years ago. The Neanderthals were either wiped out by competition from other groups or integrated into humanity through interbreeding.

Cro-Magnons

The newcomers in Europe were the Cro-Magnons, who are named after the site in France where a group of their skeletons was discovered in 1868. Their bone structure was very similar to ours today. Cro-Magnons were probably our direct ancestors. Neanderthals and modern humans may have lived side by side and even bred between themselves. Yet it was the Cro-Magnons who won the evolutionary race.

The Stone Age

Historians call this period of prehistory the Stone Age, because stone was the most important material used by the first tool-makers. These early stone-crafting techniques show surprising skill.

Neanderthal burial

Neanderthals were the first humans to bury the dead. Archaeologists have found evidence of Neanderthal burial ceremonies. The remains of tools and meat have been found in graves, showing that the dead were buried with care.

Hand axe

Scraper

Spear head

△ Stone Age tools. Both the hand axe and scraper were made from flint. Spear heads were shaped from deer antlers. The hand axe was probably the most important early Stone Age tool.

From Africa, humans began to spread to every continent – a process that took almost 1 million years. Everywhere, humans were on the move. This was the age of the great migrations.

The Great Migrations

The Neanderthals vanished from Europe, although small groups may have remained in remote places. Modern humans moved across Europe and Asia and started to explore America and Australia. A wetter climate over the entire world produced a green region of lakes and grasslands in what is now the Sahara Desert. Animals and people thrived in these surroundings.

Cro-Magnons move into Europe from the Near East.	c. 38,000 BC
People reach America and Australia from Asia.	c. 33,000 BC
Neanderthals die out.	c. 28,000 BC
Evidence of cave people in Brazil.	c. 23,000 BC
Last wet period in Saharan North Africa.	c. 13,000 BC
People reach the tip of South America.	c. 8,000 BC
British Isles cut off by rising sea levels.	c. 3,000 BC
People reach Pacific Islands by boat.	c. 2,000 BC

Nomads, or wanderers, moved constantly to find fresh food supplies. Small groups of people walked across continents, following the animals they hunted for food.

Some moved into the north of Asia and even traveled across to what is now Alaska, but most of these early peoples on the move headed toward warmer regions. They began to settle on grassy plains and close to water. Everyone lived in harmony with nature, and their lives were regulated by the seasons.

We can form an idea of what early human life was like from studies of the Australian Aborigines. Until the 18th century, these people had little contact with the world beyond Australia. A few isolated groups of people in parts of

△ Aboriginal rock artists looked "beneath the skin" to show a person's bones or organs. Paintings of people and animals are found at sites linked in Aboriginal belief to the Dream Time, when spirits created the world.

Making fires

People made fire using a simple wooden stick called a fire drill. The drill was turned quickly over a piece of dry wood until it produced enough heat to start the fire.

△ Stone Age hunters killed deer and other animals with spears, bows, and stones, often ambushing a herd on the move. The humans' intelligence, weapons, and teamwork made up for their comparative lack of strength and speed.

South America and Southeast Asia also preserved a "Stone Age" way of life into the modern age.

The Aborigines

The Aborigines probably reached Australia overland, crossing a land bridge that joined New Guinea to Australia 30,000 years ago. They had boats, so sea migrations were also possible. There is also a theory that some crossed the Pacific Ocean and landed in America.

Food, clothes, and tools

These people lived by gathering food and hunting. Along the coast, they fished with nets, basket traps, and spears. In the bush, they used fire to drive animals into traps and made poisons from leaves and roots to drug fish in pools. Women and children collected roots, fruits, insects, and honey from wild bees' nests. They wore no clothes and rubbed animal fats onto their bodies to protect themselves from cold.

Technology was simple. The Aborigines made simple stick shelters. They made stone tools and knew how to use bows and arrows as well as spear-throwing. The boomerang was used for hunting and war.

Paintings and dances

On rocks and cave walls, artists used colored earth to make paintings, telling stories of myths and legends. This rock art, and the songs and dances of the people, reveals spiritual beliefs. One of the most powerful beliefs was the notion of the "Dream Time" – this was the time when all living things were created.

△ The Aborigines used ritual boomerangs, decorated with secret symbols, in magical dances.

BC

400,000

2,000

4,000

100,000

20,000

10,000

Around 18,000 years ago, the last of a series of Ice Ages gripped much of the Northern Hemisphere. Icecaps spread southward across Europe and North America. The sea level fell, uncovering land bridges which animals and people had crossed – between Asia and Alaska for example.

The Last Ice Age

This last Ice Age had a dramatic effect on people's way of life. The spread of snow and ice reduced the size of the areas in which they could live. Many moved away to seek warmer regions. Other groups adapted to living in the freezing conditions. Clothed only in animal skins and taking shelter in caves and tents, people tried to survive around the fringes of the vast ice sheets.

Tool-making

People who kept themselves alive by hunting needed good weapons and tools. They made these from flints, choosing stones that were easily chipped or flaked to create useful cutting and scraping edges. Where good flints were found, people dug mines to hack out the stones. They set up tool-making "factories" where they made polished stone axes and other tools with great skill.

Hunters make clay figures of people and animals. — *c.* 23,000 BC

Cave dwellers made paintings about this time at Lascaux in France and Altamira in Spain. — *c.* 23,000 BC

Last Ice Age reaches its coldest point. Earliest rock art known in Asia. — *c.* 16,000 BC

Hunter-gatherers cross from Asia into North America via the exposed Bering Strait. — *c.* 14,000 BC

End of the last Ice Age. Possible first domestic animal - the dog - used for hunting. — *c.* 11,000 BC

New Stone Age begins. — *c.* 6,000 BC

▷*As well as being an important source of meat, woolly mammoths provided skins for clothing and shelter. Their bones and tusks were carved into tools and decorative ornaments.*

▷ Cave artists used natural paints made from colored earth and plant juices. Their drawings may have been made for ritual magic, to bring success to a group's hunters.

△ This Ice Age man is using a stone blade to scrape clean the skin of a hunted animal.

Tool-makers settled near their mines and traded their finished tools with other groups. The first trade routes were made by people traveling from one place to another to exchange goods. In boggy areas, the first "roads" were made – consisting of wooden walkways built from logs. Near rivers and lakes, people became skilled boatmen and fishermen, making their craft from hollowed-out tree trunks and bundles of reeds. They wove fishing nets and built lakeside huts on stilts. They made fire with friction (rubbing) techniques, using a bowdrill or striking flints. Once a fire was lit, people did their best to make sure it did not go out.

Social life

People living in groups had to find ways of working together. They developed ideas of sharing tasks between men and women, and between individuals. Expert tool-makers (perhaps women or the elderly) stayed in camp while others went hunting – and so had more time to practice their skills for the benefit of the group.

By working together, early humans were able to hunt and kill big animals such as mammoth and bison.

Hut of mammoth bones

Ice Age hunters made shelters from the bones of mammoths. They made the framework of bones and filled in the gaps with skins, turf, and moss. Groups of men drove the animals into swamps, where they became trapped and were killed with spears or rocks.

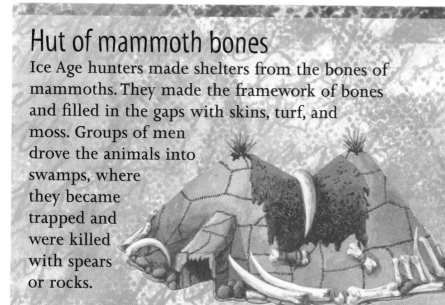

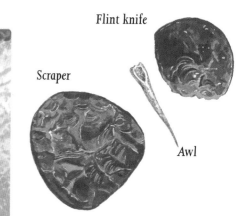

Flint knife

Scraper

Awl

△ Tools for scraping were made mainly from flint. This hard material could be chipped into tools of many different shapes and sizes. Other tools were made from bone, antlers, and tusks.

25

About 10,000 years ago the icecap had shrunk. Warmer weather made life much easier and human groups began to grow. In places, people who used to wander around looking for food found that, by gathering wild cereal plants such as rice and wheat, and sowing the seeds, they could grow new plants in the same place.

The First Farmers

People naturally chose plants with the largest grain-heads. A chance cross-breeding of wheat and wild grass in the Jordan Valley in Israel produced a new wheat with bigger grains. People found that grinding the grains produced flour, the basic ingredient in bread, an important new food. How this breakthrough in skill and diet happened is not clear, but it changed history.

Sheep may have been domesticated.	c. 9,000 BC
Start of farming in the Near East. Walls of Jericho, the earliest town, built.	c. 8,000 BC
Wheat and barley are grown in the Near East. Pigs and cattle are domesticated.	c. 7,000 BC
Farming spreads west into Europe and east into Asia. Copper in use. Pottery made.	c. 6,000 BC
First use of brick for building in the Near East.	c. 5,000 BC
First farmers cross to Britain. First plows used in Near East.	c. 4,000 BC
Invention of the wheel in Mesopotamia. Use of copper tools spreads.	c. 3,500 BC
Domestication of the horse in central Asia.	c. 2,500 BC

Settling down

People no longer wandered after herds of wild animals or in search of fresh plants to pick. Instead, some stayed in one place, making homes beside their new plots of roughly tilled and sown ground. They had become farmers.

Rivers and lakes were good places to settle. Fish could be caught in nets and water channeled along ditches to the new fields. The first farmers made new tools, such as wooden digging sticks and sickles with flint blades, to harvest their crops.

Farmers tamed animals too. Hunters had already tamed wolf cubs to help in the hunt, but now

△ Early tools were made from materials such as flint, bone, and antlers. Common ones were the flint sickle (right), the flint and wood hammer (center), and the antler pick (left).

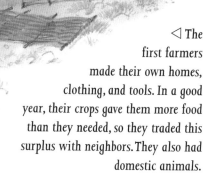

◁ The first farmers made their own homes, clothing, and tools. In a good year, their crops gave them more food than they needed, so they traded this surplus with neighbors. They also had domestic animals.

Dogs and poultry

Populations grew after the Ice Age. People could not find enough food by the old way of hunting and gathering. A new strategy was needed to survive: farming and the raising of domestic animals.

domestic dogs were trained to herd flocks of sheep and goats. Farm animals were bred from young wild animals, captured and raised among people. Domesticated animals were then bred to make them more docile and suitable for human use.

Farmers and new tools

The first farmers lived in the Near East, across a region stretching west from the Nile Valley to the Tigris and Euphrates rivers. This area became known as the Fertile Crescent. Farming also developed in other continents at this time – in China and in the Americas.

With farming came new inventions and skills. People made pottery and invented the wheel, used first to turn the clay as it was shaped. They made metal tools, first from cold-beaten copper (about 8,500 years ago), then from bronze (a mixture of copper and tin formed by heat). About 5,000 years ago, people learned how to smelt (melt and separate) iron ore from rocks. They used the iron to make tools, both for peace and for war.

Iron Age world

Farming brought new wealth. Trade grew as did warfare. The richer people clustered together to defend themselves against raids by envious enemies. Village life demanded a communal form of government. Chieftains who had once led bands of nomads became rulers of villages. Some of the villages grew rapidly into the world's first towns.

△ The first farmers began to develop new skills, which included the use of fire to make metal tools and weapons. The tools seen here are (from left to right): a sickle for harvesting crops, a knife, and a pair of pincers.

27

Civilization began with the first towns. Towns grew into cities, which became the centers of the world's first empires. Egypt, the Indus Valley, and China all had advanced societies.

The First Civilizations

Impressive civilizations also rose in central America, Africa south of the Sahara, and the eastern Mediterranean. Religion, trade, art, and lawmaking developed. So did technology – and warfare. Human life became more organized and complex.

The first towns

The oldest known town ruins are those of Jericho – its walls date from about 11,000 years ago. The ruins of Catal Huyuk, in Turkey, date from about 8,250 years ago. People built towns in Mesopotamia, Egypt, the Indus Valley, China, and Central America. Rivers were the cradles of these new civilizations, attracting farmers and traders. Towns became marketplaces, and cities became centers of government.

Kings and cities

The early city-states were led by kings, who made laws. Often kings were also priests. Powerful kings such as Sargon of Akkad

and Hammurabi of Babylon
ruled the first empires. The pharaohs
of Egypt lived in imperial splendor, in a
land made rich by farming and trade. Other
rulers built luxurious palaces such as
Knossos on the island of Crete.

The period from 5,000 BC to 500 BC produced magnificent
buildings, such as the ziggurats of Babylon and the pyramids of Egypt.
The stones of Stonehenge and the mysterious heads left by
the Olmecs in Central America show that
people in Europe and America were also
artists and builders.

New technology and ideas

This was an age of crucial new
technologies – the wheel, metal tools,
and weapons were developed at this
time. Coins were first used. Writing and
mathematics developed. The
Babylonians studied the stars. New ideas
were evolving, and spreading with the
help of trade, ready to shape the next
stage of human history.

BC
400,000
100,000
20,000
10,000
4,000
2,000

When people settled down to farm they chose to live near a water supply, often a river. Between two mighty rivers – the Tigris and the Euphrates in Mesopotamia – the world's first great civilization rose 6,000 years ago.

Mesopotamia

Mesopotamia, meaning "between rivers," lay in the country we know as modern Iraq. Northern Mesopotamia's weather was mild, with enough rain for crops to grow in some areas. In the south lay a flat, swampy plain built up from mud spread by the river floodwaters. This area was called Sumer. It had little rain and long, hot summers.

Sumer

People had lived in Sumer since 5,000 BC. They fished the rivers, hunted wild pigs and birds for food, and picked fruit from date palms. The muddy soil was rich, but crops died without rain in the burning summer heat. So farmers dug canals to channel river water to their fields of barley, wheat, dates, and vegetables. They turned over the earth with plows pulled by oxen.

Gods and grain

Farming flourished and by around 3,500 BC, new people settled in Sumer. With their arrival, cities began to grow. Food was plentiful, so farming villages grew in number and size. People lived and worked together. Their buildings of mud brick included a house – or temple – for the local god. Here they offered gifts in return for the god's care of

The weaving loom is in use by this date. Hot metal working in Near East. — *c.* 4,000 BC

Earliest map on a clay tablet shows River Euphrates. — *c.* 3,800 BC

Towns of Uruk (Eridu) and Ur in Sumer. First use of potter's wheel. — *c.* 3,500 BC

Invention of the wheel in Mesopotamia. Flax grown to make linen. — *c.* 3,500 BC

Cuneiform writing developed in Sumer. — *c.* 3,200 BC

First city-states in Mesopotamia and Near East. — *c.* 3,000 BC

Domestication of the horse in central Asia. — *c.* 2,500 BC

Destruction of the city of Ur by the Elamites. The last king of Ur, Ibbi-Sin, is taken captive. — *c.* 2,000 BC

▷ *People in Mesopotamia traded along the rivers, using small boats. By 5,000 years ago, people had invented the wheel, and carts were pulled by oxen and donkeys. Sacks of barley were traded as currency as well as being used for food.*

Jewelery

Skilled metalworkers in Sumer made fine jewelery from silver and gold. These items were inlaid with precious stones, such as lapis lazuli.

△ Some of the wedge-shaped ("cuneiform") characters in the Sumerian writing system looked like objects; others were symbols.

their families, homes, crops, and animals. Gifts of harvest crops led to the temple also being used as a grain store. Even farm animals such as oxen and donkeys were kept there, perhaps to hire out for work in the fields.

Writing and counting

Goods passing in and out of the temple store had to be checked and recorded. A system of numbers and counting was invented – as well as the world's first writing system. People skilled in writing, called scribes, were highly trained, important people.

The beginning of writing is also the beginning of human history. Sumerians used clay tablets and a sharpened reed to carve wedge-shaped characters into the soft, damp surface. The clay was baked hard, so the writing became a permanent record. Sumerian tablets can still be read. The Sumerian system of counting has lasted, too. They used units of 60 when telling the time in seconds, minutes, and hours and when measuring a circle with 360 degrees.

▷ Sumerian women wore long dresses and robes. Rich women liked jewelry, such as bead necklaces, gold earrings, and headdresses.

BC

400,000
100,000
20,000
10,000
4,000
2,000

Town life created a society with more rules in which more people did specialized tasks. The world of city-states such as Ur was one run largely by men.

Society and City-states

A man was master of his household, including his wife, children, and slaves. Women could, however, own their own property. Boys from wealthier families, such as the sons of court officials, went to school to be taught by scribes. Other children learned to do what their parents did at home.

Priest power

Priests were important because of the temple trade. They organized everyone who worked in and around the temple, from craftworkers to merchants and scribes. Villagers farmed land for the gods, under the priests' watchful eyes. Farmers paid rent to the temple, and priests also acted as tax collectors. In return, a state allowance of food was distributed to city dwellers.

As villages grew into towns and cities, temple officials played a big part in ruling them. A rich and powerful elite class emerged, living in splendid temple-palaces. Most powerful of all was the king, the gods' representative on Earth. He was responsible for law and government, for keeping order, and for defending civilization against enemies.

City-states and their rulers

Among the earliest cities of southern Mesopotamia were Eridu, Uruk, Nippur, and Kish. These cities were like small states, with their own

First cities of Mesopotamia.	3,500 BC
Cities and temples in Sumer built of mud brick.	3,000 BC
Rise of city of Ur.	2,850 BC
Gilgamesh, legendary ruler.	2,750 BC
Rise of the Akkad Empire.	2,400 BC
Sargon of Akkad is first great king.	2,350 BC
King Ur-Nammu rules Ur.	2,112 BC
King Hammurabi rules Babylon.	1,750 BC

▷ In Mesopotamia, there were hundreds of gods and goddesses, including Nanna the moon god and Inanna the goddess of love and war.

ENKI   NINHURSAG   NANNA   UTU   INANNA

△ The royal standard of Ur, a decorated wooden box, dates from about 2,500 BC. On its mosaic panels, farmers parade and soldiers march into battle.

government and rulers. Around 2,700 BC, the title "lugal," meaning big man, was used for the ruler of Kish. Uruk, which in about 2,700 BC was the first city to protect itself with a wall, had a ruler with the title "En."

Sargon of Akkad

City-states often fought one another over trade and border disputes. Sumerian soldiers fought mainly on foot, although some rode in chariots drawn by wild donkeys (onagers). When one city grew powerful enough to rule the others, it created a small kingdom, such as those of Lagash and Ur. Around 2,375 BC, Lagash and all the other city-states of Sumer were defeated by Lugalzaggisi, ruler of Umma. Sumer was united under his rule for 25 years. But from the north came an even mightier conqueror – Sargon of Akkad – the first great king in history.

Sargon created the first empire in Mesopotamia. One of his successors, the fourth king of Akkad, was Naram-Sin (he reigned from 2,254 to 2,218 BC), whose war triumphs are recorded on a famous sculpture, the Naram-Sin Stele.

△ King Hammurabi of Babylon (ruled c.1792 –1750 BC) is shown before the sun god at the top of this carved stone pillar. The king's laws were carved onto the pillar below.

Sargon of Akkad

Sargon had been cup-bearer to the king of Kish. Records say that he fought the Sumerian cities, threw down city walls, and took 50 of their rulers captive, including the ruler of Uruk. Sargon ruled for a total of 56 years. He made one of his daughters a priestess of the moon god in Ur.

△ In the city-states of Mesopotamia, scribes such as the one shown here carved the local ruler's code of laws onto clay tablets.

In Mesopotamia, as many as 300,000 people lived in a big city. Within the walls, the city was a maze of narrow streets, alleys, and marketplaces. Many buildings were made of mud brick but some houses were built from reeds. They were similar to those still used by people living in southern Iraq.

Homes and Temples

A well-to-do family lived in a two-story home with no windows. It had a flat roof where the family might sleep and a central courtyard that was pleasantly cool in the evening. Here, visitors would have their dusty feet washed by a slave. The bedrooms were upstairs; the kitchen, living room, and storerooms were downstairs. There was little furniture - only chests, stools, and tables – and most people slept on mats, although some rich people had beds. Each home had a shrine, set in the wall, and often a small family tomb.

Food and drink

The Sumerians made unleavened bread (bread that does not rise) and ate porridge made from wheat and barley grains. Vegetables, dates, milk, butter, and cheese were served at

First cities of Mesopotamia.	3,500 BC
Writing in Sumer. First use of bronze.	3,200 BC
Cities and temples in Sumer built of mud brick.	3,000 BC
Great Pyramid of Giza built in Egypt.	2,590 BC

▷ A ziggurat consisted of an enormous platform structure with an earth core, over which unglazed bricks were laid. The building was faced with fire bricks. Ramps and steps led up to the top, where the temple was erected.

Brick-makers fired bricks in kilns to produce building materials for structures that were intended to last. Kiln-fired bricks could survive the seasonal rains without needing too much repair.

mealtimes too. Cattle and sheep provided meat, and fish was a very popular food. Fish "take-out" stalls sold ready-cooked fish. The favorite drink was beer. For entertainment, people played board games, listened to stories of legendary heroes, or played musical instruments. Water and food were kept in large storage jars. Glass was made, some time before 2,000 BC, but for use in jewelery.

Temples to the gods

The Sumerians worshipped many gods and goddesses – gods of the sky, the air, the Sun, the Moon, fertility, and wisdom. Each city had its own patron god.

Slaves, taken captive in war, toiled to build Mesopotamia's splendid temples. The White Temple in Uruk, built in 3,000 BC, was made of whitewashed brick, set on top of a pyramid or ziggurat. A ziggurat was an artificial mountain, on which the people thought the local god lived, watching over the citizens he protected. The ziggurat's platform of earth was faced with bricks. Temples were built on top of the platform. The Hanging Gardens of Babylon, one of the Seven Wonders of the Ancient World, were probably built in the same way.

△ Reed houses were built using reeds cut down from the marshes around the Tigris and Euphrates rivers. The Sumerians also made canoes from these reeds.

The wheel

The wheel was first used by the Sumerians in making pottery in about 3,500 BC. About 300 years later, this invention was adapted for a startling new use – transportation.

△ Mud bricks, dried in the sun, were one of the least expensive building materials. These sun-dried bricks were made stronger with straw, but they were not waterproof.

After the fall of Ur in 2,000 BC, many cities of Mesopotamia were ruled by the Amorites, whose two strongholds were Isin and Larsa. In 1,763 BC, Larsa fell to a great army led by Hammurabi (1,792–1,750 BC). The new ruler gave the new name, Babylonia, to the kingdoms of Sumer and Akkad.

Babylonia

Under Hammurabi, all of Mesopotamia came under one rule. The king of Babylonia was also the high priest of the national god. The palace now held power over the temple. Under the king there were three classes of people: aristocrats, commoners, and slaves. Trade was no longer controlled by the city, so merchants and traders managed their own businesses.

The laws of Hammurabi

The laws of King Hammurabi applied across his empire. They covered trade, business and prices, family law, criminal law, and civil laws. Their main principle was "the strong shall not injure the weak." Hammurabi also set up a system of set prices and wages and gave his people a fair and well-run tax system. In AD 1901, his laws were found written on a stone slab in Susa, Iran where a victorious king had taken it as war booty.

One of the conflicts between the former

Hittites make iron tools and weapons.	2,000 BC
First Babylonian dynasty.	1,830 BC
Fall of Larsa. Hammurabi rules Babylon.	1,763 BC
Babylon conquers other city-states.	1,750 BC
Nebuchadnezzar fights off Assyrian invasion.	1,125 BC
Tiglath-pileser I of Assyria conquers Babylon.	1,116 BC
Babylon again invaded by Assyrians.	700s BC
Old Babylon falls.	689 BC
Rise of New Babylon.	626 BC

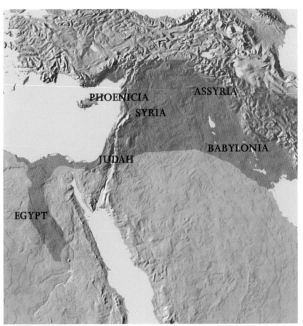

▷ This map shows the extent of the Babylonian Empire under King Nebuchadnezzar II. Under his rule, the Babylonians captured Syria and Palestine.

△ Marduk was the chief god of Babylonia. Poets praised him as kind and merciful lord of the heavens and the source of civilization and law. His sacred animals included the dragon.

The new Babylon

People entered the city through eight great bronze gates. The most magnificent of these was the Ishtar Gate, which was decorated with patterns and pictures of lions, bulls, and dragons – all in shiny, colored bricks.

states of Babylonia was over the control of river waters. In wartime, rulers dammed rivers to cause flood or drought in the land of their enemies. Sometimes a river would be diverted away from the crops of a rival city. Hammurabi now commanded the water power.

Hammurabi's city

The city of Babylon had magnificent temples and palaces. Its winding, narrow streets were lined with private houses. Most had a courtyard with rooms around it. In the city walls were gates, around which traders held markets. Traders and merchants traveled as far afield as Syria, Assyria, and the kingdoms of the Persian Gulf.

The fall of Babylon

During 700 BC, Assyrians from the upper Tigris area, north of Babylonia, invaded Babylon. The city was destroyed in 689 BC by the Assyrian king Sennacherib but later rebuilt. A new Babylonian empire began to grow in 626 BC, when the general Nabopolassae defeated the Assyrians. Under this king and his son, Nebuchadnezzar II, the Babylonian Empire controlled most of the Middle East.

△ The Babylonians produced written records by carving picture symbols onto clay tablets. The tablets carried information about astronomy and mathematics, as well as records of legal and business matters and religious texts.

▷ The ancient Babylonians were the first to study the stars, some time before 2,000 BC. They knew of five planets: Jupiter, Mars, Mercury, Saturn, and Venus.

BC

400,000

2,000

100,000

4,000

20,000

10,000

The city-states of Sumer traded across the Arabian Sea with people who lived by another great river – the River Indus, which flows through Pakistan. Here, one of the world's first great civilizations had begun, like Sumer, with farms, villages, and small towns.

The Indus Valley

Around 2500 BC, cities were planned and built. These cities remained unknown until archaeologists began excavating them in the AD 1920s. There were two main cities – Harappa in the north of the Indus Valley and Mohenjo Daro in the south. The people who lived here were farmers, tending fields and watering crops with silt-laden waters washed down when the snows melted in the mountains to the north.

Well-planned cities

Harappa and Mohenjo Daro were carefully planned and laid out on a grid system. They were large cities, over 3 miles around their outer boundary. The cities had wide roads and brick houses, most of which

Farming settlements grow in the Indus Valley.	3000 BC
First cities of the Indus Valley.	2500 BC
Aryans from the north begin to threaten Indus peoples.	2100 BC
Indus Valley civilization begins to decline.	2000 BC
Indus Valley civilization is destroyed.	1500 BC

▷ The city of Harappa. Many houses were built on mud-brick platforms to save them from seasonal floods. Most had baths, with water from a public well or a well in the courtyard.

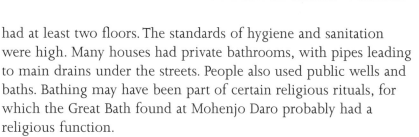

Rulers known as priest kings were found in all the great ancient civilizations. This ruler was the link between people and god, on whose will their fate depended. Both Harappa and Mohenjo Daro were probably ruled by a priest king and by a priestly elite.

△ *Archaeologists have found hundreds of artifacts during the excavation of Mohenjo Daro. Many, such as this bronze figurine of a dancing girl, have been well preserved in the sand and mud around the settlement.*

△ *The farmers of the Indus Valley used wooden carts pulled by a pair of oxen. Deep grooves made by heavily laden carts have been found in the excavated streets of Mohenjo Daro.*

had at least two floors. The standards of hygiene and sanitation were high. Many houses had private bathrooms, with pipes leading to main drains under the streets. People also used public wells and baths. Bathing may have been part of certain religious rituals, for which the Great Bath found at Mohenjo Daro probably had a religious function.

Traders used a standard system of weights and measures, and each city had a large granary stocked with grain. Farmers grew wheat, barley, peas, mustard, sesame seeds, dates, and cotton. Domesticated animals included dogs, cats, cattle, chickens and possibly pigs, camels, buffalo, and elephants. Over 100 other towns and villages have been found in the Indus Valley.

Rich from trade

All this suggests a high level of organization. Temples were smaller and less impressive than those of Mesopotamia, but the people of the Indus Valley enjoyed clean and well-run cities. Food was their main export, and trade was carried on by ship with copper producers in the Persian Gulf. Caravans from the north brought silver from Afghanistan and lead from Rajasthan. There was also trade with Sumer, and similarities in art found suggest the two cultures copied each other's fashions.

" No thing existed, nor did nothing exist:/ there was no air-filled space, no sky beyond./ What held it all? And where? And who secured it?

from THE RIG VEDA, c. 1,500 BC

The Rig Veda is a religious song about the ancient gods of fire, earth, air, and water.

The first great civilization in Europe arose in Greece, around 3,000 BC, on the island of Crete in the Mediterranean Sea. It was named "Minoan" after the legendary King Minos of Crete. In Greek myths, Minos was the son of Europa and Zeus, the king of the gods.

Crete and Mycenae

The Cretans were among the first people to make bronze tools and weapons. They were farmers and fishing people who lived in small towns or villages protected not by walls or forts but by the sea. These seafarers were the first naval power known in history.

Sailors and traders

The Cretans sailed the Aegean and Mediterranean seas in ships laden with goods produced by the island's farmers and skilled craftworkers – pottery, engraved stone seals, perfumes, metalwork, woolen textiles, olive oil, wine, grain, and grapes. Minoan pottery found its way to Egypt, where tomb paintings show Cretans bringing gifts for the pharaoh. They carried tin, gold, pearls, and ivory back to Crete. Trade made the Minoans wealthy.

Palace of Knossos

The chief town of Crete was Knossos, where the ruler lived in a luxurious hilltop palace. Courtyards, storehouses, and workshops formed part of the palace, which was also the center of government and an important grain store.

Earliest settlements on Crete.	c. 6000 BC
Stone-built villages on coasts of Crete. Trade with Egypt and Anatolia.	c. 3000 BC
Minoan Crete at height of its power. Palace at Knossos.	2000 BC
Start of Mycenean power. Mycenae becomes an important center.	1900 BC
Mycenae rivals the Minoans of Crete.	1500 BC
Volcanic explosion on island of Thera in Aegean Sea.	1470 BC
Myceneans take over Crete. Knossos is destroyed by fire.	1400 BC
Lion gate at Mycenae built.	1300 BC
Collapse of Mycenean civilization.	c. 1,150 BC

▷ The so-called "mask of Agamemnon" was found during the excavation of graves at Mycenae in the late 1800s. Modern historians think the mask belonged to an earlier king.

△ The Minoans favored goddesses in their worship, including the snake goddess who protected the home. The Cretan civilization left behind a rich legacy of religious beliefs and tales of heroes and gods.

The Minotaur

According to legend, King Minos kept a half-human, half-bull called the Minotaur in his palace at Knossos. Wall paintings there show young acrobats leaping along bulls' backs.

By about 1580 BC, Minoan civilization was spreading to other Aegean islands and to the mainland of Greece. There were palaces in other Minoan towns, such as Mallia and Phaisos. The great palace at Knossos, crushed by an earthquake in 1700 BC, had risen again in even grander form. In about 1450 BC, another earthquake hit Crete. After this, the Myceneans – a people from mainland Greece – ruled the island.

Mycenean warriors

The Myceneans were warlike people who lived in Greece, possibly from 1900 BC. By 1600 BC, they were trading in the Aegean, and, after the fall of Crete, they became the major power in the region. They had settlements from Sicily to Syria and close links with Troy, a city in the rich grain-growing area at the mouth of the Black Sea.

The Mycenean rulers lived in hilltop citadels overlooking cities protected by thick stone walls. The city of Mycenae was at the heart of their civilization. People entered Mycenae through the Lion Gate, a great stone gateway from which a path led straight to the royal palace. Graves of the ruling family, filled with treasure and personal possessions for the afterlife, were found near the gate in AD 1876.

By 1100 BC, Mycenean power was over. Raids by pirates cut off Mediterranean trade routes from the Greek mainland. Weakened by interstate warfare, the Mycenean cities were destroyed and lost.

△ Both the Cretans and the Myceneans had forms of writing, which they used in business and government. They wrote on clay tablets and possibly also in ink on papyrus, like the Egyptians. We know of two forms of writing, or scripts, called Linear A and Linear B.

◁ Like other Minoan palaces, the palace at Knossos was designed for elegant living and day-to-day business. Short wooden columns supported the decorated beams of the ceiling.

400,000
2,000
100,000
4,000
20,000
10,000

None of the civilizations in western Europe could rival those of Egypt and the Near East. However, more than 5,000 years ago Europeans were building spectacular stone monuments. Many of these are still standing today, as mysterious relics of a long-gone society.

Megalithic Europe

The huge stones of these monuments are called megaliths (meaning "big stones"). Some were set up on their own, others in groups or in circles. Some megaliths marked the burial place of an important ruler, while others seem to have had a religious meaning.

First stone structures in Europe.	4,500 BC
Passage graves built at Carnac in France.	4,000 BC
Lake villages in central Europe.	3,000 BC
Stone temples on the island of Malta.	2,800 BC
Beaker Folk begin to settle in Britain.	2,500 BC
End of New Stone Age in Britain. First use of bronze.	2,000 BC
Earliest work at Stonehenge.	1,800 BC
Stonehenge is more or less complete.	1,400 BC
Celts begin to settle in Britain.	1,000 BC

Europe's population grew as farming developed. People in the north looked southward towards the Mediterranean for new ideas. Traders from the civilized southern world came as far north as Britain, in search of tin needed to make bronze.

Most Europeans lived in small villages, ruled by a chieftain. His power was based on the number of weapons, sheep, and cattle he owned. Chieftains controlled trade and the places where people met to do business – river fords, valleys, and forest clearings where trails crossed. Travel was difficult because there were no proper roads. Clumsy ox-drawn wagons with iron-rimmed wheels creaked slowly along, carrying heavy goods.

The settlement of Britain

Before 3000 BC, few people lived in the British Isles apart from scattered groups of wandering hunters. Then, farmers and herders from

△ Stonehenge was built in stages between 1800 and 1400 BC. During the second stage, blue stones from the Preseli Mountains in Wales were hauled onto the site in an astonishing feat of organization and transport. Local stones added in the third stage weighed up to 55 tons.

Stone relics

Rock tombs, slab tombs such as this dolmen (right) and stone circles and temples lie scattered across Europe, even on the island of Malta. The work of trimming and raising the stones required skill.

mainland Europe arrived. They brought cattle, sheep, and pigs, and began to clear the forests to grow crops.

From about 2500 BC, new migrants arrived, bringing with them bronze tools and a distinctive pottery. Historians call them the "Beaker Folk." They mined copper and tin, made gold jewelry, and wove wool and linen for clothing.

Mound diggers and stone movers

People had no machines, and yet they tackled large digging works. They buried their chieftains, with treasures and food for the next world, beneath mounds of earth called "barrows." Many of these barrows can still be seen.

Tall single stones (menhirs), stone slab-tombs (dolmens), and the remains of large circles of stones and wooden posts (henges) are also still standing. In Britain, the most impressive stone circles are at Avebury and Stonehenge in Wiltshire. At Carnac, in northern France, there are avenues of standing stones.

Iron Age Europe

The Stonehenge builders had only stone or bronze tools. The Iron Age began in central Europe about 1000 BC. Early iron-using people mined salt as well as iron ore. About 1000 BC, new settlers called Celts came to Britain from mainland Europe. These newcomers were iron-makers and fort-builders.

△ Many people in Britain and Europe lived in village communities. A typical village dwelling consisted of a round wooden framework, filled in with twigs, turf, and mud, and a thatched roof.

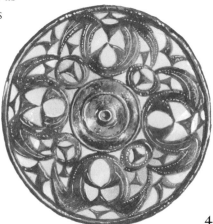

▷ The Celts were skilled craftworkers, making highly decorated ornaments from bronze and iron. Their work featured elaborate and distinctive patterns of interwoven curves and spirals.

BC

For most of a period lasting 3,000 years, Egypt was the strongest power in the world. It ruled an empire which, at its peak in about 1500 BC, included Palestine and Syria. Egyptians kings, or pharaohs, built the greatest monuments of the ancient world – the Pyramids.

Egypt

Egyptian armies fought off invaders and conquered new lands, while traders journeyed across the Mediterranean Sea and southward into Africa to bring back treasures to add to Egypt's wealth. This wealth was based on the mighty Nile River. The Egyptians called their land Kemet ("black land"). Each year, the Nile flooded and its waters spilled over the banks to spread a layer of black, fertile mud on the fields where the farmers grew their crops. This yearly gift of the Nile allowed people to enjoy a civilization of plenty.

Egypt united

The earliest peoples of Egypt were desert nomads. As they settled and grew to be farmers, they built villages and towns. By 3100 BC, Egypt had become one country. The southern kingdom of Upper Egypt conquered the northern kingdom of Lower Egypt, and King Menes made Memphis his capital.

The Egyptians regarded their king as a god. Thirty dynasties (ruling families) of these god-kings ruled from the time of King Menes in 3100 BC until 332 BC when Alexander the Great conquered Egypt. From about 1554 BC, the Egyptian kings were given the title pharaoh.

First dynastic period. Egypt is united under one king.	3,100 BC
Old Kingdom. The Pyramids are built at Giza.	2,686– 2,160 BC
A period of unrest and famine. Pyramids are robbed.	2,160– 2,040 BC
Middle Kingdom. Capital of Egypt moves to Thebes. Strong pharaohs rule.	2,040– 1,786 BC
Hyksos people from the north invade.	1,786 BC
New Kingdom. Amenhotep IV becomes king (1367).	1,567– 1,085 BC
Rameses III fights off invasions by Sea Peoples.	1,179 BC
The Late Dynastic Period. Libyan and Nubian pharaohs rule.	1,085– 332 BC
Egypt becomes part of the Roman Empire.	30 BC

△ This picture shows a pharaoh firing an arrow from his battle chariot. It is part of a decorative scene on the side of a chest found in the tomb of the boy-king Tutankhamun.

▷ The Nile not only provided Egypt's people with rich, fertile soil and plentiful water but it was also a source of food. Egyptians caught river fish to add to their basic diet. They used spears to hunt ducks on the river too.

△ The shaduf was a bucket swung from the end of a counterweighted pole. It was used to lift water from irrigation ditches, and is still used in Egypt today.

Government and daily life

Egypt was governed by officials and tax collectors, who measured the Nile's waters to predict how high it would flood each year. They could then determine how big a harvest was to be expected. Taxes were set accordingly. Most Egyptians were farmers. They grew crops of barley, wheat, fruit, and vegetables. Their diet consisted of daily meals of bread and beer, often supplemented with fish. Meat from cattle, sheep, and goats was a luxury.

Children began work at the age of five. Boys went to school if their parents could afford to spare them from work, and some girls did too. There were many slaves, but even freemen might be forced to dig irrigation canals or haul stones to building sites. Skilled workers, such as scribes (writers), stone-cutters, carpenters, metalworkers, painters, potters, bakers, and brewers, were kept busy in the towns.

The Egyptians were good at math, particularly at geometry, which they used in architecture and surveying. They drew up an accurate 12-month calendar of 365 days and used water clocks to measure time.

Picture-writing

Egyptian picture-writing is known as hieroglyphics. It was made up of about 750 signs, with pictures of people, animals, and objects. Scribes used a quick form of writing called hieratic.

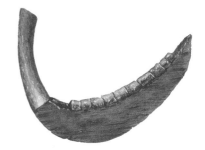

△ Egyptian farmers used sickles to harvest their crops. The harvest period traditionally lasted from March to July. Other farm equipment included ox-drawn wooden plows which were used to prepare the soil before planting time.

BC
2,000
400,000
100,000
20,000
10,000
4,000

Religion played an important part in Egyptian life. The Egyptians believed in many gods and goddesses. Their chief deities were Ra the sun god, Horus the sky god, Osiris the god of the underworld, and Isis, wife of Osiris, who represented the ideal woman.

Pyramids and Gods

This large group of gods was challenged on only one occasion, when the pharaoh Amenhotep tried to introduce worship of one supreme being, the sun god Aton.

Town gods and temples

Gods looked after every aspect of life. Every town and city had its own god, too. Temples were dedicated to a particular god or a dead pharaoh. The biggest of all these temples was the temple of Amun (a sun god who came to be linked with Ra) at Karnak. The pharaoh was the chief priest as well as a god himself. Priests in each temple cared for the statue of the god that was kept there, washing it and offering it gifts of food. Priests also prayed to the gods. Ordinary people said their prayers in the home.

The next world and mummies

The Egyptians believed in an afterlife, to which human souls journeyed after death. They thought it important that the bodies of the dead be preserved for life in the next world, so they developed techniques for making "mummies."

The dead person's organs were removed and the body was embalmed and dried,

▷ The Great Sphinx is a mysterious rock sculpture, with a human head on the body of a lion. Some historians believe it is older than the Pyramids.

First "step" pyramid at Saqqara, built by Imhotep for the pharaoh Zoser.	2,780 BC
Great Pyramid at Giza built for the pharaoh Cheops (Khufu).	2,700 BC
The pharaohs stop building pyramids. Later kings are buried in rock tombs.	1,700 BC
Start of reign of pharaoh Amenhotep III – a great age for Egypt.	1,420 BC
Temples at Luxor built.	1,400 BC
Reign of Amenhotep IV who tries to introduce the worship of one sun god.	1,367 BC
Tutankhamun rules. Egypt returns to the old gods.	1,347 BC
Temples at Abu Simbel are built during the reign of Rameses II.	1,280 BC

▷ Many Egyptian gods were pictured with animal heads. Horus, son of Isis and Osiris, was shown with a falcon's head. Anubis, god of death, had the head of a jackal.

ISIS AMUN OSIRIS ANUBIS CANOP

using salts and chemicals, and wrapped in linen bandages. It was then placed in a coffin. Even animals such as cats and monkeys were sometimes mummified. Many thousands of mummies must have been made, but only about 1,000 survive today.

Pyramids and rock tombs

Pyramids are the oldest stone structures in the world. There are more than 30, but the most famous are the three Great Pyramids at Giza. The biggest, which was built for the pharaoh Cheops, contains about 2 million blocks of limestone and is 460 feet high.

The pyramids were built as tombs, to keep the body of the dead king safe for eternity and perhaps (through their sky-pointing shape) to ease his passage to the heavens. The work of building such enormous monuments must have taken years, even with as many as 100,000 workers toiling to move the huge stone blocks up sloping ramps of sand.

Mighty as they were, the pyramids could not keep human robbers out. The treasures left inside each burial chamber with the king were invariably stolen.

△ The sun god Ra was often portrayed simply as a sun disk. He appeared in other forms too, including a cat, a bird, and a lion.

Tutankhamun

Tutankhamun became king of Egypt at the age of 9 and died when he was about 18. His tomb is one of more than 60 royal tombs around the Valley of the Kings. Its four rooms contained more than 5,000 objects – from ostrich feathers and model ships to a throne and a gold death mask.

△ Osiris, god of the dead, was often shown as a mummy on a throne, wearing the crown of Upper Egypt.

Abraham was the founder of the Hebrew people, according to the Bible. In about 1850 BC, he lived in the Sumerian city of Ur. Forced to leave his homeland because of unrest and war, he led his family northeast along the course of the Euphrates, and then west to settle in the land of Canaan.

The Jews

The Bible records that Abraham had two sons, Ishmael (the ancestor of the Arabs) and Isaac. Isaac had two sons, Esau and Jacob, and Jacob (also called Israel) had 12 sons. These sons became the heads of the Twelve Tribes, the Israelites of the Bible.

Exile in Egypt and Moses

One of Jacob's sons, Joseph, led the Israelites into Egypt after famine struck the land of Canaan. The Israelites became wealthy and influential, but under the rule of successive Egyptian pharaohs, the Israelites were forced into slavery. This slavery lasted until about 1250 BC, when Moses was commanded by God to lead the Israelites out of Egypt in what became known as the Exodus.

Moses was the great law-giver of Jewish history and religion. Jews believe that he received the Ten Commandments from God and taught his people to believe in one God. This belief in one God became the central pillar of the Jewish faith (and later of Christianity and Islam). Moses led the Israelites through the desert to Canaan, where they settled with the local Canaanites and Philistines. For a time,

BC/AD

2,000 1,750 1,500 1,250 1,000 750 500 250 1BC 1AD 250AD 500AD

Abraham journeys to Canaan.	1,850 BC
Probable date of Exodus from Egypt.	1,250 BC
Philistines conquer Israel.	1,050 BC
Saul chosen as king.	1,020 BC
King David unites the people. His son Solomon builds the Temple in Jerusalem.	1,010 BC
After the death of Solomon, ten northern tribes break away.	938 BC
Babylonians conquer Judah.	604 BC
Romans conquer Judah.	63 BC
Temple in Jerusalem is destroyed.	AD 66

▷ In this dramatic picture, the Israelites conquer the city of Jericho; at God's command the walls tumble down at the sound of the Israelite army shouting and banging drums.

▷ Moses, the leader of the Hebrew people, receives the two tablets from God. The stone tablets bear the Ten Commandments, as described in the Old Testament. They became the basis for Jewish law.

△ Jews believe that the Dome of the Rock, in Jerusalem, is built over the rock on which Abraham, on God's orders, prepared to sacrifice his son Isaac. Muslims believe that Muhammad rose to heaven from the same rock.

chosen men and women called *judges* led the tribes, but in about 1020 BC, the judge Samuel chose Saul to be the first king of Israel.

Israel and Judah

The Israelites settled in the hills of Canaan. The towns were held by their enemies, the Canaanites and Philistines. The Israelites, under King David, defeated the Philistines. After the death of Solomon, David's son, the kingdom split. Two southern tribes formed their own kingdom, Judah. The northern kingdom of Israel was more powerful but was weakened by royal squabbles and fierce religious disputes. The Assyrians overran Israel in 721 BC. It was crushed by Babylon in 604 BC, and most of the people were taken as slaves.

Exile and conquest

During this exile in Babylon, much of the Bible (Old Testament) took on the form it takes today. In 538 BC, the Persian king Cyrus, conqueror of Babylon, allowed the exiles to leave. Later, Judah became part of the Greek Empire. In 63 BC, the Romans conquered Judah, calling it Judea. In AD 66, the Jews rose in revolt, and the Romans retaliated by destroying the Temple.

King Solomon

Solomon was the son of David, the greatest Israelite king who ruled from 1010 to 970 BC. David defeated the Philistines and enlarged the kingdom, making Jerusalem his capital city. Solomon saw to the building of the Temple in Jerusalem, the most sacred place of the Jewish religion. After Solomon's death Israel split into two separate kingdoms.

△ The Dead Sea scrolls are ancient documents written on leather and copper. They contain the oldest known handwritten texts of books of the Bible.

The Phoenicians lived along the shores of the eastern Mediterranean (roughly where Lebanon is today). They were the most famous seamen of the ancient world. From 1,200 BC, Phoenicians made trade voyages across the Mediterranean and set up colonies as far away as Morocco and Spain.

Phoenicia and Assyria

The Phoenicians built strong, single-masted ships with one large sail and oars for use in windless conditions or river estuaries. When in unfamiliar territory, the Phoenicians would anchor offshore, land, and set out their goods in "silent trade" with local people.

The Phonecians' voyages took them beyond the Mediterranean, into the Atlantic Ocean. As explorers and traders, they helped to spread geographical and scientific knowledge. Their fleet was a powerful war weapon, and Phoenician ships were hired by the Persians to attack Greece.

Phoenician colonies

The most famous Phoenician colony was Carthage, in North Africa. Founded some time before 750 BC, Carthage was one of the great cities of the ancient world, with a harbor big enough for hundreds of ships. Its downfall came after a series of wars against the Greeks and final defeat by the Romans in the Punic Wars (264–146 BC).

▷ A Phoenician trading ship at a Mediterranean port. On the dockside, a scribe records the shipment as jars of oil, dye, and textiles are unloaded. In the background is a war galley with oars and a ram for attacking enemy ships.

Assyria independent under King Shamshi-Adad.	1,810 BC
Assyrian power great, then declines.	1,230s BC
Rise of Phoenicians. Tyre is an important city.	1,200 BC
First Phoenician colony in North Africa, at Utica.	1,140 BC
Assyrian power recovers. They conquer Babylon.	1,116 BC
Rise of Carthage.	750 BC
Assyrians attack Babylon.	729 BC
Sargon II starts to build palace at Khorsabad.	721 BC
End of Assyrian Empire.	612 BC
Nineveh destroyed by Medes, Babylonians, and Scythians.	609 BC

△ The Phoenicians were famous for their red-purple textiles. They used a dye extracted from mollusks. The name "Phoenician" comes from a Greek word meaning red-purple.

Ashurbanipal

From 668 to 627 BC, Assyria was ruled by a king called Ashurbanipal. He was the last great Assyrian ruler. Ashurbanipal made the city of Nineveh his capital. Here, he oversaw the building of a magnificent palace and library and ornate gardens.

The Assyrians

The Assyrians lived in the northern part of Mesopotamia (what is now northern Iraq). Their homeland was around the upper Tigris River. They were farmers who dug irrigation ditches to water their crops, the most important of which was barley. Numbers of people roamed the land more or less as bandits, and many more fought as soldiers. The Assyrians were feared throughout the Middle East as conquerors.

The rise of the Assyrians began in the 1800s BC. They expanded their trade networks as far as the Mediterranean, but were checked by the strength of the Babylonian king Hammurabi. By about 800 BC, they had a formidable army of cavalry, infantry, and archers. The Assyrians were expert at capturing towns, using wooden siege towers from which to scale or batter down the walls. They earned a reputation for extreme cruelty, slaughtering captives and looting from the peoples they defeated.

The Assyrian chief god was Assur, and the king was Assur's representative on Earth. The king was in charge of the army and the government, and he also controlled the temples and their priests. The Assyrians built on an impressive scale, constructing magnificent temples and palaces in cities such as Assur and Nineveh. Their greatest building was probably the citadel of King Sargon II, in Khorsabad, built in late 700 BC.

◁ Assyrian artists made wall relief sculptures showing winged spirits, hunting scenes, lions, and bulls. For sport, the Assyrian king and his nobles would kill captive lions released into special enclosures.

People had already lived in China for at least 500,000 years when farming began in the valleys of the Huang He (Yellow) and other rivers, more than 5,000 years ago.

China's Early Rulers

From a hazy mixture of history and legend, we learn that China's first ruling family was the Hsia. The legendary first emperors are said to have tamed the rivers, so that farmers could grow millet and wheat.

The first rulers known from archaeological evidence were the Shang. From about 1500 BC, they controlled the best farmland around the Huang He valley, and from there their power spread.

Shang slendor

The Shang kings were cruel, ruling in barbaric splendor. They built China's first cities. Shang bronzesmiths were experts at making cooking pots, tools, and weapons. Slave workers sweated to dig enormous pit tombs for dead kings, who were buried with treasures, chariots, and horses, and dozens of slain servants and soldiers to accompany their master into the next world. Farmers supplied food to the local nobleman, in return for protection.

The Zhou invaders

Shang rule lasted until 1122 BC. By then, according to Chinese history, the rulers had become tyrants. The Zhou from the west invaded and overthrew the last

▷ Ordinary people lived in villages, growing grains and raising chickens, pigs, sheep, and cattle. They used oxen and water buffalo to pull plows and dug ditches to water their fields.

BC

400,000
2,000
100,000
20,000
4,000
10,000

First farming villages in river valleys.	c. 3,000 BC
Traditional date for the discovery of silk by the wife of a Chinese emperor.	2,690 BC
Legendary dynasty of Hsia.	2,200 BC
China's first kings, the Shang. Use of bronze tools.	1,500 BC
The city of Anyang becomes the capital of China.	1,500 BC
Zhou dynasty.	1,122 BC
Period of unrest and civil wars.	770 BC
First emperor, Shih Huang-di of the Qin.	221 BC
Work starts on Great Wall to keep out the Hsiung-nu (Huns).	214 BC

△ Fierce warriors helped to keep the Shang rulers, China's first dynasty, in power for more than 400 years.

△ This food vessel, from the time of the Shang dynasty, is decorated with intricate animal motifs. It is in the form of a tiger protecting the body of a man.

Chinese writing

An example of Chinese writing on silk. The Chinese wrote in picture signs and made up about 50,000 characters. The first important work of Chinese literature, a collection of poems, dates from before 1000 BC.

Shang king. The new kings were backed by powerful nobles. Nobles built forts and walled towns to defend their lands against one another. They also fought off fierce nomads who swept down from the northern steppes on sturdy horses.

Warring states

No Zhou ruler was strong enough to control all China. For 500 years, small warring states fought for power. Yet China still prospered. Farmers grew more food, and metalworkers mastered the new skills of making iron tools. Potters, jewelers, tailors, and chariot-makers were kept busy. Scholars attended the nobles' courts, seeking work as government officials. Trade grew, and people began to use money.

The first emperor

The Qin ruler Shih Huang-di fought his way to power as first emperor of all China in 221 BC. He crushed the power of the nobles, handing over the government to hired officials (who did what he told them). He ordered everyone to speak the same language and to use the same weights and measures. Thousands of people were forced to build new roads and canals, and the emperor also built the Great Wall, which linked up older walls to create the biggest frontier defense on the earth.

◁ The Shang kings were superstitious. They consulted "oracle bones" before making any important decisions. A soothsayer would read the signs in animal bones cracked by heat, and advise the king accordingly.

BC

400,000

2,000

4,000

100,000

10,000

20,000

War has been a part of life for as long as humans have existed. Prehistoric people fought for territory and food, using rocks and sticks as weapons. Later, they used stone-tipped spears and bows and arrows.

War and Weapons

The discovery of bronze in about 3500 BC brought the first revolution in weaponry. Bronze swords and spear points were sharper than stone and bone weapons. Iron was even stronger still. Peoples of the Near East, such as the Hittites, were the first to master iron-making.

Armies and armor

Each of the ancient Near East superpowers rounded up civilians to serve in armies for the conquest of other countries, and for defense against enemies. To protect themselves, soldiers began wearing armor on their bodies. By the time of the Trojan War, about 1200 BC, armor was made from metal plates fastened with leather thongs. Soldiers

A sculpture shows an Egyptian king pictured defeating an enemy.	3,100 BC
Sumerians make bronze war axes and spear points.	2,500 BC
Body armor used by Egyptians and Mesopotamians.	2,000 BC
Chariots in use in Egypt and Near East. Sickle-shaped swords of bronze.	1,500 BC
First iron swords. End of Trojan War.	1,200 BC
Assyrian armies include infantry, cavalry, and chariots.	800 BC
Chainmail made from iron links replaces bronze armor.	500 BC
Sparta has the first full-time army in the Greek world.	400s BC

▷Assyrian troops used wheeled siege towers with iron-tipped rams to batter down the walls of enemy towns.

54

△ Egyptian soldiers fought with *spears, axes, clubs, javelins (throwing spears), swords,* and *bows and arrows.* Trumpeters blew signal calls to direct the troops.

△ Axe heads were made from bronze (shown here) and iron. A popular weapon, particularly among Chinese troops, was a halberd, a long spear with an axelike head.

Hittite charioteers

The Hittites, a fierce people from Anatolia (modern Turkey), were the first to use chariots in war. Hittite archers fired their arrows from these chariots, giving them a great advantage over the enemy.

wore metal helmets to protect the head, and carried shields (usually round or rectangular). Some warriors scorned armor – the Greeks and Celts sometimes fought practically naked.

The first organized armies

Kings had small bodyguards of trained soldiers, including chariot-drivers, but they still relied on untrained peasants as foot soldiers. The Assyrians organized the first "professional" army, and were greatly feared because of its ferocity. An Assyrian army included cavalry (soldiers on horses) and infantry (soldiers on foot).

Assyrian soldiers wore chainmail armor and fought with iron swords and spears. Archers rode into battle on chariots, then sheltered behind basketwork shields to fire and reload. Slingers hurled stones, often farther than a javelin.

Infantry and cavalry

In China, soldiers traditionally fought on foot and in huge armies (as many as 100,000 men). Facing marauders on horseback, the Chinese had to become horse-soldiers too. The Chinese composite bow of wood and bone had a longer range than a simple bow. Chinese archers also used crossbows.

There was the clash of shields, of spears and the fury of men cased in bronze... then there were mingled the groaning and the crowing of men killed and killing.

from THE ILIAD, HOMER (8TH CENTURY BC)

Nothing is known about Homer for certain. Tradition states he lived near Greece and wrote two great poems about the Trojan wars: The Iliad and The Odyssey.

Other civilizations of Africa were developing to the south of Egypt. These peoples traded with the land of the pharaohs and with each other along the rivers and across the mighty Sahara Desert.

African Civilizations

Before 6000 BC, the Sahara had a wetter climate than now. The herders and hunters who lived among its lakes left rock paintings showing a Saharan grassland and wildlife very different from the desert of today. About 3500 BC, the Sahara began to dry up, but people still followed old trade routes across the spreading desert.

A network of trade routes linked the peoples of West Africa with others in the Nile Valley and in North Africa. In Africa, the Stone Age and Iron Age overlapped. Herders became ironsmiths, moving with their herds and tools and spreading the use of iron across Africa.

Kingdom of Kush

The kingdom of Kush was in Nubia (modern Sudan). It lay in the shadow of Egypt and was at first ruled by Egyptians. Its chief cities were Napata on the River Nile, and later Meroe, a city which grew in importance because iron was mined close by. Meroe was impressive, with stone and brick palaces, baths, and the temple of the Kush lion-god Apedemeck. Kushite kings were buried in pyramid-shaped tombs beside the Nile.

Rivers and lakes in Sahara start to dry up as climate changes.	3,500 BC
Origins of Kush.	2,000 BC
Sahara is a desert. Egyptians invade Kush.	1,500 BC
Iron-working in northern Africa.	1,000 BC
Traditional date for founding of Carthage.	814 BC
Kush throws off Egyptian rule. Kushites conquer Egypt.	750 BC
Nok culture in West Africa. Iron-working spreads into east Africa.	500 BC
Kushite city of Meroe at its finest.	300 BC

△ Many of the African kingdoms and peoples traded with the Egyptians to the north. Egyptian traders wanted copper, ivory and ebony, animal skins, cattle, and slaves. They paid for these goods with gold, barley, wheat, and papyrus.

△ *A section of a wall painting from a tomb of ancient Egypt. It shows a group of Nubians offering various gifts to the Egyptian pharaoh.*

Carthage

The city-state of Carthage had two large harbors, crammed with naval and trading vessels. It was overlooked by the Byrsa, a huge walled fortress on the hill above.

The Nok people

South and west of the great desert, trade caravans carrying salt and slaves across the Sahara gathered at small towns. The market towns grew into cities and some, such as Djenne in Mali, still thrive.

The Niger River valley was the home of the Nok people. Their society developed from about 500 BC. Most people were farmers, but others were merchants, ironsmiths, and craftworkers. Each town had its own king. He ruled over a community of large family groups, in which three or four generations lived together. Temples honored ancestors and heroes. Nok artists made elegant clay heads and figures of people.

The city-state of Carthage

Before the rise of Rome, the city-state of Carthage, in what is now Tunisia, ruled the Mediterranean. Traditionally founded in 814 BC by Phoenicians from Tyre, Carthage grew rich on trade.

The Carthaginians were daring seamen, sailing their oared ships across the Mediterranean and into the Atlantic. An explorer named Hanno is said to have sailed as far south as the Guinea coast of West Africa. Carthage remained rich and powerful for 600 years, until it challenged Rome in three costly wars and lost.

Carthage had wealth and power; and it had skill and ferocity in war. Juno is said to have loved Carthage best of all cities in the world.

THE AENEID, VIRGIL (70-19 BC)

Virgil's Aeneid *tells the story of Aeneas, who visited Carthage before he founded the city of Rome.*

△ *Nok sculptures are made of terracotta, a kind of earthenware. Some are life-size. There are figures of people, animals, and heads.*

BC

400,000

2,000

100,000

4,000

20,000

10,000

The first people to settle the Americas, crossed from Asia and lived as wandering hunters or settled along the coasts in fishing communities. Groups of people traveled farther south, through the forests and prairies, across the jungles and mountains of Panama, and into the grasslands, rainforests, and mountains of South America.

The Americas

Many of these first settlers of the Americas continued to live as hunter-gatherers. Some became farmers and settled in villages which grew into towns. Two groups developed the Americas earliest civilizations – in Mesoamerica (Mexico and Central America) and in Peru on the west coast of South America.

The Olmecs of Mesoamerica

The Olmecs flourished between about 1200 and 400 BC. They made pottery and cleared the jungle to grow crops. They traveled along rivers on rafts and canoes and settled near rivers. These villages grew to become the first towns in Mexico and Central America. The Olmecs believed in nature gods of the forest and of fertility, and in their towns, they built earth mounds with straw and mud temples on top to worship these gods.

Farmers grew corn, chilis, beans, and squash. People also collected shellfish and hunted forest animals with spears and nets. Olmec society was ruled by a small group of priest-nobles, who carried out temple ceremonies, owned the best farmland, and controlled trade in valuable raw materials, such as jade.

▷ The Olmec people constructed large stepped pyramids from earth. They held religious ceremonies and worshiped their gods in temples built on top of these pyramids.

Stone Age hunters move into the Andes Mountains.	8,000 BC
People in Peru grow beans, corn, and other crops.	7,000 BC
Cotton weaving begins in Peru.	2,500 BC
First Mayan languages – in Mexico.	.2,500 BC
Religious centers, with stone temples, built in Peru.	2,000 BC
First use of iron in South America.	c. 1,500 BC
Growth of settlements in Olmec region.	1,200– 900 BC
Rise of Chavin civilization.	1,000 BC
Gold-working is widespread in South America.	800 BC

▷ In modern Peru, craftworkers carry on the traditions of their Chavin ancestors, producing colorful handwoven textiles. Designs such as these have been produced in Peru for approximately 3,000 years.

Stone heads and sacrifices

The most remarkable Olmec remains are huge stone heads, some 6.5 feet high, and other carvings of human figures with flattened features. They may represent human sacrifices. Prisoners taken in war, or contestants in a ritual ball game, may have been killed as sacrifices to the Olmec jaguar-god. Carvings show priests wearing jaguar masks. Some symbols cut into stones may be numbers, suggesting the Olmecs had a calendar.

Civilizations of Peru

In South America, people living in the Andes foothills had become farmers by about 1000 BC. They built the first towns in South America. One of the earliest civilizations of the Andes was Chavin de Huantar in Peru.

Like the Olmecs, the Chavins were ruled by priests, who later became nobles serving a king. They set up rows of stone pillars that look like ceremonial routes. They also carved stone heads and sculptures of jaguars, snakes, and condors. The Chavins used wool from alpacas and vicuñas to weave textiles. Although they had only stone tools, they made beautiful gold, silver, and copper jewelry.

△ The mysterious stone head sculptures made by the Olmecs may have been totems, made to protect the people from enemies or natural disaster. Using stone chisels and hammers, the Olmec people worked on their sculptures in teams.

Chavin farmers

The Chavin people grew corn, potatoes, and peppers. They cut terraces into hillsides and became expert at irrigation (channeling water) to cultivate the dry land and mountain slopes. Families kept llamas, guinea pigs, and dogs for meat.

△ An Olmec figurine carved from jade. Skilled craftworkers made carvings and sculptures from stone, clay, and jade.

By about 1000 BC, the civilizations of North Africa and the Near East had begun to exchange ideas. These civilizations were linked by trade routes. New ideas traveled between civilizations as groups of people moved around the world, for trade and also for conquest.

Empires East and West

People moved overland with their animal herds or set sail in ships to settle in new lands. In Egypt, China, India, and Mesopotamia civilization had introduced new ways of life. These involved farming, living in towns, trade, organized religion, and government by kings. The people who shared these common experiences were more likely to adapt to life under a common ruler, and this encouraged the growth of new empires.

Building empires

These empires brought together different peoples who spoke different languages and sometimes lived far apart. Strong rulers, backed by powerful armies, struggled to win empires and then hold them together. Sometimes the unifying force in building an empire was the will of a dynamic ruler, such

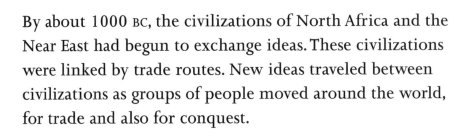

as Alexander the Great. At other times it was the power of armies, religious zeal, or the attraction of a way of life that offered greater peace and prosperity for all.

America, Australasia, and Africa south of the Sahara were still untouched by the civilizations of Europe and Asia. However, as contacts between the empires of the East and the West grew, the chain of civilization added new links. By about AD 100, when the Roman Empire was at its height, civilization in one form or another existed from western Europe across to China in the East.

Cultural areas

The empires of Greece, Asoka's India, Han China, and Rome created "cultural areas" that were larger than any earlier in history. Inside these empires ideas, knowledge, religious beliefs, and culture could spread and take root. Their effect on the history of the world has been to leave behind a cultural legacy that is still very much part of our lives today.

Persia grew from the rubble of the defeated Assyrian Empire. In 612 BC Nineveh, the Assyrian capital, fell. This left Babylon and Media to wrestle over the remains of the empire.

The Persian Empire

In 550 BC the Persian king Cyrus defeated the Medes and made himself ruler of a new empire. It was known as the Achaemenid Empire, after an ancestor of Cyrus who was named Achaemenes.

The Persians

The Persians were Iranians, whose ancestors had ridden on horses from the plains of central Asia. Many Persians lived as nomads, but their rulers built mighty cities with stone palaces. The greatest Persian city was Persepolis, built to the orders of the king, Darius I, in about 518 BC. A Persian man could have several wives, but the king could marry only women selected from six noble families.

The god of light

The Persians believed in sun and sky gods, and gods of nature. They built no temples, but worshipped on the tops of mountains. The chief

Medes set up a kingdom in what is now Iran.	700 BC
Cyrus the Great rebels against the Medes. Achaemenid Empire founded.	550 BC
Cyrus conquers Lydia.	545 BC
Cambyses, son of Cyrus, defeats the Egyptian king Psamtik III.	525 BC
Darius I becomes ruler of Persia.	522 BC
Battle of Marathon halts Persian invasion of Greece.	490 BC
Battles of Thermopylae and Salamis. Greeks defeat Xerxes, son of Darius I.	480 BC
Alexander the Great conquers Persia.	331 BC

△ The ruins of Persepolis, the capital of the Persian Empire, lie near the modern city of Shiraz, in southwest Iran. Part of the ruined palace of Darius I is still standing.

△ Ten thousand soldiers called the Immortals formed the core of the Persian army. Each spearman or archer was instantly replaced if killed or sick.

Mithra

Although Ahura Mazda was the chief god of Persia, many people also worshipped Mithra, seen here killing a bull as a sacrifice to renew life. Later, Mithraism was popular among the Romans.

god of Persia was Ahura Mazda, a winged god of light. Many people followed the teachings of the prophet Zarathustra (Zoroaster), who lived between 1400 and 1000 BC. He taught that life was a struggle between good (light) and evil (darkness).

War and empire

The Persians were good fighters, with cavalry and iron weapons, and their military energy proved too strong for their neighbors. The great soldier Cyrus conquered Lydia and the Greek colonies in Asia Minor, and won control of Babylon, too. When he died, his son Cambyses conquered Egypt. Civil war broke out after Cambyses' death, but order was restored by Darius, a relative of Cambyses.

△ Darius I ruled Persia from 521 to 486 BC. He encouraged trade through the use of coins and new canals.

The wars with Greece

Darius was an able administrator. He organized the empire into provinces, each governed by a satrap. A satrap was like a king, but the king of kings was the emperor himself, whose word was final. Darius and his son Xerxes tried to bring Greece within the empire, but failed. The Greeks beat the Persians at the battle of Marathon in 490 BC, and the naval defeat at Salamis was a major setback. But Persia stayed rich and powerful until 331 BC, when it was conquered by Alexander the Great.

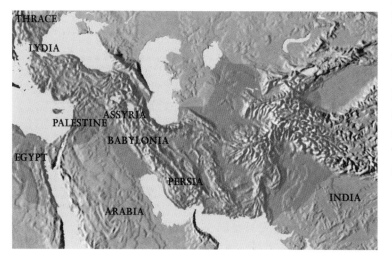

◁ The Persian Empire stretched from North Africa as far as the Caucasus Mountains in the north, and the borders of India in the east.

BC

Ancient Greece, practically cut off by sea from Asia Minor (Turkey), had escaped conquest by the warlike empires of the Near East. In this land of mountains and plains, small city-states grew up independent and proud.

The Rise of Greece

Farmland was so scarce that many Greeks left home and wandered in search of new lands. They built fine oared ships, and Greek colonists and traders could be found from one end of the Mediterranean Sea to the other.

Greek cities

Living in their small cities, the Greeks developed a remarkable system of government. Each city was enclosed by a wall for protection. Inside the city was a fort, called an *acropolis*, on a hill or mountain top. An open space, the *agora*, was used as a market and meeting place, where the men of the city met to agree how the city should be governed.

Athens and Sparta

The two states of Athens and Sparta became rivals. Athens was rich and cultured. Its citizens included astronomers, mathematicians, thinkers, writers, and artists. This was a society with slaves, but its finest rulers, such as Pericles (from about 495 to 429 BC) had vision, and its government was the first real democracy – although only men could take part.

Mycenean culture draws to a close in Greece.	1200 BC
First recorded Olympic Games.	776 BC
Nobles overthrow kings in city-states.	750 BC
Greeks found colonies around the Mediterranean Sea.	500s BC
Athens becomes a democracy, with a council of 500 men to govern it.	508 BC
Greeks defeat Persian invasions.	490–479 BC
Start of Athens' Golden Age under Pericles.	477 BC
War between Sparta and Athens, won by Sparta.	431–404 BC

▷ In 480 BC the Greek fleet defeated the Persians at the battle of Salamis. Arrows, stones, and spears rained between the ships, but the Greeks' key weapon was the ramming power of their galleys, driven at speed by banks of rowers.

△ Greek foot soldiers were called hoplites. A man had to buy his own armor, made of bronze. On the march, a slave would carry the heavy armor for his master.

Phalanx

In battle, hoplites (foot soldiers) marched in a tight group called a phalanx. Each rank kept in formation, with shields before them and their long spears pointed at the enemy as they advanced.

Athens had the best navy in Greece. Sparta had the best army. Sparta's economy, like that of Athens, was based on slave workers. There was no democracy. Sports were encouraged, and girls as well as boys were expected to be fit and athletic. Sparta was like an army camp, in which everyone was expected to obey. Boys as young as seven were taken from home and trained to be soldiers.

War with Persia

Only fear of foreign invasion made Athens and Sparta fight side by side, as they did to drive off the Persians. First Darius of Persia, and then his son Xerxes, tried to conquer Greece.

The Greeks fought desperately, at Marathon and at Thermopylae, where a small Spartan rearguard held off the Persian army. The naval victory at Salamis and the land battle of Plataea saved Greece from becoming part of the Persian Empire.

Under Pericles, Athens enjoyed a "Golden Age". The city was rebuilt, and the Parthenon temple was erected on the Acropolis. But still Athens and Sparta could not live together in peace. A war between them, called the Peloponnesian War, lasted 27 years. Athens was brought to its knees and was never the same again.

△ Broken pieces of pottery were used for letter-writing in the Greek world. Clay fragments are still found today, with business notes written on them.

"Herodotus... here displays his inquiry so that great and marvelous deeds – some displayed by Greeks, some by barbarians – may not be without their glory.

THE HISTORIES, HERODOTUS (c. 485-45 BC)

Herodotus aimed to record the causes of these wars, as well as the wars themselves.

In many ways, ancient Greece was the birthplace of Western civilization. In the small Greek cities, and especially in Athens, people gathered to discuss new ideas. The word "philosophy" comes from two Greek words meaning love of wisdom, and it is to the Greeks that we owe many of our ideas about beauty, justice, and government.

Greek Art and Science

First record of Olympic Games.	776 BC
Iliad and Odyssey stories first collected.	700 BC
Start of Athens' Golden Age.	477 BC
The Parthenon in Athens is completed.	432 BC
Birth of the philosopher Plato.	429 BC
Writings of Herodotus, called the "Father of History."	400s BC
Death of Socrates.	399 BC
Birth of philosopher and scientist Aristotle.	384 BC

The Greeks were never united as one nation, but they shared the same language and religion, and many similar ideas about the world.

Science and philosophy

The ancient Greeks were pioneers in medicine, mathematics, and science. They looked at the world in the light of logic and reason and made some fundamental discoveries. In the 400s BC Democritus declared

△ In a Greek theater the actors performed on a flat platform called the orchestra. Audiences sat in the open air, on a hillside, although there were seats, and some people brought their own cushions. Audiences might watch four plays in a single day.

that everything was made of atoms. Aristarchus of Samos (200s BC) knew the Earth was round, and even suggested that it traveled around the Sun.

The names of great Greek scientists such as Archimedes are familiar to this day. Socrates, Plato, and Aristotle were three of the greatest philosophers of that, or any other, age. But the common people were often suspicious of their questioning and free thinking. Socrates was sentenced to death in 399 BC for his views.

The gods

The Greeks believed in many gods. Each city had its own protector god or goddess, and families made offerings to household gods too. The gods were thought to live on Mount Olympus, under the rule of Zeus, the king of the gods. Greek gods were immortal, but they had human characteristics too – such as displaying love and jealousy.

Art and literature

The Greeks built many beautiful temples to their gods. They developed an elegant architecture based on mathematical rules and the use of three styles for the stone columns that are a feature of many Greek buildings.

Greek sculptors portrayed the human body in superb lifelike detail. Music also flourished, often accompanying dances or stories. The most famous stories were the heroic tales of Homer, but the Greeks also invented theater as we know it, and some of their plays are still performed, in many languages other than Greek.

△ The Parthenon in Athens was built to honor the city's protector, the goddess Athene. Her gold and ivory decorated statue was inside the great hall, enclosed by columns which supported the roof like a forest of stone trees.

△ Greek actors wore masks to show what kind of character (comic or tragic) they played. The finest play-writers were the Athenian dramatists Aeschylus, Sophocles, Euripides (who wrote tragedies), and Aristophanes (who wrote comedies).

Olympic Games

The Olympic Games were first recorded in 776 BC. People from all over Greece came to take part in or watch the Games, held every four years at Olympia. Sports such as running and discus throwing were to honor Zeus. The winners received crowns of olive leaves.

The Greek way of life spread around the Mediterranean, as traders and colonists settled in new places. The Greeks were scornful of foreigners, calling them "barbarians". Yet Greek culture could be found across southern Europe and North Africa, far away from Greece itself.

Daily Life and Trade in Greece

Greeks begin to settle in colonies outside Greece.	750 BC
Colonists found city-states in Sicily, Crete, Cyprus, and along the coast of Africa.	750–600 BC
Greek colonists establish the city of Massilia (modern Marseilles).	c. 600 BC
Greeks begin to use coins minted from silver.	500 BC
Classical period of Greek civilization.	500–336 BC
The Peloponnesian War between Athens and Sparta.	431–404 BC
Macedonians defeat the Greeks.	338 BC

Greek homes were built around a central courtyard, cool and airy, where the family slaves prepared food on an open fire and there was a small shrine to the household god. Many houses were made without windows in the outer walls. This design kept out both the hot sun and thieves.

Business in the town

Greek towns were a center for government, religion, and trade. In the town's marketplace, farmers sold produce such as cheese, wheat, meat, eggs, sheepskins, and olive oil. Fast-food sellers did a brisk lunchtime trade in sausages and pancakes. In the dusty lanes around the

△ In a Greek country house, the family relaxed in a shady courtyard during the heat of the day. People ate with their fingers, lying on wooden couches, as slaves brought in the dishes and a musician played on pipes or the lyre. Men and women wore a chiton, a cloth square draped over the body and fastened by a pin at the shoulder.

△ Much of what we know about how the Greeks lived comes from pictures on vases. The pictures show wars and stories from mythology, but also daily activities such as hunting, farming, and fishing.

Cargo ships

Greek ships were wooden, with one square sail. Cargo ships were rounder and slower than war galleys, and often had no oars. In ships with no deck, skins or cloths covered the cargo.

marketplace, skilled craftworkers carried on their businesses. They included sandal-makers, potters, tanners (who prepared animal skins), armorers, blacksmiths, and jewelers.

Farming and fishing

Wherever they settled, Greek farmers relied on three main crops: grapes, olives, and grain. Oxen pulled wooden plows, but much of the work of sowing and harvesting was done by hand. Grapes were made into wine. Wine and olive oil were stored in large two-handled jars called amphoras. Olive oil was used for cooking, as a fuel in lamps, and for washing (the Greeks did not use soap).

Most colonies were near the sea, and fishermen sold freshly caught fish in the market. Greek colonists enjoyed stories about sea creatures, sea gods, and the heroic legends of "the old country" – the peninsula of mainland Greece.

Traders

Greek traders sailed into the Black Sea and along the coast of North Africa. Merchant ships probably went beyond the Mediterranean, as far north as Britain. Trade with the "barbarians" (people who spoke no Greek) was done by silent exchange of goods, more being offered until both parties were happy with the deal.

△ A portrait of a Greek woman on a fragment of pottery. Greek women spent most of their time around the home, organizing the household and supervising the family's slaves.

Thucydides the Athenian wrote the history of the war fought between Athens and Sparta in the belief that it was going to be a great war.

HISTORY OF THE PELOPONNESIAN WAR, THUCYDIDES

The Greek historian Thucydides fought in the Peloponnesian War before writing his history.

One man took the Greek world into a new age, looking east towards Asia. He was Alexander of Macedonia, known to history as Alexander the Great.

Alexander the Great

Alexander was the son of the soldier-king Philip of Macedonia and Olympias, princess of Epirus. Philip's power had grown while Athens and Sparta were at war. He made his small northern kingdom a power to be feared. The Macedonian army joined with the Greeks in 338 BC to defeat the Persians.

The victory against the Persians brought unity, but in Philip's moment of triumph he was cut down by an assassin. His son Alexander, only 20, became king. Alexander had been taught by the wise scholar Aristotle and had shown a love for learning. But his greatest gift was ruthless generalship. His first act was to crush a revolt by the people of Thebes to secure his grip on Greece.

Alexander's campaigns

In just 13 years, Alexander led his army out of Europe and into Asia. He started off with 35,000 men. First, he crushed the might of Persia and swept through Syria into Egypt. There he was welcomed as a liberator from Persian rule. He founded the city of Alexandria, which became one of the great cities of learning and trade of the ancient world.

From Egypt, Alexander marched into Mesopotamia and Babylonia. The Persians had regrouped, but he defeated their army at Gaugamela. Alexander burned the Persian city of Persepolis, and shortly

▷ On his horse Bucephalus, Alexander leads his troops into battle at Issus in 333 BC. The horse was said to be too spirited and wild until tamed by Alexander.

Philip II becomes king of Macedonia.	359 BC
Birth of Alexander.	356 BC
Philip defeats Persians at battle of Chaeronea.	338 BC
Philip is murdered. Alexander becomes king of Macedonia.	336 BC
Battle of Issus. Alexander defeats the Persians.	333 BC
Alexander conquers Persian Empire.	331 BC
Alexander's army enters India.	326 BC
Death of Alexander.	323 BC
Separate states emerge across the empire.	311 BC

△ *Alexander, shown here, believed that the Greek hero Achilles was his ancestor. He learned by heart the account of Achilles' deeds in the epic poem, the Iliad.*

Alexandria

The city of Alexandria in Egypt was founded in 332 BC. It became famous for its library, established in the 200s BC by the Egyptian kings Ptolemy I and Ptolemy II. Its lighthouse was one of the Seven Wonders of the Ancient World.

afterwards the Persian king Darius was killed by his own side.

Afghanistan and India

This astonishing campaign took Alexander's army eastward into Afghanistan and as far north as Tashkent in central Asia, before he turned south toward India. In 326 BC Alexander entered what is now Pakistan and defeated the Indian king Porus. He hoped to find the mythical river Ocean, which encircled the world, but his troops would go no farther. They endured a terrible return journey across the desert of Gedrosia.

△ *Alexander imposed a single system of money throughout his lands. He was keen to promote trade and commerce across the empire too.*

The world empire

Alexander decided to make Babylon the capital of his new "world empire." He married a Persian princess and hired soldiers of all nationalities. Everywhere he went, Greek ideas went too. Alexander was planning new conquests when he became ill and died in Babylon, just before his 33rd birthday.

Without Alexander's genius, his empire soon broke up into smaller states ruled by his generals. The strongest of these were Macedonia, Egypt, and the Asian kingdom of Seleucus Nicator.

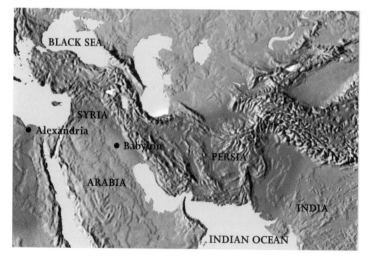

◁ *Alexander's empire stretched from Greece to North Africa and as far east as India and Afghanistan. He ruled most of what was then thought of as "the civilized world." After his death, Alexander was buried in the city of Alexandria.*

71

By about 600 BC India was a jigsaw puzzle of kingdoms and tribal states. In the state of Kapilavastu, Gautama Buddha, founder of one of the world's great religions, was born in about 566 BC.

New Empires in India

Most people in India at that time followed the ancient religious beliefs of Hinduism. However, the teachings of Buddha found favor with powerful rulers, and Buddhism spread quickly in India.

The rise of Chandragupta

By the 400s BC the most powerful state in India was the kingdom of Magadha, which had its capital at Patna. Yet its control was weakening.
It is said that while Alexander the Great was marching into India in 325 BC, he met a young Indian ruler named Chandragupta Maurya. Chandragupta also had ambition. He seized the throne of Magadha and took

Birth of Buddha.	566 BC
Chandragupta rules small kingdom of Nanda.	321 BC
Alexander the Great invades India.	326 BC
Chandragupta wins control of Greek-held lands in India and Afghanistan.	303 BC
Bindusara succeeds his father Chandragupta.	297 BC
Asoka Maurya becomes emperor.	272 BC
Asoka conquers Kalinga (Orissa) and becomes a Buddhist.	261 BC
Death of Asoka.	232 BC

△ A detail of stone carving on the Buddhist stupa at Sanchi in India, dating from the 100s BC. It shows a parade with musicians and a ruler being driven in a two-horse chariot.

△ Buddhism is still one of the world's foremost religions, with devotees all over the modern world.

△ The extent of the Mauryan Empire during the reign of Asoka. He extended the limits of the empire until most of India was under Mauryan rule.

△ The carved stone lions on the pillar at Sarnath have become a national emblem for India.

Asoka

Asoka was probably the greatest ruler of ancient India. He became a vegetarian after adopting Buddhism and tried to follow Buddha's teachings of non-violence. After years of soldiering and killing, Asoka believed that everyone should respect all living things. He travelled in his empire, hearing the ideas and problems of his subjects.

advantage of the upheaval caused by Alexander's campaigns to seize a large chunk of territory in the north.

The Mauryan Empire

So began the Mauryan Empire. Chandragupta's son Bindusara continued and extended his conquests. The old capital of Patna (then called Pataliputra) was now the center of an empire that stretched from the Arabian Sea in the west to the Bay of Bengal in the east. Only the southern tip of the Indian subcontinent lay outside its territory.

Emperor Asoka

Chandragupta's grandson Asoka was the greatest emperor of ancient India. He took government very seriously, reforming taxes, encouraging trade and farming, and building walled cities with pleasant houses and paved streets. His officials traveled the country, building roads (including what Indians now know as the Great Trunk Road) and collecting taxes from peasant farmers in villages.

Asoka was born a Hindu, but he became a Buddhist. He then gave up war, sickened by the slaughter he had seen during his conquest of Orissa in the southeast. He urged his people to be tolerant of others and to respect all life.

Asoka's laws

Asoka made new laws and had them inscribed on stone pillars set up all across his empire. There are ten still standing today, the most famous at Sarnath near the Hindu holy city of Benares (Varanasi). The tall pillar at Sarnath is topped with four carved lions and four wheels. The wheel, often referred to as the "wheel of life," is an important symbol of Buddhism.

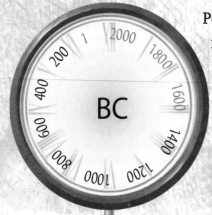

Peoples all over the world formed systems of beliefs in powers greater than their own. The earliest religions were connected with the forces of nature – the sun, the moon, wind, water, rocks and trees – and with animals.

Eastern Religions

The great religions of the world all began in Asia. Three of them – Judaism, Christianity, and Islam – began in the same area of west Asia. Hinduism and Buddhism began in India.

In the civilizations of the ancient world, the king was often seen as the gods' representative. The god-king defended his people. The Egyptians believed in many gods, and in a life after death. One pharaoh, Akhenaton, tried to replace the old gods with a 'one-god' faith based on sun worship. The experiment was short-lived.

Rig Vedas, earliest Hindu holy songs, written in India.	1500 BC
Jews leave Egypt (the *Exodus*). Moses receives the Ten Commandments.	1200 BC
Hindu *Upanishads,* or holy books, name a supreme spirit called Brahman.	700 BC
Zarathrustra (Zoroaster) in Persia.	*c.* 600s BC
The scholar Confucius teaches in China.	500s BC
Lao-tzu writes the *Tao Te Ching,* about the unity of all things in nature.	500s BC
Jainism, in India, founded by a wise man named Mahavira.	500 BC
Buddhism spreads in India after Asoka becomes a Buddhist.	200s BC

△ Buddhism was taught by a prince named Gautama Buddha. In this picture he is shown meditating under a shady bodhi tree in an Indian village.

74

△ Hindu sculptures of gods and goddesses are full of energy. The four-armed Vishnu is the preserver of the Universe. He is one of Hinduism's two main gods – the other is Shiva.

India

Hinduism is the oldest of the Asian beliefs. There are many Hindu gods, and many rules that govern foods, behavior, festivals, and even which jobs people may do.

Buddhism began in India in the 500s BC and was later spread by missionaries to Burma and China. In its birthplace of India, Buddhism practically died out. It was different from other religions in having no god or gods. Its followers were taught to escape the sufferings of life by desiring nothing. Another Indian religion, Jainism, forbade its followers to kill any living thing, even an insect.

Judaism

The Jews were the first people in Europe and Asia to put their faith in one god. They believed that they were a chosen people, who owed their escape from slavery in Egypt and Babylon to a supreme God whom they called Yahweh (the Lord). God gave the Ten Commandments (laws) to Moses, and prophets delivered messages from God. Jews believed that God would send a messiah, or saviour, to bring justice and peace. Later, followers of Jesus Christ, a Jew, believed he was the Messiah (the Son of God).

Confucius

In China, people worshipped their ancestors and nature spirits. In the 500s BC, a scholar named Confucius taught a system of "right behavior" which has influenced Chinese government and society ever since. He taught loyalty to the family, worship of ancestors, and obedience to the laws of society.

△ A bronze statue of Buddha. The name Buddha means "the enlightened one."

The first emperor of China, Shih Huang-di, created enormous upheaval. The building of the Great Wall was just one sign of this upheaval, for the emperor was a ruthless tyrant. Millions of poor Chinese were forced to work as laborers on the Great Wall and other vast building projects.

Han Rule in China

Only four years after the emperor's death, the army and the mass of peasants were up in arms. From this rebellion emerged a new dynasty, the Han. The first Han emperor was Liu Pang, a minor official turned soldier, whose parents had been peasants themselves.

BC/AD

End of the Qin dynasty.	206 BC
Liu Pang becomes the first Han emperor.	202 BC
Start of Wu-ti's reign. Wars against the Hun.	140 BC
Wang Mang becomes emperor, briefly founding the Hsin dynasty.	AD 9
Huns raid China and burn Chang-an.	AD 23
Han dynasty restored by emperor Liu Hsiu.	AD 25
Buddhism has reached China by this time.	AD 100
Han power begins to decline.	AD 125
End of the Han dynasty.	AD 220

The Han emperors

The Han rulers made the city of Chang-an their capital. It was defended by thick walls, 60 feet high in places. The emperor lived in a magnificent palace, among his wives, concubines, courtiers, and guards.

Chinese rulers were superstitious, employing court magicians and fortune-tellers. During the period of Han rule, large stone statues were placed outside tombs. There were also enormous figures of Buddha, for Buddhism reached China in the first century AD.

Most ordinary people lived in one-room shacks and were very poor. Merchants were not allowed to live within the city walls. They were considered inferior to wheat farmers or women who reared silkworms.

China's trade links

It was during the Han dynasty that Chinese traders first had regular

△ A bustling street in the Chinese city of Chang-an (modern Xian). Traders regulated by city officials sold everything from livestock to jewelery. Scribes, artists, and craftworkers were kept busy in what was, in the 100s BC, probably the world's biggest city.

△ These soldiers are part of the huge army of terracotta figures buried near the tomb of the first Chinese emperor, Shi Huang-di. As well as thousands of warriors, the burial army also included clay horses and chariots. The figures were placed in three pits inside the large complex surrounding the emperor's tomb.

The Silk Road

The Silk Road stretched 2,500 miles across central Asia. Chinese traders traveled along this route, bringing their brightly colored silks to sell to merchants in the ports and cities of Europe.

contact with the West and with an empire as large as China's — Rome. From Chang-an, traders followed the Silk Road, crossing the smaller empires of Kushan and Parthia to reach the Mediterranean shores and the Roman world. Chinese silk fetched a high price, for the secret of making silk was unknown in the West.

Attacks from the Huns

Fearing attack from the Hsiung Nu or Huns, fierce horsemen from the north, the Chinese at first tried to buy them off with bribes. Under the strong Han emperor, Wu-ti (149–87 BC), the Huns came back to attack the Chinese capital of Chang-an, and there was savage fighting.

Wu-ti sent his armies west into central Asia to punish the Huns. While there, the Chinese reinforced their defenses. They rounded up large, fast horses for their cavalry. They added new stretches to the Great Wall to keep out the Huns. But over the years the Huns' repeated attacks weakened China. In AD 23, the nomads poured into China again and burned Chang-an. Han emperors reigned until AD 220, but their power was weakened. After Han rule ended, China, without a unifying ruler, split into several smaller kingdoms.

Green is the grass on the riverbanks/ Dense are the willows in the garden/ Fair is the woman upstairs/ Bright as the moon at her window.

ANONYMOUS HAN DYNASTY POEM c. AD 100

△ The Chinese so much admired the swift horses of the central Asian steppes that they made bronze statuettes of "flying horses."

People from mainland Asia had settled on the islands of Japan by 7000 BC. The original inhabitants may have been the Ainu, about 15,000 of whom still live in Japan.

Japan

The early Japanese lived by hunting and fishing. Farming began around 1000 to 500 BC, when the Japanese learned to grow rice, a skill learned from China. They also began to make metal tools and to make pottery using a potter's wheel. The site in Tokyo where pottery from this time was first found gives this period of Japanese history its name: Yayoi.

Village life

The Yayoi farmers dug ditches to irrigate their rice fields. They built thatched homes and storehouses on stilts for their rice crop. Farmers lived together in villages, and each village was led by a chief who was often a woman shaman, or magician. The women shamans of Japan were powerful figures. In the 200s BC a shaman named Himiko used her authority to end a civil war between numerous small states. According to legend, Japan had its first emperor in the 600s BC but there is no historical evidence of his existence.

Contact with China

About AD 240, the Chinese sent ambassadors to the islands of Japan. These visitors wrote reports on what they saw,

Timeline (BC/AD)

1000 BC	Rice farming begins in Japan.
660 BC	Traditional date of Japan's first emperor, Jimmu Tenno.
250 BC	Start of the Yayoi period. Bronze and iron tools.
AD 240	Chinese visit Japan and report on its way of life.
AD 300	Growth of Yamato power in Japan.
AD 350	Japan probably unified under one ruler around this time.
AD 400s	New ideas are brought from China. Japan rules part of Korea.
AD 500s	Yamato power declines. Japan loses its grip on Korea.

▷ *A typical Yayoi farming scene, showing their thatched homes, storehouses on stilts and the ditches to irrigate their rice fields.*

▷ The Chinese sent ships to report on what was going on in Japan. They called Japan "Wo," and regarded it as a subject country. Relations between the two countries seem to have been friendly, since Japan posed no threat to China.

△ A modern Ainu elder in traditional dress. A few Ainu people still live in separate village communities, following their traditional way of life, but most have integrated into modern Japanese society.

giving historians the first detailed view of life in Japan at this time. The Chinese saw large towns and cemeteries - the Japanese buried their dead in large pottery jars or in stone coffins. The Japanese admired the Chinese and copied the way the Chinese wrote, the Chinese calendar, and the teachings of the scholar Confucius.

Warlords and emperors

By the AD 300s the Japanese had become expert in making iron tools and weapons. Shaman chiefs still ruled the villages, but there were now powerful warlords who led bands of warriors. These warrior-bands or clans (related families) fought for power.

Warlords were buried in huge tombs, beneath earth mounds, some of which were shaped like keyholes. The body of the dead ruler was laid to rest dressed in armor, with his weapons beside him, and with rich gold and jade jewelery.

By AD 400 one clan, the Yamato, had become supreme. They controlled central Japan and parts of southern Korea. The Yamato chiefs were the first real emperors and are regarded as the ancestors of Japan's present royal family.

Burying the dead

During Japan's Yayoi period, from 250 BC the dead were often buried inside wooden coffins or stone tombs. Stones were used to mark out the area of a burial site. Sometimes burial rites involved placing the body inside a double jar made of pottery, such as the one shown here. The tallest of these Japanese burial jars was more than 6.5 feet high.

△ The Yayoi people made bell-shaped objects called dotaku out of bronze. They were decorated with pictures of animals or scenes from daily life.

BC

The Celts came from central Europe, although their previous origins are unclear. Around 500 BC, perhaps to escape wars with their Germanic neighbors, they began to move westward. Groups of people settled in what are now Spain, France, Britain, and Ireland.

Celtic Europe

Some Celts, known to the Romans as Gauls, invaded Italy and others went as far east as Greece and Asia Minor. The Celts were warlike and their arrival usually led to fighting. In the British Isles, Celtic invaders sometimes drove out the local Britons, but elsewhere settled peacefully alongside them. They brought with them their languages, which became the Welsh and Gaelic still spoken more than 2,000 years later.

Warriors in hillforts

Celtic warriors fought in horse-drawn chariots and on foot, often with wild bravery. They were quarrelsome and often fought among themselves. But they were also skilled in farming and using iron to make tools and weapons.

To protect themselves and their farm animals, the Celts built forts on hilltops. Large family groups lived in or around these hillforts, taking shelter inside if attacked. The hillforts were oval or round, with earth ramparts topped by wooden stockades. The biggest, such as Maiden Castle in Dorset, had two or more ramparts and gateways defended by walls that curved out like horns, giving defenders a clear shot at anyone trying to break down the gate.

700 BC	Evidence of Celts in Austria, from graves.
500 BC	Celts spread westwards across Europe, and also to the south and east.
390 BC	Celts attack and loot Rome.
192 BC	Romans counterattack and invade Cisalpine Gaul in northern Italy.
100s BC	Gauls and Romans fight for control of Massilia (Marseilles) in France.
75 BC	The Belgae, a Celtic tribe, move across the English Channel to settle in Britain.
55 BC	Julius Caesar tries to invade Celtic Britain, but withdraws.
54 BC	Caesar invades Britiain again. Celts agree to pay tribute (tax) to Rome.

△ A Celtic hillfort was surrounded by a ditch and an earth rampart topped by a wooden stockade. The round houses inside had conical thatched roofs and walls made of woven sticks plastered over with mud. The settlement's gateway was well defended against attack.

△ *Around the campfire at night, Celtic poets, storytellers, and musicians would pass on tales of the gods and of events in the history of the Celtic people.*

Druids

Celtic priests called druids performed mysterious rites in sacred groves of trees. The Moon, the oak tree, and mistletoe were all magical to the Celts, and so too were many animals.

Art and legend

The Celts were artistic people. They loved stories and music, and they made beautiful jewelery and metalwork decorated with abstract designs and animal shapes.

They had no written language, passing on their legends of gods and heroes in stories around the fire. Most of what we know of the Celts comes from the writings of their enemies, such as the Romans. The Celts themselves left a legacy of art and legend, and language – Welsh, Breton, Cornish, Irish, and Scottish Gaelic are all Celtic languages.

Loyalty and sacrifice

The Celts were led by chiefs. Each warrior swore loyalty to his chief, who rewarded his followers with feasting and booty after victory. The various tribes never came together in a lasting state.

The Celts believed in many gods, some of whom were rather unattractive, such as potbellied Dagda, whose club could deliver either life or death. Celtic religion involved human sacrifice, although most reports of bloodthirsty practices come from the Romans, who thought the Celts were brave but barbarous.

△ *The Celts were expert metalworkers, making fine objects out of gold, silver, and bronze. Their work featured geometric designs, animals, and human faces.*

"Tempest on the plain of Lir/ Bursts its barriers far and near/ And upon the rising tide/ Wind and noisy winter ride –/ Winter throws a shining spear.

STORM AT SEA, CELTIC POEM"

Rome grew from a small kingdom in Italy. It became a republic and one of the mightiest empires of the ancient world, with an empire stretching the length of the Mediterranean Sea.

The Rise of Rome

According to tradition, the city of Rome was founded in 753 BC. Legends say that early Rome was ruled by Etruscan kings, of whom Romulus was the first. Romulus and his twin brother Remus were suckled by a she-wolf after being abandoned by their wicked great-uncle. They founded Rome, but the brothers quarreled and Remus was killed.

The Etruscans, who came from Etruria in northern Italy, chose a strong position for their city on the top of seven hills. To the south lived the Latini, or Latins. In time both peoples became simply Romans.

The republic

In about 510 BC, the Etruscan kings were driven out of Rome, which became a republic. The Roman Republic was ruled by the Senate, which consisted of a group of elders who elected two consuls each year to lead them. The senators advised the consuls, but the consuls were powerful in their own right.

The typical Roman citizen was a peasant with a small farm. About 200 BC large estates owned by townspeople began to grow up, using slave labor.

Traditional date for founding of Rome.	753 BC
Roman Republic founded after overthrow of King Tarquinius Superbus.	510 BC
Plebeians (workers) revolt against patricians (aristocrats).	494 BC
Work starts on the Appian Way.	312 BC
Rome defeats Gauls, Samnites, and Latins in Third Samnite War.	298 BC
Patricians and plebeians share equal rights in Rome.	287 BC
Start of Punic Wars between Rome and Carthage.	264 BC
Carthaginian general Hannibal crosses Alps to attack Italy.	218 BC

△ A busy street in ancient Rome. Some buildings had several stories, and citizens collected water from a communal trough. Roman shops opened onto the street. Wine and oil sellers, butchers, and bakers did good business, and at times laws were passed to stop traders cluttering up the sidewalk.

△ Etruscan warriors. The Etruscans, the masters of central Italy in the 500s BC, were defeated by the Romans.

Roman Villa

A Roman villa was a large comfortable, country home, with hot-air central heating and a courtyard for fine weather. The family had servants to run the house and slaves to work on the farm.

The power of the army

Rome rose to power thanks to its fertile farmland, its army, and its key position in the middle of Italy. One of its earliest roads, the Appian Way, was built in 312 BC so that soldiers could travel southward. The Roman army was the best in Europe. By 200 BC Rome was Italy's leading power. It was able to challenge and defeat rivals such as Carthage for control of the Mediterranean world.

Everyday life in town and country

The Romans believed town and countryside should be organized and peaceful. They built walls around their towns for protection. Within the walls were shops and houses, both large and small. There were blocks of flats too. Rich and poor went to the public baths to wash, relax, and meet friends. Every town had its temples dedicated to protector gods and goddesses. Business was done in the forum, originally the town marketplace.

In the countryside, Romans lived with their servants in villas on big estates. Some villas were run as large farms. The owners kept sheep and cows, and vineyards were also profitable. The owner and his family lived in a comfortable house with its own garden.

△ Part of a carved stone relief depicting a Roman funeral procession. The pallbearers carry the dead person on a raised bier, followed by the mourners.

> He succeeded in founding his city, and installing the gods of his race in the Latin land... that was the origin of the Latin nation and the proud battlements of Rome.

THE AENEID, VIRGIL (70–19 BC)

Virgil was a Roman poet. He wrote his poem The Aeneid *to tell the mythical history of the founding of Rome by the poem's hero, Aeneas.*

Having destroyed the power of Carthage in 201 BC, the Romans began to build an empire. The Celts, the Seleucid kings, the Greeks, and the Egyptians all fell before Roman power. Only the Parthians in the east and the Germanic tribes in northwest Europe defied the mighty Roman army.

The Roman Empire

Rome was a republic, with a form of democracy, but strong leaders were ambitious for sole power. In 49 BC Julius Caesar (100–44 BC) attacked Gaul. Like all successful Roman leaders, he knew that victory would bring booty, captives, and cheers from the people in Rome.

In 44 BC Caesar was murdered by plotters who feared he might become king. Civil war broke out. After the war Caesar's great-nephew Octavius, thereafter known as Augustus, became Rome's first emperor.

The empire

At its peak, the Roman Empire stretched from Britain in the west to Mesopotamia in the east. The army defended this empire. As well as fighting, Roman soldiers built roads, forts, and aqueducts. They guarded the borders while Roman ships patrolled the Mediterranean trade routes. A network of roads criss-crossed the empire, linking towns and forts.

Roman peace

Most people accepted Roman rule for the benefits it brought, letting them farm and trade in peace.

▷ Gladiators were trained to fight in the arena. Some carried a shield and sword; others fought with a net and a long three-pronged spear, or trident.

After conquering Gaul, Julius Caesar invades Britain.	55 BC
Caesar is murdered.	44 BC
Romans conquer Egypt. Cleopatra and Mark Antony are defeated.	31 BC
Octavius becomes emperor and calls himself Augustus.	27 BC
Romans invade Britain.	AD 43
Volcanic eruption buries town of Pompeii in Italy.	AD 79
Roman Empire at its greatest.	AD 100
Barbarian attacks on Roman Empire increase.	AD 180
Visigoths attack Rome.	AD 410

▷ The Circus Maximus in Rome was packed with fans of chariot racing. Races were fast and furious, with frequent violent crashes, and winning drivers became rich superstars.

△ Part of the complex of Roman baths in the city of Bath, in England. Romans would visit the public baths to bathe in hot and cold pools, and also to relax and talk with their friends.

Towns grew, even in remote corners of the empire such as Britain. Wherever they went, the Romans built towns with baths, temples and theaters, and in the countryside, comfortable farmhouses called villas, many of which even had central heating.

To keep the mass of the people amused, Roman rulers presided over religious holidays, victory parades, and games in the arenas where mock battles and fights between gladiators were staged before vast, noisy crowds. Chariot racing was also popular, with heavy betting on races.

The Roman way

People throughout the Empire adopted Roman ways. Latin was widely used as the language of government, along with Greek, the language of scholars. Many people took to wearing Roman clothes and thought of themselves as Romans.

The Romans were great borrowers – they adopted many gods from other cultures, and they copied Greek styles in architecture and art. But they were also inventors. The Romans were the first to make concrete, and they used the arch to make roofs that spanned large inside spaces, without the need for columns.

A vast empire

Rome benefited greatly from its position in the middle of Italy. Through their economic power and by winning wars against their neighbors, the Romans were able to create one of the largest empires in history.

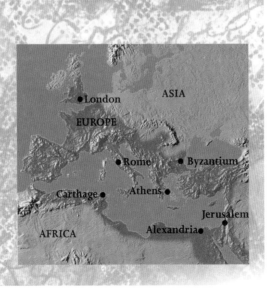

△ Slaves made up about a third of Rome's population. At the slave auctions, slaves wore tags advertising their skills and good character.

AD

At this time the Roman Empire was governed by the personal will of the emperor, but the emperor's power rested on the army. Weak or bad emperors were sometimes overthrown by army generals. Some emperors ruled well – Hadrian, for example, traveled widely to inspect building projects. Others, such as Nero and Caligula, were cruel or mad.

War and Government

Caligula is emperor.	AD 37–51
Claudius is emperor.	AD 41–54
Romans invade Britain.	AD 43
Colchester becomes a "colony" for retired Roman soldiers.	AD 49
Nero is emperor. Rome burns.	AD 54–68
Birth of Tacitus, a Roman historian who wrote about the conquest of Britain.	AD 56
Boudicca leads a revolt against the Romans in Britain.	AD 60
Vespasian, a former soldier in Britain, is emperor.	AD 68–79
Trajan is emperor. There are 31 legions, the highest number yet.	AD 98–117
Hadrian is emperor.	AD 117–138
The empire is divided.	AD 395
Rome is captured and burned by the Visigoths.	AD 410

The Romans were such good organizers that the empire usually kept working even when there was a fool at its center. It was divided into provinces, such as Britannia (Britain), each ruled by a governor or legate (chosen person). The governor had a staff of officials, who looked after finance, army matters, law-making, trade and all the other affairs of government.

The legions

The Roman army's main fighting troops were its legions. Each legion had up to 5,000 men, whose training and discipline were usually a match for any enemies they faced.

A legionary soldier wore armor to protect his body. On the road he marched at a steady pace, carrying his kit hung on a pole over one shoulder. He carried clothes, a food dish, cooking pot, rations, and tools.

▷ Most Roman soldiers fought on foot, although cavalry were used for patrols and in battle. Cavalrymen were sometimes recruited from foreign countries.

▷ Emperor Trajan (ruled AD 91–117) built a monument 100 feet high to the Roman army. Its carved reliefs show soldiers doing all kinds of tasks, from storming a fort to building a camp. This section shows Roman legionaries, who were builders as well as fighters, constructing a fort.

△ Octavian, a great-nephew of Julius Caesar, took the title Augustus as first emperor (27 BC to AD 14). The month of August was named in his honor.

Taking control

As soon as a new province was conquered, the army set up bases to control it. In Britain, the Romans invaded in AD 43, and having defeated the southern tribes, began building forts and roads.

When the eastern Britons rose in revolt under Queen Boudicca, the Romans were at first defeated, then regrouped and won a decisive victory. The Romans took revenge, burning farms and villages, but soon saw this was a mistake. They changed to "Romanizing" – making conquered Britain prosperous so that its people would no longer want to fight Rome. By AD 100, the Romans controlled England and Wales as far north as Hadrian's Wall in northern England.

Rome's power weakens

In the end, not even the Roman army could control such a huge empire. From AD 200 the army was stretched to defend the frontiers, especially in the east (Balkans) and northwest (Germany). Barbarian attacks increased. Britain was abandoned in the early 400s, soon after the empire had split into eastern and western halves. The western half crumbled, leaving the Eastern Empire, at Constantinople (now Istanbul Turkey), to preserve the legacy of Rome into a new age.

Hadrian's Wall

Hadrian's Wall was built in AD 122 to defend the northern frontier of Roman Britain. It acted as a checkpoint on movement between England and Scotland. The wall took eight years to build and stretches for 73 miles.

△ A Roman coin stamped with the head of the Emperor Hadrian. During his reign, he personally visited nearly every province in the Roman Empire.

BC/AD

2000
1750
1500
1250
1000
750
500
250
1AD
1BC
250AD
500AD

The Greeks believed in many different gods, chief among these were a family of supernatural beings who lived on Mount Olympus and watched over humanity. Certain gods looked after the harvest; others cared for wild animals, the sea, war, and so on. The Romans took over many of these Greek gods and gave them Latin names.

Ancient Gods

The Greeks believed the gods could and did interfere in human affairs, bringing success or disaster. The king of the gods was Zeus, whom the Romans called Jupiter. The Greeks also believed that the Universe was a sphere. The upper half was light and airy, the lower half dark and gloomy. The Earth was a flat disc, floating between the two halves. When people died they went to the Underworld, which was ruled by Hades, the brother of Zeus.

Monsters and heroes

The Greeks also told stories about all kinds of nature spirits – magical beings often half-animal and half-human, such as centaurs (half-human and half-horse). There were fearful monsters that turned people to stone (such as Medusa), but even these horrors could be defeated by heroes, with the help of a friendly god or goddess. Some heroes in Greek myths, such as Odysseus and Jason, even became part of Western culture.

First Olympic Games honor Zeus.	776 BC
Temples on the Acropolis in Athens are built.	400s BC
Socrates is sentenced to death for showing disrespect to the gods.	399 BC
Greece conquered by Rome. Romans adopt many Greek gods and myths.	146 BC
Probable year of Jesus's death. Christianity spreads into the Roman world.	AD 28
Many Romans switch from the old religion to new beliefs.	AD 100s
Persecution of Christians in Rome, during the reign of Diocletian.	AD 200s
Constantine makes Christianity the official religion of the empire.	AD 312

◁ The Romans adopted Greek gods including Minerva (Athena, Greek goddess of wisdom and war). The Roman god Mars was identifed with Ares, the Greek god of war.

Mars   Minerva

▷ *A funeral procession passes along a Roman street. The body was carried on a litter for burial, followed by mourners and musicians. Noble Romans in particular honored their dead ancestors.*

△ *Ruins of Greek and Roman temples can be seen across Europe, the Near East, and North Africa. Every town had its own temple, dedicated to a protector god or goddess.*

Gods and god-emperors

The gods of the Greeks and Romans were unpredictable and too much like humans in many ways. People tried to please the gods by building statues and temples in their honor and by offering gifts. Each city had its own protector god or gods. Athens was watched over by the goddess Athena. In Rome a huge temple to Jupiter stood on the Capitoline Hill. The gods were honored by processions and sacrifices carried out by a priest.

The Romans borrowed gods from all parts of their empire – from Greece, Egypt, Asia Minor, even Celtic Britain. Many soldiers became followers of Mithras, a Persian god. Several emperors were worshipped as gods while still living.

New and old ideas

Most Romans had no clear idea about what happened to people after death, although they were afraid of ghosts, and had a deep respect for ancestors. They were generally tolerant of new beliefs, but the Roman emperors did for a time persecute the new religion of Christianity. By the AD 300s many Romans had adopted the new faith, with its promise of an afterlife in heaven.

Sea god

Poseidon was the Greek god of the sea and is often shown carrying a three-pronged spear, called a trident. The Greeks believed Poseidon to be the brother of Zeus, the king of the gods, and Hades, god of the underworld. He was also associated with horses, and the Greeks thought that he was the father of the winged horse, Pegasus.

△ *Zeus, king of the Greek gods. The first Olympic Games, which took place in 776 BC, were held in his honor. Zeus was head of a family of gods and goddesses called the Olympians.*

The period from AD 500 to AD 1500 in Europe is known as the Middle Ages. It is called "middle" because it falls between the two worlds of ancient history and modern history, yet the term "Middle Ages" has no historical meaning in other parts of the world.

The Early Middle Ages

In China, for instance, history is described in terms of dynasties (ruling families), while the history of America is often divided into before Columbus (that is, before the arrival of European settlers) and after.

The world after Rome

Roman rule had created a common cultural framework across much of Europe, North Africa, and the Middle East. After the collapse of the Roman Empire, Roman ways continued to influence many people; Roman law, for example, became the basis for much European law. Latin, the language of the Romans, was used by scholars and in government. The Roman Catholic Church used Latin in its services until modern times.

So Roman culture lived on. Historians used to refer to the period after the fall of the Roman Empire as the "Dark Ages." Fine cities did fall into ruins, the old Roman roads crumbled, the Roman peace no longer existed. This was a time of movement, uncertainty, and violence. Yet it was not

all darkness. Great works of art were created, achievements were made in science and architecture, and people performed great feats of heroism and exploration.

The new Europe

Although the Roman Empire in the West had fallen, the Empire in the East held out for a few hundred years. In Europe, the Christian Church was the force that held Europe together. The popes ruled from Rome, like the emperors of old. Christianity spread slowly across Europe, and in monasteries scholar monks preserved many Greek and Roman books for future generations.

A time of change

The early Middle Ages were a time of change. In the Middle East, the new and fast-growing faith of Islam became the backbone of new empires. In Asia, the empires of India and China continued to enjoy a civilization that was more advanced than any in Europe. People were on the move. Arabs and Turks expanded into new lands, Saxons and Angles moved across the North Sea to England. From Scandinavia, the Vikings set out in their longships across the seas to trade, farm, and fight.

The period covered by this book ends with the first millennium – and the Norman conquest of England in 1066. This marked a turning-point in the history of Britain, signaling an end to the ancient world. It opened the door to the second half of the Middle Ages, beyond which lay the Renaissance, the Age of Discovery and the dawn of the modern world.

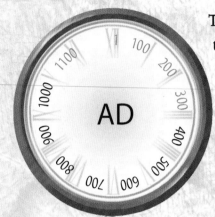

The Roman Empire split in two in AD 395. After the collapse of the western half in AD 476, the eastern part survived. Its capital was Byzantium (now Istanbul in Turkey), a city founded by the Greeks.

The Byzantine Empire

The Roman emperor Constantine gave the city of Byzantium a new name, Constantinople. It became the home of eastern orthodox Christianity, and the capital of the Byzantine emperors.

Roman Empire divides into East (Byzantium) and West (Rome).	AD 395
Emperor Theodosius repairs and rebuilds the city walls.	AD 408
Fall of the Western Roman Empire.	AD 476
Justinian and Theodora rule Byzantine Empire.	AD 527–565
Byzantines conquer southeastern Spain.	AD 554
Wars with Arabs and religious quarrels weaken Byzantine power.	AD 700s
Byzantine Empire recovers.	AD 900s
Death of Basil II is followed by further period of weak rule.	AD 1025

Byzantium was "Rome in the East." Here, artists and scholars carried on the traditions of ancient Greek and Roman culture. The Byzantines loved music, poetry, and art, and decorated their churches with beautifully colored wall paintings, or frescoes, and mosaic pictures. Mosaics are pictures made from small pieces of glass or stone set in patterns.

Wars and laws

The Byzantine Empire was strongest in the AD 500s. The Emperor Justinian had a mighty general, Belisarius, who won many battles. He also had a clever wife, the empress Theodora. Justinian's laws, which gave new rights to women and children, became the framework for later legal systems in many countries in Europe.

A magnificent city

Most of the people of the Byzantine Empire were farmers. They came to the city to sell goods and to marvel. Foreigners visiting Constantinople were amazed by its magnificence. Its

△ Chariots raced around the track in the Hippodrome. Entrance was free (the emperors knew that the races kept the mob amused). *As well as thrilling and often dangerous races, there were animal fights, dancing girls, and circus acts to entertain the huge crowds.*

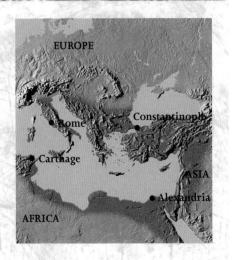

Eastern empire

The Byzantine Empire swallowed up Turkey, the Balkans, parts of Spain and North Africa, Egypt, and the western coasts of the Mediterranean. The Empire was at its height under Justinian.

△ *A 19th-century print of the emperor Justinian and his influential wife Theodora. Through war and diplomacy, Justinian made Byzantium the greatest power in the eastern Mediterranean.*

port was packed with ships, its markets swarmed with people of many nations. Richly dressed noblewomen were carried on litters by servants along streets in which slaves and soldiers jostled sailors and merchants.

The city was dominated by the enormous church of Hagia Sophia, to which the emperor and his retinue paraded to celebrate Christian festivals. Built in only six years, between AD 532 and 537, by order of Justinian, the huge domed building is one of the gems of world architecture. Inside the vast Hippodrome, crowds of 60,000 roared with approval or scorn for the chariot racers. Nobles and rich merchants lived in comfortable houses with central heating. Poor families crammed into multi-story tenement blocks.

As strong as its emperor

The Byzantine empire needed strong rulers. After Justinian's death in AD 565, few rulers came near to matching his power, and the empire was weakened by wars. Only vigorous soldiers were able to rally its forces and maintain a grip on its lands and trade.

Byzantium managed to fight off its enemies and survive into the second millennium. Its end came finally in 1453, when the city of Constantinople was captured by the Turks.

△ *Byzantine traders used gold coins called bezants. These coins have been found across Asia as far as China and as far west as the British Isles.*

Justice is the constant and perpetual wish to render to everyone his due.
EMPEROR JUSTINIAN (*c.* 482–565)

Most Native Americans were nomads, hunting for food. Yet in North and South America, and especially in Central America, people lived as farmers and built towns and cities.

Civilizations in the Americas

The most spectacular builders of North America were the Anasazi people, who lived in the southwest region of what is now the United States. They lived in cliffside "apartment blocks" called *pueblos*. Their descendants took the name of Pueblo. The Anasazi and their neighbors, the Hohokam, grew corn, wove cotton cloth, and made clay pottery.

Teotihuacan (Mexico) begins its rise to power.	AD 350
The city of Tiahuanaco (Bolivia) and Huari empire (Peru) are flourishing.	AD 600
In what is now the southwest U.S., the Anasazi build multi-story houses.	AD 700
The Mayan civilization is at its most powerful for the next 200 years.	AD 700
The city of Teotihuacan is destroyed. Tiahuanaco also declines about this time.	AD 750
Rise of the Toltecs in Mexico. They build a city called Tula.	AD 900
Chichén Itzá is the most important Mayan city and religious centre.	AD 900
The Mississippian people develop a farming culture in North America.	AD 1000

Teotihuacan

In Mexico, there stood one of the biggest cities in world. It was called Teotihuacan, or "City of the Gods," and it grew in the Teotihuacan valley from AD 350 to 750. The city had wide avenues, squares, palaces, and temples. These temples were built as step pyramids, and towered more than 195 feet high. The two largest are the Pyramid of the Sun and the Pyramid of the Moon. We know little about the city and what happened in it. It was conquered by the Toltecs who built their own temple-city at Tula.

Great mountain city

Over two miles high in the Andes Mountains, not far from Lake Titicaca, was the city of Tiahuanaco. It thrived between AD 500 and 1000. The kingdom of which it was part was ruled by priest-kings, who grew rich from farming and trade with nearby states such as Huari in Peru.

△ The Maya played a ball game in which players tried to knock a rubber ball through a stone ring. The game was both a sport and a religious rite, with the ball possibly representing the sun.

A Mayan priest wears an elaborate feathered headdress. The Maya worshiped many gods. Priests led ceremonies in the pyramid-temples. Sacrificial offerings were made to please the gods, who included the jaguar.

△ A temple in the Mayan city of Chichén Itzá. The city's natural well, called a cenote, was used for sacrifices. Many Mayan treasures have been recovered from the well, which was surrounded by pyramids, temples, and other buildings, including a ball court.

The Maya

The Maya were at their most powerful from AD 200 to 900. Their calendars date back to before 3000 BC, and they remained powerful until conquered by the Spanish in the AD 1500s.

The Maya lived in city-states, ruled by kings who ruled over a society of priests, nobles, warriors, skilled craftworkers, and peasant farmers. Each city had its own sign, or emblem. Hunters in the forests brought birds' feathers, which were made into headdresses, and also jaguar skins, which were highly prized.

Mayan farmers grew beans, corn, and squash. They kept turkeys for meat and bees for honey, but they had no domestic animals that were big enough to pull wheeled carts.

Cities and sacrifices

The Maya built large cities. The biggest was Tikal (Guatemala), where about 60,000 people lived. Religious ceremonies and sacrifices (involving animals and sometimes humans) were at the center of Mayan life. Priests skilled in maths and astronomy studied the stars, the Sun and the Moon. The Maya used sign writing, and wrote on thin pieces of bark.

△ Chac, the Maya rain god. Carved stone figures called Chac Mools have been found in Mayan temples. They were probably used to make sacrificial offerings.

Give us a steady light, a level place
a good light, a good place,
a good life and beginning.

from THE POPUL VUH, ANONYMOUS MAYAN POEM

AD

In the first centuries after Christ, Christianity spread from Palestine into North Africa, Asia Minor, and across Europe. Further east, many people in the Arabian peninsula were still pagans, worshipping ancient gods. In this region, during the 600s, there arose a new religion – Islam.

The Rise of Islam

Islam had its roots in the Hebrew-Christian belief in one God, and its prophet was Muhammad (AD 570–632).

Muhammad's life and vision

Muhammad was born in Mecca (now in Saudi Arabia), an important trading town. After his parents died, he was raised by an uncle and became a merchant and caravan manager.

Muhammad was angered by the evils he saw around him in Mecca: injustice, selfishness, and the worship of pagan idols. Many religious

Probable date of Muhammad's birth.	AD 570
Muhammad begins preaching in Mecca.	AD 610
Flight to Medina, the Hegira.	AD 622
Muslims defeat the Meccans at Badr.	AD 624
Muhammad's teachings are written down in the Koran, the holy book of Islam.	AD 625
Meccans besiege Medina.	AD 627
Muhammad leads an army into Mecca and smashes the pagan idols there.	AD 630
Muhammad dies. Abu Bakr becomes the first caliph. Islam spreads beyond Arabia.	AD 632
Ummayad dynasty rules the Islamic world from Damascus.	AD 661

△ The old mosque at Mecca. Muhammad used to pray in the courtyard of his home. As a result, Islamic mosques have an open space where people gather five times a day to pray.

▷ The Muslims built mosques and minarets wherever the new religion took hold. One of the oldest Islamic monuments is the Dome of the Rock in Jerusalem (right), which was completed in AD 691. According to Muslim belief, Muhammad ascended to heaven from here to speak with God.

△ The people of Arabia traded by camel caravans, which broke their journeys at oases. Muhammad knew this life well. As a young man he worked as a manager for the caravans. He married his employer, a widow named Khadija.

ideas were talked over by travelers of many beliefs (including Jews and Christians) who met in the town to do business. Old beliefs were being questioned.

Muslims believe that the angel Gabriel came to Muhammad in a vision. The angel told Muhammad he must bring people to belief in the one true God, Allah, and to submission (Islam).

The birth of Islam

Muhammad began preaching and soon got into into trouble with the authorities in Mecca. In AD 622 he left the city, hid from his enemies in a cave, and then traveled across the desert to the town of Medina. This journey, known as the Hegira, begins the Muslim calendar. The Medinans welcomed him and adopted the new faith.

Many people in Mecca were determined to crush Islam. But in AD 630 Muhammad's forces entered the city in triumph. He broke up the pagan idols in the Kaaba, or shrine, but spared the Black Stone, which is still there. The Meccans submitted and Muhammad continued to preach and live frugally, until he died in AD 632.

Mecca became the holiest city of Islam. Muhammad's teachings were written down in the Koran, the holy book of Islam.

Astronomy

Astronomy was a respected science in the Islamic world, and Baghdad and other cities had flourishing scientific communities. Arab astronomers added their own observations to those of the Babylonians and Greeks and named many of the brightest stars.

△ Beautifully decorated tiles adorn the walls, domes, and minarets of mosques throughout the Islamic world. The brightly colored tiles feature geometric and arabesque patterns.

From the AD 500s, Japan was influenced more and more by Chinese ideas. The teachings of Confucius and Buddhism were brought to Japan. Prince Shotoku, who ruled from AD 593 to 622, strongly encouraged Chinese ways.

Fujiwara Japan

Shotoku believed that the Japanese emperor should be all-powerful, like the ruler of China. He made Buddhism the national religion, but the old Shinto religion continued to be strong, preserving a distinct Japanese identity.

Prince Shotoku's changes

Shotoku reorganized the Japanese court into 12 ranks, and set out rules which governed the behavior of everyone from ruler to lowliest peasant. Shotoku's successors divided Japan into provinces, governed by local officials who reported directly to the emperor. In AD 794 emperor Kammu made Kyoto (then called Heian) his capital.

The Fujiwaras

In AD 858, however, the emperor lost control to a strong noble family called the Fujiwaras. The Fujiwaras had built up their power in the countryside, where they owned huge estates. Other nobles too had built up small 'empires' of their own.

The Fujiwaras gradually won control of the emperors, and of government, by marrying their daughters into the imperial family. The emperor had little real power. His Fujiwara "adviser" gave the orders.

Reign of Prince Shotoku, called the founder of Japanese civilization.	AD 593
Shotoku sends first Japanese embassy to China.	AD 608
Earliest written works in Japanese.	AD 700
Emperor Kammu makes Kyoto his capital.	AD 794
Bronze sculptures of Buddha made at the temple of Horyuji.	AD 800s
Fujiwara family gains control over the emperor.	AD 858
The Tale of Genji was probably written about this date.	AD 1008
Feuds weaken Fujiwara control. Power shifts to the daimyos.	AD 1000s

△ At the court of the Fujiwaras, richly dressed men and women spent much of their time strolling in ornate gardens with flowering trees, artificial hills, and ponds.

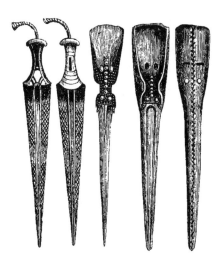

Samurai warriors

Japanese soldiers used iron swords and wore heavy armor. The bands of soldiers who served the land-owning loard, became known as the Samurai, the "knights" of medieval Japan.

△ *Japanese daggers. Iron weapons were made in Japan from the AD 300s, and were buried in nobles' tombs, with armor and models of servants and animals.*

The Fujiwaras held onto power in Japan for 300 years. During this time the great estates grew bigger and stronger, until the lords ruling them were almost like kings. By the AD 1000s, these lords, who were called daimyos, led private armies of heavily armored soldiers. These soldiers were called samurai.

Elegant court life

Fujiwara rule was based on life at court. Here, elegant courtiers wandered through beautiful gardens, or listened to poetry and stories. One of the most famous books in Japanese is *The Tale of Genji*, a long novel written by a court lady-in-waiting called Murasaki Shikibu in the early AD 1000s. Japanese writing was done with great care and skill, using a brush. The Japanese adopted Chinese writing to create their own written language, using characters to represent sounds. Only a few educated people could read Japanese.

Few ordinary people knew anything about this elegant life, unless they worked as servants at court. Most Japanese lived in small villages, as peasant farmers. They grew rice and vegetables, and caught fish from the sea. Small trading craft sailed between Japan and China, but otherwise Japan had little contact with the outside world.

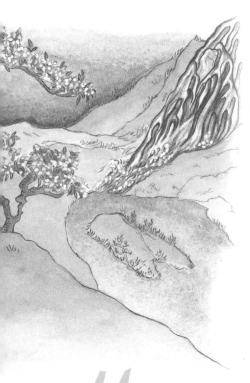

△ *A wooden gate, or torii, is the symbol of Shinto, and stands outside Shinto temples. Shinto (meaning "the way of the gods") was the traditional religion of Japan.*

"Lady Koshosho, all noble and charming, she is like a weeping willow at budding time. Her style is very elegant and we all envy her manners.
DIARY OF MURASAKI SHIKIBU (C. AD 975–1031)"

After the end of Han rule in AD 220, China was weak and divided until AD 581 when Yang Chien founded the Sui dynasty (a series of rulers from the same family). He ruled from the city of Chang'an and governed well encouraging agriculture and foreign trade.

Chinese Dynasties

Chinese cities were a wonder to foreign visitors. Chang'an had more than one million citizens, yet its cleanliness was startling. There were public baths, and hot water was sold in the streets for washing. Toilet facilities in houses were fairly basic, emptying into cesspools, but waste was collected in carts every evening and taken away. The Chinese habit of using toilet paper came as another surprise to visitors.

The Tang and Sung dynasties

The second Sui emperor, Yang Di, was less prudent than Yang Chien. He taxed people heavily to pay for expensive projects, such as rebuilding the Grand Canal and constructing new imperial palaces and gardens. Discontent flared into revolt. The emperor was killed and a government official named Li Yuan seized power. He founded the Tang dynasty, which lasted for almost 300 years until it was overthrown by the warlord Chu Wen in AD 907.

End of Han dynasty is followed by a period of weak rule known as Six Dynasties.	AD 220
Start of Sui dynasty.	AD 581
The printing press may have been invented in China as early as this.	AD 600
Start of Tang dynasty. Period of prosperity and progress in arts and sciences.	AD 618
Northern rebellion is led by a soldier named An Lushan.	AD 755
More rebellions, leading to the fall of the Tang dynasty in 907.	AD 875–907
The Five Dynasties and Ten Kingdoms — leaders struggle for power in China.	AD 907–960
Sung dynasty founded. China's population tops 100 million.	AD 960

△ The wheelbarrow was a Chinese invention and was used by farmers, market traders, and construction workers. This typical barrow has a central wheel, not unlike today's garden barrows.

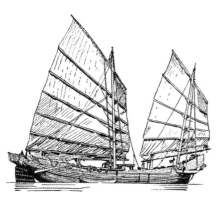

△ A two-masted Chinese junk. Chinese ships had watertight compartments and stern rudders. With easily handled sails, they were less sinkable and more easily steered than Western vessels.

△ The oldest printed book known is the Diamond Sutta, a Buddhist scroll made from sheets of paper printed with woodblocks. It was made in China in AD 868.

△ By AD 1100 the Chinese were using magnetic compasses such as this one, with an iron needle and marked points.

Making paper

A paper-maker at work, spreading wet pulp over a mesh frame. The invention of paper was announced by the director of the Chinese imperial workshops in AD 105. The Chinese began to use paper money under Sung rule.

For a time China was then split into five dynasties and smaller kingdoms, but in AD 960, the Sung dynasty reunited China and made their capital at Kaifeng. The Sung ruled until AD 1279. They were not as strong as the Tang emperors, but they were more technologically advanced.

Chinese culture

The Tang and Sung periods were good times for China. Painters and poets flourished. China was united and prosperous. Painters created beautiful calm landscapes, to show the harmony between people and nature. Poets such as Wang Wei, Li Po, and Tu Fu wrote about love and war. Potters made delicate pottery, known as porcelain. The Chinese were the first people to print books, using wood blocks.

Trade in China moved by road and along the impressive canals. The Grand Canal connected the main rivers. Most canals were dug in level ground, so avoiding the need for locks, but in the AD 900s Chinese engineers developed the pound-lock, with gates at either end, which could be emptied or flooded to let boats pass through.

New technology

The Chinese were fascinated by machines. They invented the wheelbarrow for carrying loads, and even fitted barrows with sails to make pushing easier. They used waterwheels to mill rice and drive hammers to beat metal into shape. They knew about the magnetic compass, and their ships had stern rudders (still unknown in the West). Chinese soldiers had the best crossbows in the world, and also a range of smoke and fire weapons. Most alarming of all to an enemy were rockets, which began to be used in the 900s, and "fireguns" – bamboo tubes filled with gunpowder.

The advance of Islam seemed unstoppable in the late 600s. The Byzantine and Persian empires could not halt the armies of Islam, nor could Egypt. By AD 700, Muslims controlled most of the North African coast, and ships patrolled the Mediterranean Sea and Indian Ocean.

Muslim Empires

Muslims from Morocco invaded Spain, but the advance of Islam into western Europe was stopped in AD 732 by the Frankish army of Charles Martel.

Life under Ummayad rule

Under the rule of the Ummayad family in Damascus there were four classes of citizens: Arabian Muslims; new converts; Christians, Jews, and Mandaeans (a Persian sect); and slaves. The new converts included people from Egypt, Syria, Persia, and Asia Minor. They adopted Arab ways but brought to the Arabs a wealth of new learning in philosophy, medicine, art, and science.

Islam had been born in the desert. The Ummayad court was a more sophisticated world where music and gambling were tolerated. One caliph married a Christian. Another spent most of his time horse racing.

The Abbasid Empire

Ummayad rule grew weaker but lasted until the mid-700s. Then Abu al Abbas, a descendant of Muhammad, founded a new dynasty – the Abbasids. His followers raised an army in Persia and rallied the supporters of the dead caliph Ali to their cause. After a terrible battle lasting nine

▷ A scene from The Thousand and One Nights, a collection of stories set in the Baghdad court of Harun al-Rashid, the most famous of the Abbasid rulers. In these stories, collected from around the eastern world, characters such as Sinbad and Aladdin appear.

Abu Bakr becomes first caliph.	AD 632
Caliph Omar is murdered and is succeeded by Otham, leader of the Ummayad.	AD 644
Othman is murdered and the Shiite leader Ali becomes caliph.	AD 656
Ali is murdered. The Islamic capital moves from Mecca to Damascus.	AD 661
Caliph Abdalmalik sets up new government system for the Islamic empire.	AD 685–705
Franks defeat Muslims at battle of Poitiers to halt their advance into Europe.	AD 732
The Abbasid dynasty is founded.	AD 750
Harun al-Rashid unites the Islamic empire.	AD 786
Turkish Seljuks seize power in Baghdad.	AD 1000s

▷ *Arab trading ships sailed across the Indian Ocean to India and Indonesia and farther eastward as far as China.*

△ *An Arab astronomer's drawing of the star group, or constellation, of Orion (the Hunter). Like the Greeks, Arab scientists drew constellations as human figures, animals, or objects.*

days, they captured Damascus. Most of the Ummayad ruling family was murdered, and the new rulers soon moved their capital to Baghdad (in what is now Iraq).

Arabic was the common language throughout most of the Islamic world. By AD 786, the court of the caliph Harun al-Rashid at Baghdad was one of the most splendid in the world. Trading ships sailed to and from China, and the warehouses along the River Tigris were stocked with rare and wonderful goods from Africa, India, and the Far East. Medicine and science were ahead of anything known in Europe. There were slaves from Africa and even Scandinavia.

Rival rulers, however, claimed independence in various parts of this empire. Baghdad itself came under threat in the 11th century from invaders.

The Seljuk Empire

The Seljuks were descendants of nomadic Turks from central Asia. They took their name from a chief named Seljuk. They charged into the western Islamic world in the early AD 1000s. Their leader Toghril Beg captured Baghdad. His nephew Alp Arslan attacked the city of Constantinople and defeated the Byzantine army in AD 1071.

The Seljuks

The Turkish Seljuks were superb horsemen, riding with stirrups and firing bows at the gallop. Known as "the men of the sword," they added new strength to Islam, which was governed by "the men of the law."

△ *The crescent moon and star became important symbols in Islam and were often incorporated into architecture and other designs. The Islamic year calendar is based on the cycle of the Moon.*

After the fall of the Roman Empire, the Christian church provided the only stable government in Europe. It was weakened by its division, between the west (Rome) and the east (Constantinople) and faced growing pressure from the spread of Islam.

Monastic Life

The Christian faith spread slowly among the pagan peoples of western and northern Europe, who were called "heathens" by Christians. Its teachings were spread by missionaries, such as Patrick, Augustine, and Boniface. Missionaries traveled to the British Isles, Germany, Scandinavia, and Russia, converting the local rulers and building churches. It was a slow business, and parts of northern Europe were not Christian until the beginning of the second millennium.

Christian communities took on the work of teaching faith, education, and healing, at a time when governments themselves had very little power. In this work, monasteries came to play an important part.

Saint Benedict's rules
In the early Christian world, very religious people had sometimes gone off to live on their own as hermits, to

Egyptian missionaries preach in Ethiopia.	AD 350
St. Patrick preaches Christianity in Ireland.	AD 450
St. Columba founds a monastery on the island of Iona.	AD 500s
St. Benedict of Nursia sets the rules for Western monks.	AD 480–543
Monte Cassino in Italy is the first abbey in Europe.	AD 529
Pope Gregory sends Augustine to convert the English.	AD 596
Augustine founds the first English Benedictine monastery at Canterbury.	AD 596
Boniface preaches to the Saxons in Germany.	C. AD 700
Edward the Confessor starts to build Westminster Abbey.	AD 1042

▷ A monk at work on an illuminated manuscript (handwritten book). The work was slow and painstaking but worthwhile because it was another way to show dedication to God.

△ The monastery at Mont Saint-Michel in France was built by Benedictine monks in AD 966. It stands on a tiny island in Normandy, linked by causeway to the French mainland.

△ Monks spent part of their time teaching young boys, who would in time become monks themselves. A monk's day was regulated by hours of work, rest, and worship.

△ An "illuminated" letter from the page of a medieval manuscript. Monastery artists and scribes decorated the pages of their books with these beautifully colored "illuminations."

Celtic Christians

Elaborate carvings were made on Celtic crosses, the distinctive symbol of the Celtic Christians. They founded monasteries in the north of Britain. One of the first, at Lindisfarne, was founded in AD 635 by a monk named Aidan.

meditate and pray. Others formed strict communities, where they lived apart, praying and studying the Bible, hoping to avoid the "sins" of town life. These communities became monasteries.

In the AD 500s, an Italian named Benedict of Nursia drew up a set of rules for monks (people in monasteries). All monks must be poor, unmarried, and obedient. Monks wore simple robes, shaved their heads, and shared all their the daily tasks.

Monasteries were for men only. Religious women joined orders of their own and became nuns. Each monastery was led by an abbot, and the largest ones became centers not only of religious life but also of local power. Some abbots had as much power as any nobleman, controlling farms, trades, and even private armies.

The daily round

Monks went to eight church services every day. They ate their meals in the refectory, the dining room, often in silence while one monk read from the Bible or some other religious book. They grew their food, reared farm animals, baked bread, and brewed beer. They made their clothes and furniture and built their own churches. They also looked after the sick.

There is no salvation outside the Church.

Love the sinner but hate the sin.

Love and do what you will.

ST. AUGUSTINE OF HIPPO (AD 354-430)

St. Augustine was born in what is now Tunisia in Africa. He was one of the most important men in the early Christian Church.

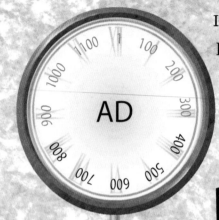

In the late AD 300s, the Roman army was hard pressed to fight off waves of barbarian invasions. Troops in distant outposts, such as the British Isles, were needed to defend the empire, and by AD 410, the last Roman soldiers had left England for mainland Europe.

Britain After the Romans

The Romans had hired warriors from northwest Europe (Germany and Denmark) to help defend the coasts of England against pirates and raiding bands (many of whom were Germans themselves). Without the Roman army to protect them, the Roman Britons of England were unable to prevent these mercenaries, and any new bands of invaders, from taking over land they wanted.

Roman army has left Roman Britain by this date.	AD 410
Possible date of "King Arthur," leader of the Britons.	AD 500
Augustine arrives to convert the English to Christianity.	AD 597
Death of Redwald, king of East Anglia. Sutton Hoo ship burial.	c. AD 627
Lifetime of English monk Bede, who wrote a history of the English people.	AD 673–735
Offa of Mercia is overlord of all England.	AD 780
First Viking attacks on England.	AD 787
Kenneth MacAlpin is first king of a united Scotland.	AD 843
Rhodri Mawr is Prince of Wales.	AD 844

The newcomers were a mixture of peoples – Angles, Saxons, Jutes, Frisians – who became known as the "English." There were also raiders from the north, Picts and Scots, who attacked northern England.

The Saxon settlement

The invaders came to England to find land to farm. They were well armed and tough and drove away many Britons, who moved into western England and Wales, taking their Christianity with them. The pagan newcomers took over their farms but also set about clearing new land. They felled trees, plowed the land, and built wooden houses.

The new English were suspicious of Roman-British civilization and avoided the towns. Gradually these towns fell into decay. Roads were no longer used, and Roman villas, their owners gone, became ruins – empty reminders of a vanished way of life.

△ A Scots warrior. The Scots' leader, Kenneth MacAlpin, was the first king to rule the land we now call Scotland.

Sutton Hoo

Artifacts from the Sutton Hoo burial site include a gold belt, a sword, and a shield. There are also several pieces of jewelery. Finally, there was a scepter and standard which must have belonged to the dead King Redwald.

The English kings

By AD 600, the English had set up several small kingdoms. These included Kent, East Anglia, Essex, Sussex and Wessex ("the lands of the East, South, and West Saxons"), Mercia, and Northumbria.

The most powerful ruler among the English kings was acknowledged as "bretwalda," or supreme king. The Sutton Hoo ship burial, discovered in AD 1939, is almost certainly the monument to King Redwald of East Anglia, who was bretwalda in the AD 620s, and who died in AD 627. The strongest English king of the AD 700s was Offa of Mercia.

Western and northern Britain

In Wales, there were four British kingdoms: Gywnedd, Dyfed, Powys, and Gwent. These were independent under their own princes. In the west of England was the kingdom of Dumnonia. In the far north, the Picts ruled Pictavia and fought the Scots who ruled in the west. By the AD 800s, the Scots, under Kenneth MacAlpin, claimed to rule the Picts as well.

△ Saxon farmers harvested grain with sickles and pitchforks. The Saxons tilled old Roman fields and plowed new land but abandoned the Roman villas.

At this period … Britain, being deprived … of all her warlike stores, and of the flower of her army, was exposed to the ravages of her enemies on every side.

ECCLESIASTICAL HISTORY, ST. BEDE (AD 731)

Bede was a monk in the AD 700s. He wrote an important book called the Ecclesiastical History of the English People.

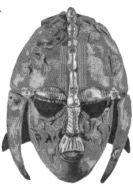

△ The iron helmet found in the ship burial at Sutton Hoo is one of many treasures unearthed by archaeologists at the site in Suffolk.

AD

The Franks emerged from the ruins of the Roman Empire in AD 476 as the dominant people of western Europe. Their leader Clovis enlarged his lands around the River Rhine (Germany) by wars. By AD 540, the Franks ruled most of the old Roman province of Gaul (France, named after the Franks).

The Franks

Clovis becomes king of the Franks.	AD 481
Franks defeat the last great Roman army in the West at the battle of Soissons.	AD 486
Franks control most of Gaul and Germany.	AD 540
Pepin the Short founds the Carolingian dynasty.	AD 751
Charlemagne born.	C. AD 742
Charlemagne rules the Franks.	AD 771
Charlemagne fights Muslims in Spain. The Frankish army is attacked at Roncesvalles.	AD 778
Charlemagne is crowned emperor of the West by Pope Leo III.	AD 800
Charlemagne dies.	AD 814

The first Frankish ruling family is known as the Merovingian dynasty, after Clovis's grandfather Meroveus. Clovis became a Christian. He made Paris his capital city. Most of the Franks were peasant farmers, who lived on lands ruled by nobles. The peasants raised food, doing the seasonal tasks of plowing, sowing, and harvesting. They also had to fight for their lord when he went to war. Frankish lords fought to win new land and shared the spoils of conquest with their soldiers. This Frankish system of land-holding and service was the beginning of the feudal system in Europe.

The Carolingians

The Merovingian kings actually had less power than their "mayors of the royal palace," officials who traditionally came from two families. The winner of a power struggle between these families was Pepin of Herstal, who ruled the

▷ Charlemagne was very tall and a man of enormous energy. He could not write, but he did learn to read Latin. He liked to listen as books were read to him.

▷ Frankish soldiers head for battle. Under Charlemagne, the Frankish Empire expanded greatly, taking in neighboring Bavaria and Lombardy. The Franks finally conquered Saxony after about 30 years of bitter fighting.

△ The sword of Charlemagne. The favorite weapons of Frankish soldiers were the lance and the sword.

Franks even though he was not their king. Pepin's son was Charles Martel, whose army defeated the Muslim invaders of southern Europe in AD 632. Charles Martel's son was another Pepin, Pepin the Short, and he made himself king.

Pepin the Short's son Charles became the most famous of all Frankish rulers. He was called Carolus Magnus (Charles the Great), or Charlemagne in old French. The "Carolingian" dynasty is named after him.

Charlemagne's empire

When Pepin died, his sons Carloman and Charlemagne shared power until Carloman died. Then Charlemagne set out and won new wars of conquest in the Netherlands, Germany, and Italy. When he defeated pagans, such as the Saxons of Germany, he forced them to become Christians like himself.

Charlemagne wanted to govern well. His capital of Aachen, called "a second Rome," was rich and dazzling, yet he chose to live simply. No other ruler in Europe was so famous or magnificent, and on Christmas Day in 800, the pope crowned Charlemagne Holy Roman Emperor.

New writing

This is a sample of Carolingian script, the clear and more easily written style of writing that was introduced during the reign of Charlemagne. The actual text is written in Latin.

△ The horn of Roland, a Frankish hero killed at the battle of Roncesvalles in AD 778.

The power of the English kingdoms ebbed and flowed as first one, then another, became dominant. By AD 800, the strongest English kingdom was Wessex. But it faced a threat from yet more invaders, the Vikings, who saw England as a good place to settle.

Alfred the Great

The Vikings came from Norway, Sweden, and Denmark. The first Viking ships appeared off the southern English coast in AD 787, according to the history known as the Anglo-Saxon Chronicle, which was begun in the reign of Alfred.

Northern Britain, too, felt the fury of these marauding Norsemen, or Danes as the English called them. Vikings raided and looted the rich monasteries of Northumbria. Ships loaded with families and farm animals also crossed the North Sea, and Viking farmers and traders settled in Orkney, in Ireland, and the Isle of Man.

A fight for survival

In AD 850, a huge fleet of 350 Viking ships appeared in the River Thames. That winter a Viking army camped in southeast England for the first time. Such mass attacks posed a threat to the survival of the English kingdoms.

East Anglia, Northumbria, and Mercia were all ravaged by Viking armies in the AD 860s. The Christian king of East Anglia, King Edmund, was murdered for refusing to give up his faith. In AD 871, Wessex was attacked. Its new king was the young and untested Alfred, the fifth of four brothers, each of whom had been king before him.

Alfred's wars and peace

Alfred's first campaigns were failures, and he had to retreat and hide in the

△ Alfred had fought at sea himself and ordered the building of ships for the first English navy. The new ships were similar to the Viking longships, but bigger and faster.

First Vikings land in England.	AD 787
Alfred is born.	AD 849
A great army of Vikings attacks England.	AD 865
Vikings kill King Edmund of East Anglia.	AD 869
Alfred becomes king of Wessex.	AD 871
Alfred captures London and fortifies the city.	AD 886
Alfred dies. His son Edward becomes king (to AD 924).	AD 899
Athelstan, Alfred's grandson, rules English and Vikings in England.	AD 924
Reign of Edgar, the high point of Anglo-Saxon rule in England.	AD 959–975

△ *Alfred is said to have made candle clocks to time his working day, which was divided between government, prayer, and learning.*

The Danelaw

The lands in eastern England settled by the Vikings became known as the Danelaw. The English at the time referred to the invaders as "Danes." In places, Viking settlers mingled with the local people.

marshes of Somerset. Rallying his forces, he defeated the Vikings at the battle of Edington and made a treaty with them. The Viking leader Guthrum agreed to become a Christian. In return, Alfred allowed the Vikings to settle in East Anglia.

Alfred was now recognized as king of all the English. He set about making his kingdom strong enough to resist future Viking attacks. He built a navy. He built forts and fortified towns called burhs to protect the countryside. He rebuilt the defences of London. He organized a system of "call-up" in time of war – a farmer had to supply two soldiers for every plow on his land. The army was divided into two groups: one armed and ready to fight, the other working on farms and guarding the forts.

Law-maker and scholar

Alfred issued new laws, to end the feuds which caused bloodshed between families and to give more protection to the weak against the strong. He divided his kingdom into shires governed by eldermen.

Alfred invited foreign scholars to his court. He was determined to educate his people, and he spent many hours translating books from Latin into English. For his many achievements, he is the only English king honored with the title "the Great."

△ *The Alfred jewel was found near Athelney in Somerset in AD 1693. It may be part of a bookmark. On it are the words "Alfred had me made" in Latin.*

> Then began I ... to turn into English the book that is named in Latin *Pastoralis* ... one-while word for word, another-while meaning for meaning.

ALFRED THE GREAT (AD 849–899)

Alfred was the most important lawmaker among England's early kings.

The Vikings came from Scandinavia (Norway, Denmark, and Sweden). Their homeland of mountains, fjords, and forests offered little spare farmland for a growing population. So, many Vikings went abroad in search of new lands to settle.

The Vikings

The Vikings were farmers, but also fierce warriors, and their first impact on western Europe was a violent one. Norwegians and Danes began to sail across the North Sea in the late AD 700s, raiding the coasts of Britain and mainland Europe. They raided churches and towns, carrying off loot and slaves. Their raids caused panic, and rulers tried to buy off the invaders with gold. This only encouraged the Vikings to come back for more.

Trade and home life

Viking towns such as Kaupang in Norway and Hedeby in Denmark flourished on deals in furs, reindeer antlers, and walrus ivory. These materials were exchanged for weapons, jewels, and pottery.

Viking home life was based on farming and fishing. Several generations (including uncles and cousins) often shared one single-roomed house made of wood, stone, or turf. A good sword was passed down from father to son.

Many of the Vikings' gods were the same pagan gods of the Germans and English. The most important was one-eyed Odin, but most people's favorite was Thor, the thunder god who brandished his hammer.

△ Ships lie beached beside a Viking town, with wooden houses thatched with straw. Vikings made long journeys by ship and overland to trade.

The trading town of Hedeby in Denmark is founded.	AD 790s
First reported Viking raid on England.	AD 787
Vikings begin to settle in the Baltic region and Russia.	AD 860
Vikings reach Iceland.	AD 874
Vikings are given Normandy to prevent further attacks on France.	AD 911
Danish Vikings become Christians.	AD 960
Erik the Red discovers Greenland.	AD 982
Leif Eriksson lands in North America.	AD 1003
A Dane, Cnut, becomes king of England.	AD 1016

AD

Longships

The Viking longships were fast and strong enough to cross oceans. They had a long, slender hull with a single mast and sail.

△ Both Viking men and women dressed in hard-wearing clothing made from linen or woolen cloth. They wore shoes made from leather.

Intrepid voyagers

Sailing west into the Atlantic Ocean, Norwegian Vikings settled in Iceland (AD 874) and Greenland (AD 982), and they landed in North America in AD 1003. Swedish Vikings crossed the Baltic to the important trade towns of Kiev and Novgorod and traveled on eastward to the Black Sea. Greek and Arab merchants called the northerners "Rus" – which is how Russia got its name.

Vikings could be found in Sicily, Baghdad, and Constantinople. Trade goods from such faraway places have been found in Jorvik (York) in England and in Dublin in Ireland.

Leaders and government

The leader of each community was the richest landowner, or jarl. He shared his wealth, entertaining his warriors and servants with feasts and songs in his great hall. The most powerful leaders called themselves kings. They tried to settle blood feuds between enemies, which were very common.

Viking free men met in assemblies called "things" to settle disputes about crimes or land disagreements. Laws passed down from generation to generation. A person who refused to obey the rules of the "thing" was an outlaw, and anyone might kill him.

Since tonight the wind is high/ The sea's white mane a fury/ I need not fear the hordes of Hell/ Coursing the Irish Channel.

ON THE VIKING RAIDS, ANONYMOUS

△ Decorative brooches such as this were used by both Viking men and women to hold their outer garments (cloaks and tunics) in place.

By the AD 1000s, trade routes between Europe and Asia were well established. Much of this trade went by sea. People traded in slaves and furs, gold and silver, ivory and precious stones, silk and carpets, glass and leatherwork.

Trade and Towns

Arab dhows sailed to India and East Africa, Chinese junks to the islands of Indonesia and Japan. Viking ships crossed the Atlantic to Iceland, Greenland, and North America. The Vikings founded small settlements. In Iceland, settlers met in the Althing – Europe's oldest democratic assembly.

By land and sea

Many sea craft were small, with oars and could navigate rivers; river towns were often busy ports, like London and Viking Jorvik (York), for example. There was regular trade between Vikings in Jorvik and Dublin in Ireland, with Viking towns in Scandinavia.

Few poor people ever left their home village except perhaps to go to market. But scholars, soldiers, merchants, and kings traveled far, even though roads were poor. Charlemagne traveled widely around his empire. King Alfred went from England to Rome as a boy. Most journeys were made on foot, or on horseback, and were slow. Travelers followed well-used

△ Merchants exchange goods in a busy street in Viking Jorvik (modern York) in England. These men are trading in furs, which were one of the main exports of Jorvik at this time.

Paper-making spreads from China into the Islamic world.	AD 750
Porcelain is first made in China.	AD 900
Trade treaties are made between Kiev and Constantinople.	AD 907
An Arab scholar, Al-Masudi, travels the East African coast as far south as Mozambique.	AD 916
Rise of the kingdom of Ghana in Africa and its chief city Kumbi Saleh.	AD 920
Woodblock printing of inexpensive books in China.	AD 950
First Viking sighting of North American mainland.	AD 1000
Ghana kingdom controls trade routes across the Sahara in Africa.	AD 1000
Leif Eriksson lands in North America.	AD 1003

▷ *Caravans carrying gold, salt, and slaves followed the long trails across the Sahara Desert. There was trade between the cities of West Africa and those of North Africa, Egypt, and Arabia. The routes taken by Muslim pilgrims to Mecca in Arabia were also important.*

trade routes, where some safety from bandits might be expected. The most famous was the Silk Road, the long trade route overland from China to the west.

How peoples saw themselves

By AD 1000, the Christian peoples of Europe were taught to see themselves as belonging to "Christendom" – the Christian world. In its empire, Islam had unified peoples who shared not only a religion but also language, science, and art.

To an Easterner, Western civilization appeared much less sophisticated. An Arab ambassador seeing Vikings in Russia thought them impressive ("as tall as date palms"), but uncivilized – they ate like animals, lived in crude houses, and worshipped idols.

Civilizations apart

With their canals, fine houses, markets, and restaurants, Chinese cities were unrivaled. Yet, China remained aloof, caring little for what went on in the barbarian world beyond its frontiers. The peoples of North and South America, too, remained outside the growing cultural exchange.

△ *Odin, the god of battle and death, was one of the principal gods worshiped by the Vikings. He was the ruler of Asgard, the heavenly home of the gods.*

Silk traders

For many years, the Chinese were the only people that knew how to make silk. European traders would make the long journey to China to take silk back to Europe, where it was an expensive luxury.

△ *A pottery figure of an Armenian merchant, made in China during the Tang dynasty (AD 618–907).*

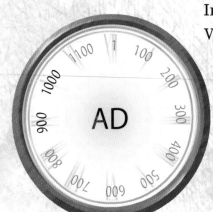

AD

1100 · 1 · 100 · 200 · 300 · 400 · 500 · 600 · 700 · 800 · 900 · 1000

In the AD 900s, England was again attacked by Vikings. King Ethelred (AD 978–1016) tried to buy off the invaders with bribes. His people had to pay higher taxes to raise the money. But the idea of bribes did not work either.

Norman Conquest

In AD 1013, the Danish king Sweyn Forkbeard made himself king of England, and the unpopular Ethelred fled to Normandy in France. In AD 1016, Sweyn's son Cnut became king. During his reign, which lasted until AD 1035, England was ruled as part of Cnut's empire, which included Denmark and Norway. Cnut was a good king, but his two sons had brief reigns, and England's next ruler brought confusion.

Viking leader Rollo is given Normandy. Normandy is later ruled by dukes.	AD 911
King Cnut, ruler of England, Norway, and Denmark, dies.	AD 1035
Death of Harthacnut, last Danish king of England.	AD 1042
King Macbeth of Scotland is killed by Malcolm Canmore, who later becomes king.	AD 1057
Harold, son of Godwine, and his brother Tostig fight the Welsh.	AD 1063
Harold is shipwrecked in Normandy.	AD 1064
Edward the Confessor sees the completion of Westminster Abbey.	AD 1065
Harold is king. Normans win battle of Hastings. William becomes king.	AD 1066

Edward the Confessor

The new king was Edward, known as the Confessor, son of the exiled Etheltred. He was more Norman than English and very religious. He built the first Westminster Abbey.

Power was in the hands of the English earls, like the scheming Godwine of Wessex. Edward married Godwine's daughter, but they had no children. So when Edward died in AD 1066, there was no obvious heir. The witan, or council, of England chose Earl Godwine's son, Harold, as king.

Rivals for a crown

There were two other claimants. One was Harold Hardrada, king of Norway. The other was William, Duke of Normandy, a distant relative of Edward the Confessor. William claimed that Harold had sworn to

△ The Normans built castles to defend their newly won lands and subdue the conquered English. Each castle stood on an earth mound, or motte. A wooden tower was built on top. At the foot of the mound was a stockade, or bailey, inside which were stables, houses for soldiers, stores, and a kitchen.

△ *William of Normandy ruled England from AD 1066 to 1087. He claimed that Edward the Confessor promised him the throne in AD 1051. He also said that Harold (who was shipwrecked in France in AD 1064) had sworn to accept this.*

Domesday Book

In AD 1085, William I ordered a survey of land in England. The findings were written down in the *Domesday Book* (means "Day of Judgement"). It is the best record we have of life in England between AD 1066 and 1088, naming about 13,000 towns and villages.

back his claim. This may or may not be true. Hardrada and William were both tough soldiers, and both prepared to attack England to seize the throne.

Two battles and a conquest

The Norwegians landed first, in the north of England. Harold defeated them at the battle of Stamford Bridge near York on September 25 AD 1066. Both Harold Hardrada and Tostig were killed. Then news came that William's ships had landed in Sussex, and Harold at once rushed south to fight them.

The crucial battle was fought only 19 days later, on October 14 at Senlac Hill, north of Hastings. The English, who fought on foot, resisted bravely as the Norman cavalry charged their wall of shields, and archers fired showers of arrows at them. In the end, Harold was killed, the shield wall broke, and the Normans won.

The Normans rule

William declared himself king. He was crowned in Westminster Abbey on Christmas Day. The English nobles lost their lands. French became the language of government. William and his barons built castles to guard their new land. A new age was beginning.

▷ *The story of William's invasion and the battle of Hastings is told in 72 scenes in the Bayeux Tapestry. The embroidery is about 20 in. wide and 76 yards long. It was made on the orders of William's half-brother.*

The people who lived during the late Middle Ages did not, of course, think they were "medieval" at all but modern. The term "medieval," which comes from the Latin word meaning "of the middle age," was only invented much later on, by historians and other scholars.

The Late Middle Ages

The late Middle Ages stand in the gap between the Norman Conquest of England, in 1066, and the modern period, which begins with the Renaissance.

In many ways this time seems puzzling and remote to us today, full of armored knights, saints, pilgrims, gloomy castles, and muddy villages. The only heat came from open fires, and the only light from oil or candles. Time meant little, for there were very few clocks in use.

Life and faith

The vast majority of people all over the world lived and worked on the land. They depended entirely on what they could grow or catch, and if crops failed or hunting was bad, they would simply starve. Hunger was always a threat, and so were disease and war. In this world of fear and death, religion had a very important place.

Richard I

By about AD 1000, Christianity had taken hold across nearly all of Europe, while the religion of Islam had spread across the Near East. These two faiths governed every part of people's lives and gave out harsh treatment to anyone who dared to question them.

Familiar sights

Yet the late Middle Ages also included many things that are familiar to us today. The first great cities, such as Venice and Constantinople, were growing, and many modern nations were forming. The idea of rule by parliament was developing, and the earliest universities were founded. People were beginning to introduce systems of banking. We can still see many fine medieval buildings today, from the cathedrals and castles of Europe to the temples and palaces of faraway Asia.

How did a medieval king control his realm? In Europe, few monarchs were rich enough to keep a standing army ready to put down a rebellion. Besides, most of their subjects lived in remote areas where bad roads made traveling slow and difficult, especially for large bands of soldiers.

Lords and Peasants

System of feudalism develops in Western Europe.	c. 750
William of Normandy invades England. Normans build timber castles.	1066
Domesday census of land and people of England is completed.	1086
Feudalism across much of Western Europe. Fiefs pass land on from father to son.	c. 1100
Richard I builds massive Chateau Gaillard in France, at a great cost.	1198
Peasants' revolt in England against poll tax. Tax riots in Paris.	1381
Decline of castles begins, as new warfare methods make them easier to conquer.	c. 1400
Feudalism begins to decline.	c. 1400

The answer was to share the land among royal supporters. The king gave grants of property, called fiefs, to his most powerful noblemen – the bishops, barons, and other strong knights. In return, the nobles promised to obey the king and to raise troops to fight for him whenever they were needed. Historians refer to this system of fiefs (or "feus" in Scotland) as "feudalism."

Feudalism touched every part of society, from top to bottom. The nobles granted portions of their estates to lesser lords or knights, who in turn rented plots of land to small farmers and peasants. The peasants paid the rent by laboring on their landlord's fields and giving him a share of what they grew themselves.

Peasants

The life of a peasant was hard – and often short. (The average lifespan of a European peasant in 1300 was only 25 years.) Peasants had to work every day except for Sundays and "holy days" (holidays), tending their animals and crops. Markets were usually far away, so if they didn't grow enough food they would probably starve. There was also the danger of death from disease or violence.

△ This stronghold of a Norman lord is well protected against attack. Around the lower area, called the bailey, runs a palisade (fence) of pointed stakes. The wooden tower (an early form of castle) above is built on a flat-topped mound called a motte.

△ *The medieval peasant owned almost nothing. The landlord owned the land and buildings in the manor, as well as all the animals and crops. He even owned the peasants' clothes.*

In the fields

These peasants are working in the fields surrounding their lord's castle. They are breaking up the soil with a plow pulled by an ox. At this time, the large majority of Europeans were peasants.

The manor

There were very few big towns in early medieval Europe, and at least 90 percent of people lived and worked in the countryside, on manors or estates belonging to their landlord. The farmland in the manor was divided into three sections, and the families were given plots in each one.

The lord of the manor had complete control of his little community. He took rent from the peasants living in his manor, in the form of produce and labor. He was the judge in the manor court, with the power to fine or imprison wrongdoers.

The castle

At the center of the manor was the lord's home. This might be simply a large house, built strongly of stone. A richer and more powerful lord might live in a castle, with room for knights and other soldiers. Kings and barons sometimes built a series of castles to impose their control over a wide area. More than 25,000 castles were built in Western Europe alone during the Middle Ages.

If an enemy army approached, the villagers could take shelter inside the castle, bringing their livestock and food stores with them.

△ *A highly ornate gold drinking goblet. Only a very wealthy person could afford costly items like this. Poorer people drank out of leather tankards or earthenware cups.*

> A good man was ther of religioun,/ And was a poore Person of a town,/ But riche he was of holy thought and werk.

THE CANTERBURY TALES, GEOFFREY CHAUCER

Chaucer was a poet who lived at this time. The Canterbury Tales is his most famous work.

121

Palestine lay at the eastern end of the Mediterranean Sea. This was the Holy Land, the most important place in the Christian religion, where Jesus Christ had been born and lived. When it was captured by Muslim armies in the 11th century the Christian powers in Europe set off to recapture it.

The Crusades

Seljuk Turks seize holy city of Jerusalem.	1078
First Crusade ends in retaking of Jerusalem (1099).	1096
Second Crusade ends in Christian defeat and loss of Jerusalem again.	1147
Saladin becomes leader of the united Seljuks.	1187
Third Crusade. Christians fail to regain Jerusalem.	1189
Crusader troops sack Constantinople.	1204
Children's Crusade ends in tragedy.	1212
European interest in recapturing the Holy Land begins to fade.	1291

Arab Muslims had conquered Palestine in about AD 660, but they had still allowed Christian pilgrims to visit. However, when the Seljuk Turks swept down from central Asia and invaded Iran, Iraq, and then Palestine, they persecuted Christians. By 1078, they had seized the Holy City of Jerusalem and were even threatening Constantinople itself.

The First Crusade

The Byzantine emperor, a Christian monarch who lived in Constantinople, needed help. He turned to the pope, who in 1095 called for all Christians to start a holy war against the Seljuks.

Thousands rushed to join the Crusader armies. They crossed into Palestine and recaptured the important cities of Nicaea and Antioch. Jerusalem fell in 1099 after a desperate siege lasting six weeks, and the Crusaders took terrible revenge by slaughtering thousands of Muslims.

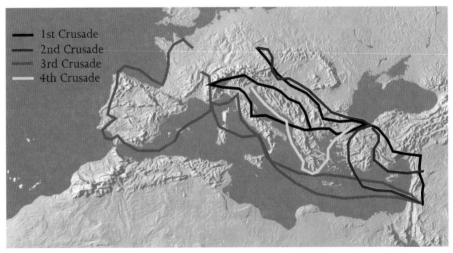

△ The routes taken by the First, Second, Third, and Fourth Crusades to the Holy Land, spanning a period of more than 100 years.

▷ Standards flutter in the breeze as Crusader knights board galleys and sailing ships in a Mediterranean port. Servants carry on baggage and supplies for the voyage to the Holy Land.

△ At the end of the First Crusade, many knights stayed to guard the conquered land. They built fine castles and settled down to lead comfortable lives as colonists.

The Second, Third, and Fourth Crusades

The easy existence of the newly victorious Christian forces made them weak. The Turks meanwhile grew strong again and struck back in 1144 by taking Edessa. Alarmed, the German and French kings answered the threat by leading fresh armies on the Second Crusade in 1147, but the Muslim forces quickly defeated them.

By 1187, the Muslims were united under a new leader – the wise and gallant Saladin. He launched his own holy war, or "jihad," against the European invaders, driving them out of Jerusalem. Once again, a Crusader army sailed for the Holy Land but failed to retake Jerusalem. In 1202, the Pope called for yet another expedition to seize Jerusalem. This was a greater disaster, because the Crusaders never reached Palestine. Greedy for money and loot, they decided to attack Constantinople instead. The capital of the Byzantine Empire was taken by storm and sacked in 1204, and the Christian emperor, whose plight had inspired the first Crusade, was killed.

The Children's Crusade began in 1212. Fifty thousand children set off from France and Germany for the Holy Land. Many died on the journey; many more were captured and sold as slaves in Africa. The Pied Piper legend may be based on the story of these children.

Richard I

Richard I of England and Philip II of France led the armies of the Third Crusade, setting sail for the Holy Land in 1189. Despite early success, the two leaders began quarreling and never recaptured Jerusalem. Richard was forced to make a treaty with the Muslim leader, Saladin, and return home.

△ The seal of the Christian knights who settled on the island of Sicily. They pledged to shelter and protect pilgrims traveling to Palestine.

In 1167, a child called Temujin was born on the desolate plains of Mongolia. When the boy was nine, his father was murdered and his family was left poor and friendless.

The Mongol Empire

From this grim beginning, Temujin grew up to become one of the world's greatest conquerors. He was hailed by the Mongols as Genghis Khan – the "Universal Ruler."

The great khan

The Mongols were tough and violent and splendid horse riders. For centuries, the many Mongol clans, or groups, had fought among themselves. As Genghis Khan rose to power, he united these clans and organized them into a fearsome army.

In 1206, Genghis Khan became leader of all the Mongol people and began to build his astonishing empire. First, he defeated the neighboring Tanguts to the south. Then, in 1213, his massive army swept over the Great Wall into China. After destroying the troops of the

Birth of Temujin.	1167
Temujin becomes leader of all Mongols, with the title of Genghis Khan.	1206
Mongol armies begin invasion of China.	1213
Mongol armies invade and devastate Khwarizm.	1218
Death of Temujin.	1227
Ogodei, son of Temujin, becomes new khan.	1229
Mongol armies suffer first defeat at Ain Jalut.	1260
Kublai, grandson of Temujin, conquers southern China.	1276
Failure of Mongols' attempt to invade Japan.	1281

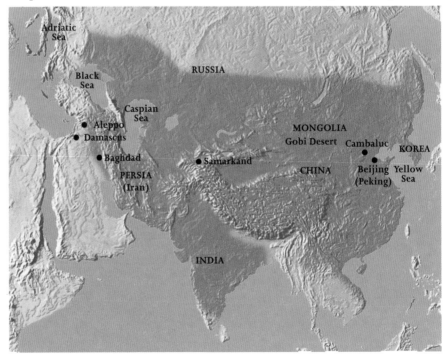

△ The mighty empire of the Mongols stretched from the Danube river in Europe in the west, across eastern Europe and Asia, to China in the east.

Mongol life

The Mongols lived on the flat, grassy steppes of Asia, wandering with their herds of sheep, goats, and cattle. They carried their tentlike felt homes, called yurts, around with them.

△ *Genghis Khan was a ruthless warrior, destroying entire cities and their populations during his conquests. Yet he succeeded in keeping the peace across his vast empire.*

△ *A Mongol warrior. With their tight discipline, nimble horses, and rapid shooting of arrows, the Mongols were terrifying enemies.*

▷ *A group of Arab merchants take shelter from the fierce midday heat. Their camel train is carrying goods from ports on the Red Sea to the Mediterranean coast.*

Chin emperor, they marched on to Beijing. The emperor fled south, leaving the whole of northern China to the Mongols. When the Sultan of Khwarizm (modern Iraq and Afghanistan) killed a party of Mongol merchants in 1218, Genghis Khan's troops raged through Khwarizm, burning cities, plundering, and killing.

Into Europe

Genghis Khan died of a fever in 1227, but the Mongols continued to build the empire. The new khan was Ogodei (Temujin's son), who strengthened his hold on Khwarizm and China. Within 50 years, all of China's vast lands were under Mongol rule.

In 1236, Ogodei's son Batu set out on the most ambitious adventure yet. With an army of 150,000 men, he crossed the River Volga and invaded Russia. From here, Batu rampaged into Poland and Hungary and reached the shores of the Adriatic Sea. The Mongol Empire now stretched right across Asia and into Europe.

Batu was poised to sweep on into Western Europe, but events at home forced him to turn back. Ten years later the Mongols came west again. They sacked the cities of Baghdad, Aleppo, and Damascus, but again their leader was summoned back home.

"For God's sake, let us sit upon the ground and tell sad stories of the death of kings," says Richard II of England in Shakespeare's play. Being a medieval ruler was a dangerous business, especially in Britain.

Medieval Monarchs

Richard II himself was deposed in 1399 and savagely murdered, as was Edward II 50 years earlier. Henry II (1189) and Richard I (1199) were killed in battle, and John (1216) and Edward I (1307) died of disease.

The power of the barons

European kings saw themselves as chosen to rule by God, and they were crowned in magnificent religious ceremonies. They believed that they had complete power over their subjects and that anyone who rebelled against them was defying God's wishes. All the same, a king who was weak, unjust, or stupid could soon get into trouble with his powerful barons.

Many barons grew so strong that the monarch could not control them, and some even built up their own fiefs into small independent realms within a kingdom. They raised private armies, which they sometimes used to attack their neighbors and plunder their possessions and land.

The king's court

A wise king summoned his barons to court, where he could keep an eye on them. The royal court was the center of the kingdom, where the monarch showed off his wealth and power. Many courts were scenes of great magnificence. Frederick II, the Holy

△ The magnificent coronation of Charles V. He became king of Spain in 1516 (he was the grandson of King Ferdinand and Queen Isabella of Spain), and three years later he was crowned Holy Roman Emperor. During his reign Charles ruled more countries than any other monarch in Europe.

AD
1100 / 1200 / 1300 / 1400 / 1500 / 1600 / 1700 / 1800

c. 1170 — Henry II of England holds special court sessions to settle disputes.

c. 1180 — Andreas Capellanus writes a book called The Art of Courtly Love.

1215 — English barons force King John to sign the Magna Carta.

c. 1225 — The Roman de la Rose, the most famous troubadour poem, is written.

1241–1270 — Reign of "ideal" monarch, Louis IX of France.

1264 — English "commons" are summoned to the King's Council for the first time.

1295 — King Edward I of England calls first recognizable parliament.

c. 1400 — English Commons gain the right to introduce bills to Parliament.

△ *Jousting in medieval times. Clad in a full suit of armor, knights on horseback competed in jousting matches, trying to knock each other to the ground with lances.*

Magna Carta

In 1215 the English barons forced the unpopular King John to sign a document now called Magna Carta (Great Charter). It protected the rights of nobles, and made sure no one was imprisoned without trial.

Roman Emperor (1220–1250) had a castle with golden floors, dancing girls, and exotic animals. Charles V of France (1364–1380) entertained 800 guests at his palace in Paris with a feast of 40 dishes.

However, the court was also the seat of government. The king's ministers and officers collected taxes and made laws. The monarch himself might also preside over special sessions to settle disputes between nobles and decide on grants of land.

Love and war

There were many pastimes for the royalty and nobles at court. The courtiers watched mock battles, or "tourneys," in which groups of knights fought each other. Not all games were so violent. On wet days, lords and ladies might sit indoors playing chess or backgammon, while card games (which were invented in China or India) became popular in Europe in the 1200s. A more daring pursuit was "courtly love," a sort of artificial love game with very strict rules. A knight declared his passion for a lady (probably married to someone else) and wrote her worshiping poems but rarely pursued his interest any farther.

"No free man shall be taken or imprisoned or dispossessed, or outlawed or exiled ... except by the lawful judgement of his peers or by the law of the land.
MAGNA CARTA (1215)

△ *King John, who was forced to sign the Magna Carta. Copies of the document, which tried to put an end to the king's abuse of his power, were distributed across England.*

AD

During the Middle Ages, England became the dominant power in the British Isles. Yet for most of the period, her rulers were not English but French. The Normans came in 1066 and quickly formed England's ruling class.

Kingdoms of Britain

After the Normans came the Plantagenets, whose first king, Henry II, was crowned in 1154. The biggest part of Henry's realm was in France. His son, King Richard I, spent less than six months of his reign in England.

Henry II brought peace to England after years of civil war and unrest. He curbed the power of the barons and reformed the legal system. He also led several expeditions to France to try and expand his territories there. There were also closer neighbors to deal with. The English kings needed to stop invasions into English territory. In addition, control of the other nations of the British Isles allowed the English to earn more money by raising taxes.

Ireland

Henry II invaded Ireland in 1169, entered the capital Dublin, and forced the Irish rulers to accept him as overlord. After this, English settlers gradually took over the eastern part of the island, seizing land from Irish chieftains. English rule brought increased trade and prosperity to

Malcolm III becomes first king of a united Scotland.	1057
William I becomes first Norman king of England.	1066
Henry II becomes first Plantagenet king of England.	1154
English soldiers invade Ireland.	1169
Llewelyn II rules over most of Wales.	1256
Edward I completes conquest of Wales and begins castlebuilding.	1282
Edward I invades southern Scotland.	1296
Robert the Bruce defeats English at Bannockburn.	1314
English recognize Scottish independence.	1328

△ Robert the Bruce, leader of the Scots, inspired the Scots to a great victory against the English at Bannockburn in 1314. Over 10,000 English soldiers were killed.

△ *Robert the Bruce. After the victory at Bannockburn, he drove the English out of Scotland by 1328, forcing them recognize Scotland as an independent country.*

△ *An Anglo-Irish cavalryman. By 1300 most of Ireland was under the control of the English.*

Ireland. This situation lasted until 1315, when a Scottish army landed in Ulster. After a long war, Ireland lay in ruins. England's power was weakened and never properly recovered, and the Irish chieftains won back most of their lands.

Wales

Norman barons had settled in the south of Wales, but in about 1215, the Welsh drove them out. They were united by Llewelyn the Great, their first national leader. By the 1250s, his grandson, Llewelyn, ruled most of the north and center of Wales. Edward I was determined to take control of the Welsh. Within ten years of coming to the throne, his armies had defeated Llewelyn and conquered most of Wales.

Scotland

The Scots caused the biggest problems for the English. In the 1200s, Scottish armies had made several border raids into northern England. Edward I was eager to conquer this dangerous and prosperous country. In 1296, he invaded and crushed the Scots at Dunbar. By 1305 he had defeated and killed the freedom fighter William Wallace. Defeat at Bannockburn by Robert the Bruce finally ended English success.

Now's the day, and now's the hour; See the front o'battle lour!
See approach proud Edward's power – Chains and slaverie.

SCOTS, WHA HAE, ROBERT BURNS

Robert Burns was a poet that lived in the 1700s. He wrote many patriotic Scottish poems.

△ *The lion was seen as a symbol of English power. For over 200 years, English kings tried to impose their rule on the other nations of the British Isles.*

The 14th century was filled with wars: in southeast Asia, the Siamese invaded Cambodia; Timur Lang, the last great Mongol leader, sacked Baghdad; the Ottoman Turks swarmed into eastern Europe; the Austrians fought the Swiss; the Portuguese fought the Castilians; and, in Germany, the nobles fought each other.

The 100 Years' War

The longest and most exhausting of these wars was between England and France. It lasted, off and on, until the middle of the 1400s and is known as the Hundred Years' War.

Two rivals

The conflict was a very complicated one. The Plantagenet kings of England also ruled a large part of France, while the rest belonged to the king of France. Both monarchs wanted to be the sole ruler of a united country. The French began to move into the English lands, seizing Normandy in 1204 and later taking charge of Gascony in the southwest.

There were plenty of other reasons for war. The French supported the Scots in their struggle against England. The English, in turn, claimed the throne of France when Charles IV died in 1328 and left no heirs.

The first phase: 1337–1360

Edward III of England dispatched his army to Normandy in 1337. He won a great sea battle at Sluys in 1340, as well as two land battles – at Crecy in 1346 and at Poitiers in 1356. He

▷ Edward, the oldest son of Edward III, was known as the Black Prince because he wore a suit of black armor. At the age of 16, he led a wing of the English army at the Battle of Crecy.

Edward III invades Normandy.	1337
English victory at the battle of Crecy.	1346
Treaty of Bretigny brings brief halt to the war.	1360
War breaks out again, and English lose territory in France.	1369
Henry V defeats French at the battle of Agincourt.	1415
Treaty of Troyes makes Henry V heir to French throne.	1420
Beginning of series of French victories, inspired by Joan of Arc.	1429
French drive English from all of France except Calais.	1453

AD

▷ English troops lay siege to the French town of Troyes. The city gates have been shut and barred against them. English officials are trying to persuade the leaders of Troyes to surrender.

△ English and Welsh longbowmen could shoot as many as ten arrows per minute. It took much longer to reload the French crossbows.

took the port of Calais and captured the new French king, John the Good. But the English army was smaller than the French one, far from home and ravaged by disease and lack of food. Edward made a treaty with the French in 1360, granting him control of Gascony in return for giving up his claim to France's throne.

Mercenaries and rebels: 1360–1413

The peace lasted only nine years. In 1369, the war flared up again when English armies tried to establish a hold on Gascony and Aquitaine. They sacked the city of Limoges, slaughtering its inhabitants. But Edward slowly lost most of the land he had gained.

The final phase: 1413–1453

In 1413, England had a new and warlike king – Henry V. He renewed the English claim to the French throne, launching a fresh invasion in 1415. He won the battle of Agincourt against a much bigger French army. When Henry V died in 1422, the tide turned again. The French, inspired by Joan of Arc, won a series of battles. By 1453, they had driven the English from Maine, Gascony, and Normandy and the war was won.

Joan of Arc

The French troops were inspired by a young peasant girl called Joan of Arc. She claimed to hear voices from God, telling her to free the French from English rule. Joan was finally captured, tried by the English, and found guilty of witchcraft and heresy. On May 30, 1431, she was burned at the stake.

△ A longbowman's quiver of arrows. Other weapons used in the Hundred Years' War were crossbows, halberds (combined spear and axe), and cannons.

During the early part of the Middle Ages, few kings had permanent armies. In time of war, they ordered their barons and other nobles to call up people from their estates. Military service was one of the ways to pay the rent. The result was often a rabble of unskilled and terrified peasants.

The Age of Armor

The only quality troops were the knights and men-at-arms who fought on horseback. By the 1300s, however, many tenants had begun to pay their rents in cash. Kings and lords could use this money to hire professional soldiers, who were properly trained.

A knight usually came from an upper-class family. He began his training as a squire at the age of 14, learning to ride horses, wrestle, and fight with the sword and the lance. At about 21, the squire was made a knight at a special ceremony, where he promised to fight for good and punish evildoers.

More extensive use of mail armor. Knights cover their arms and legs.	c. 1100
First recorded use of a stone-throwing trebuchet at the siege of Lisbon, Portugal.	1147
Rockets first used in warfare (in China).	1232
Mail armor now often covered with steel plates.	c. 1300
First recorded use of a cannon by Arab troops.	1304
Knights wear full suits of jointed armor to cover the entire body.	c. 1400
First steel crossbows in use.	c. 1420

▷ When striking a castle, attackers battered at the gates with a heavy ram. They also constructed machines like cranes, which could lift soldiers over the walls and into the castle.

△ *A knight in full armor. It was made of metal plates joined with straps and rivets to allow easier movement.*

Coat of arms

Each knight decorated his standard or shield with the heraldic symbols of his own coat of arms. This made it easier to identify the knight in full armor. Each coat of arms had its own unique design, made up of different colors, patterns, and objects or figures.

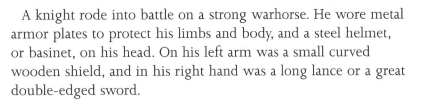

A knight rode into battle on a strong warhorse. He wore metal armor plates to protect his limbs and body, and a steel helmet, or basinet, on his head. On his left arm was a small curved wooden shield, and in his right hand was a long lance or a great double-edged sword.

The footsoldier

Footsoldiers had to be very tough. Unlike the mounted men, they would have to march as much as 19 miles a day, carrying all their equipment. Their simple leather boots soon grew soggy in wet weather, and lasted only a few weeks. Food was often scarce, as a large army soon ate everything in the surrounding countryside. Footsoldiers fought with narrow swords, short axes, or slashing blades set on long poles, called glaives.

△ Some footsoldiers wore coats of mail, but most made do with a padded canvas tunic and a leather or metal helmet.

Siege weapons

When the enemy took refuge inside a castle, there were two main ways of breaking down the defenses. One was to smash holes in the castle walls, often with the help of a battering ram hung from chains inside a shelter. The other was to dig a tunnel under the walls. The miners supported the roof of the tunnel with wooden beams. When it was complete, they built a big fire inside and ran away. As the props burned away the tunnel collapsed, bringing with it the foundations of the wall above.

◁ *This siege engine, known as a mangonel, was used to catapult stones at the walls of an enemy's castle.*

△ *An elaborate spearhead. In the mid-1300s, a new weapon came into use — a simple cannon that fired metal darts or stone balls.*

"We see death coming into our midst like black smoke," wrote a Welsh poet in 1349. Bubonic plague was a deadly disease which brought death to most parts of Asia, North Africa and Europe. There was no known cure for this plague.

The Black Death

The plague started as a bloody swelling in the armpit or groin and quickly invaded the whole body. It was highly infectious and killed uncountable millions of people. Another writer of the time called it "the end of the world."

The Black Death begins

The infection probably began on the steppes, the grassy plains, of Asia. It was carried by fleas that lived on the fur of marmots and other rodents. Any hunter who had contact with one of these animals would almost certainly be bitten by the fleas and catch the plague. The steppe peoples were wanderers and soon spread the disease.

First reports of the epidemic came from China in 1331. Within 20 years, more than 30 million Chinese had died, and the plague had begun moving westward, reaching central Asia and India by 1340.

Into Europe

By now the fleas had found a new home, the fur of the black rat. The holds of most medieval cargo ships were full of rats, and so the plague began to spread even faster, by sea.

Traders sailed from the Black Sea across the Mediterranean, and then out into the Atlantic, taking the disease with them. In

First outbreak of bubonic plague recorded in China.	1331
Plague reaches central Asia.	c. 1340
Genoese fleet brings plague to Europe.	1347
Plague reaches France and Britain.	1348
Spread of plague slows down.	1351
Second major outbreak throughout Europe and Asia.	1361
Beginning of third epidemic.	1375
Recurring outbreaks of plague in cycles of two or three years.	c. 1430

△ Crowded medieval towns, with their cramped streets and open sewers, were ideal breeding grounds for disease. Corpses were left out in the road for people to collect, thus spreading the disease further. The doors of infected houses were locked and marked with a cross.

△ Medieval paintings often depicted death as a skeleton, dancing and leading victims to their end.

The Black Death spreads

Between 1347 and 1350, the Black Death raged across Europe and the Muslim world. As many as 1,000 people died daily in the port of Alexandria.

this way, it reached places as far apart as Sweden, Egypt, and Libya. In 1347, a Genoese fleet brought rats with the plague to the port of Messina in Sicily. Within a few weeks, thousands there had died. In terror, the citizens drove the ships out to sea again, but it was too late. The infection had taken hold.

Out of control

At the height of the epidemic, the daily death toll in Cairo, one of the world's largest cities, may have reached 7,000. In France and the British Isles, at least a third of the entire population perished. Everywhere there were scenes of chaos and horror. Wood for coffins was scarce, and victims had to be buried in mass graves, or "plague pits." When there was no space for graves, the rotting corpses were stacked in piles at the side of the road.

The plague returns

The epidemic began to slow down after about 1351. It had killed at least 25 million people in Europe and the Near East – one in three persons. In 1361, a second great outbreak swept across the land, followed by several more at intervals of two or three years. It was not until after another outbreak in the 1600s that the threat of the Black Death faded at last.

△ Fleas living in the fur of the black rat carried the deadly plague virus across Europe. The rats lived close to humans, in the thatched roofs of people's homes.

> Many died daily or nightly in the public streets: many others died at home.
>
> ## GIOVANNI BOCCACCIO, ITALIAN POET, 1351
>
> Boccaccio was an Italian poet and diplomat who lived between 1313 and 1375.

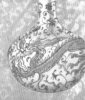

The Mongols completed their conquest of China in about 1270. For the first time the large country was united under the rule of a foreign power. The emperor was Kublai Khan, one of the grandsons of Genghis Khan, who governed very strictly.

Ming China

Kublai Khan forbade the Chinese from marrying into the Mongol race or speaking their language. They could not carry weapons, join the army, or hold positions of power. However, Kublai did give many important posts to foreigners. Among these was an Italian, Marco Polo, who arrived in Beijing in 1275.

Marco Polo

Marco Polo was one of the first Europeans to visit the Mongol court. He impressed the khan, who appointed him governor of the city of Yangchow.

In his famous account of his adventures, Marco Polo described the wealth and prosperity which Kublai brought to China. There were huge granaries stocked with grain and a grand canal for bringing goods to the capital. The Yangtze River became a great highway for shipping, where boats were loaded with silk, gems, and other treasures ready for the Persian Gulf. However, some modern scholars believe that Marco Polo never actually went to China but wrote his account based on reading other peoples' descriptions.

▷ *Kublai Khan receives Marco Polo at his court in Shangdu. Marco spent over 20 years in the khan's service, traveling all over China before returning home to Venice in 1295.*

Kublai Khan extends Mongol conquest of China.	1270
Marco Polo arrives in Beijing.	1275
Death of Kublai Khan.	1294
Chu Yuan-chang becomes first emperor of Ming dynasty.	1368
Death of Chu. His son Yung-lo becomes emperor.	1398
Seven exploratory voyages led by Zheng-ho.	1405–1433
End of the Ming dynasty.	1644

△ Running from the Pacific coast to central Asia, the Great Wall stretched for nearly 4,000 miles across China's northern border. Millions of men were forced to build it and thousands died.

Forbidden City

Beijing's Forbidden City was an area of elaborate palaces where only the servants of the emperor could enter.

The Ming emperors

After Kublai's death in 1294, Chinese people began to rebel against the harsh Mongol rule. By 1368, they had driven the foreigners out and the Ming dynasty had taken control. The first Ming emperor was Chu Yuan-chang, who had been a bandit, a soldier, and a monk. He restored Chinese pride and kept the country unified.

Chu and his successors turned Beijing into one of the greatest cities in the world, with the "Forbidden City" at its center. In the countryside, more land was plowed to grow more grain for food and cotton for clothing.

Walls and canals

The Chinese also had to protect themselves from further invasions from the north. They strengthened and extended the Great Wall as a barrier against attacks, fortified by garrisons of soldiers. To feed the troops, the Ming emperors also extended the Grand Canal, which carried 20,000 barges full of grain and other supplies over 1,000 miles.

The Chinese navy

Chu's son Yung-lo spent huge sums of money on exploration by sea. Fleets of 60 or more vessels made seven voyages into the Indian Ocean between 1405 and 1433.

By the 1430s, however, the Ming had grown suspicious of foreigners and travel. They ended the great voyages and banned overseas trade. Anyone who was caught dealing with foreign merchants was sentenced to death. China had closed itself off from the outside world once again.

△ Under the Ming emperors, art and literature flourished in China, most notably the making of the blue and white pottery still famous today as Ming porcelain.

There had been great cities in ancient times, such as Athens, Rome, Babylon, and Beijing. Most of these had fallen into ruin during the Dark Ages. Trade stopped between many towns, and thousands of people moved to the countryside to work on the land.

Towns and Trade

The later Middle Ages saw a return to the idea of living in cities. Peasants needed a market to sell their surplus produce. Craftworkers needed places to make and sell their goods. Merchants needed ports to receive cargoes. Bankers needed somewhere they could collect or lend out money.

Goods galore

Towns grew because trade grew. Goods traveled between East and West by ship or by the slower camel or horse transport overland. From China and the Indian Ocean came precious cargoes including silk, porcelain, and spices. From western Europe came iron, coal, cloth, and timber.

Ports such as Venice and Genoa became major trading centers. Their ships took goods all over the Mediterranean as far as London and Flanders. They also took part in the thriving trade in slaves, carrying men and women from Asia and Russia to be sold in North Africa and Europe.

▷ Inside a medieval shop, a butcher weighs customers' purchases on his scales. Anyone who cheated might find themselves in the stocks or fined.

1209 London Bridge is the first stone bridge across the River Thames.

1238 Trading port of Gdansk founded.

1252 The first pure gold florin is minted in Florence.

1277 Milan becomes a city-state, governed by local nobles.

c. 1280 Paris, with population of 150,000, is Europe's biggest city.

1380 Venice defeats Genoa to gain control of eastern Mediterranean trade.

1425 Building of London's Guildhall, for all guild members.

1442 Founding of first important bank in France by Jacques Coeur.

△ *Banking probably developed in northern Italy, where moneylenders did their business from benches, or "banks." They charged customers interest for these loans.*

Gold florins

The bankers of the Italian city of Florence issued their own gold coins, called florins. This one is stamped with a lily, the city's emblem. It is the size of a fingernail. Cash was often too heavy and unsafe to carry around.

Freedom from feudalism

Towns, like villages, began as part of a lord's estate. Townspeople had to work for the lord and pay him rent. But as towns grew bigger and wealthier, the people wanted to be free from the old feudal ties. In England, the monarch gave citizens the right to govern themselves in return for a yearly payment. Such towns became boroughs, or burghs, able to make their own local laws and raise their own taxes.

Elsewhere, this struggle for freedom was more violent. In northern France and Belgium, there were armed rebellions against royal power. The free cities, or communes, often had to fight each other to keep their independence.

△ *Each occupation, including these blacksmiths, had its own guild. The guilds fixed prices and standards of work, and they made sure their members were well paid.*

The guilds

The boom in prosperity and freedom was good for a town's craftworkers, and their numbers grew. Some cities had separate streets for each kind of trade – one for shoemakers, one for butchers, and so on. Each trade formed its own association, or guild. All workers in a guild trade had to go through a long and difficult training program. The guilds soon grew rich and powerful as they were able to set the prices that all the tradesmen in the guild were allowed to charge.

◁ *The port of Constantinople, with its unique position between the continents of Europe and Asia, was an important trading center. Many of the rich trade routes between the Persian Gulf and the Black Sea passed through the city.*

AD

The Ottoman Empire

In about 1300, a Turkish leader called Osman ruled a small kingdom in Anatolia (modern Turkey). His family name in Arabic was "Othman" and is better known to us today as Ottoman. Osman and his descendants were to build up one of the most important and long-lasting empires in world history.

The Ottoman Turks began to take over parts of the weak Byzantine Empire. The new empire was a strong Muslim answer to the power of Christian Europe in the west.

Osman founds small kingdom in Anatolia.	*c.* 1300
Ottoman clan gains control of all Anatolia.	1302
Beginning of Turkish advance. They capture Bursa, making it their capital.	1326
Ottoman Turkish armies cross into Europe, invited by Byzantine emperor.	1346
Turks defeat Crusader armies at battle of Nicopolis.	1396
Death of Timur Lang ends Mongol threat to Ottoman Empire.	1405
Mehmet II conquers Constantinople after a long siege.	1453

Beginnings of an empire

In 1346, a Byzantine leader hired some Ottoman troops to fight for him. This was a disastrous move. It allowed the Turks to cross the Dardanelles into Europe, where their fierce horsemen swiftly defeated the Bulgars and Serbs. In 1389, they crushed the Slav armies in Kosovo.

This greatly alarmed the Pope, who called for yet another crusade to turn back the Islamic threat to Europe. But the Ottomans massacred the crusading army at the battle of Nicopolis in 1396. They now ruled an area which stretched from Hungary to the Near East.

Timur Lang

When the Ottomans tried to expand eastward, there was a nasty shock in store for them. One of the rulers here was Timur Lang (Timur the Lame), who claimed to be a descendant of Genghis Khan. He had already conquered Persia and ravaged much of central Asia, including Russia and India, before the Ottomans attacked.

△ Sultan Mehmet II sent an army of over 150,000 soldiers, together with 300 ships and an array of huge cannons, to capture the city of Constantinople. Only 8,000 Byzantine troops were left to defend the capital. After eight weeks, the Turks broke through the massive city walls and completed their victory.

△ *An intricately carved doorway marks the entrance to an Ottoman mosque. After the fall of Constantinople, the city's Hagia Sophia church became a mosque.*

Timur Lang

Timur Lang was a ruthless leader. When he seized the city of Isfahan in 1387, he ordered his men to execute all 70,000 citizens and pile their heads in huge mounds outside the city walls.

Timur fell on the Turks like a hurricane, sacking their chief city in Anatolia, wiping out their army and capturing their leader. Then he began to loot their empire and break it up. That might have been the end of the Ottoman story, but in 1405, Timur died and the last of the Mongol kingdoms fell apart.

Rebuilding

Gradually the Ottoman dynasty put its empire together again. Under Sultan Murad I, the Turks regained parts of Greece and reached the borders of Hungary and Poland. The Ottoman army was now a highly trained force, led by troops of "janissaries," who were Christian slaves, and "spahis," or skilled mercenary soldiers.

After Murad died in 1451, his son, Sultan Mehmet II, nicknamed "the Conqueror" and "the Drinker of Blood," became sultan. Mehmet wanted, above all, to conquer the ancient city of Constantinople.

The fall of Constantinople

The fall of Constantinople in 1453 marked the end of Byzantine power and the start of a great Turkish advance. The city became the new Ottoman capital. Within 30 years, Mehmet had conquered most of southeastern Europe, including Greece and parts of Italy.

"The empire of the world I say must be one. To make this unity, there is no place more worthy than Constantinople.

SULTAN MEHMET II

△ *This Turkish battle standard would have been carried by the Ottoman armies. At the top is a crescent moon, the symbol of Islam.*

After about 1450, the great nations of Europe began to emerge. For most of their history, they had consisted of small warring states, or had been invaded by powerful neighbors. Now, things were changing fast.

New Nations

The connection between France and England was broken at last. Spain and Portugal grew stable enough to found their great seagoing empires. Germany (part of the Holy Roman Empire) had strong leaders from the Habsburg dynasty.

Wars of the Roses

With the end of the Hundred Years' War in 1453, England was plunged into a fresh series of civil wars. The rivals were the two branches of the Plantagenet dynasty, York and Lancaster. In 1455, the ill Henry VI of Lancaster let his brother Richard of York rule as protector. When Henry recovered, Richard clung onto power but was defeated and killed.

In 1461, the Yorkists deposed Henry and Edward IV became king. In 1470, Edward fled and Henry became king again. In 1471, Henry was murdered. Another Henry reunified England when he defeated Richard III of York in 1485 and became Henry VII, the first Tudor monarch.

AD

1424 — Cosimo de' Medici establishes his family as rulers of Florence.

1450 — Sforza family seizes power in Milan.

1455 — Beginning of power struggle in England between houses of York and Lancaster.

1477 — Death of Charles the Bold allows Louis XI to seize Burgundy.

1478 — Ivan III of Russia begins expansion of his kingdom by seizing Novgorod.

1479 — Ferdinand II becomes king of Aragon.

1485 — Henry Tudor wins battle of Bosworth to take the English crown.

1492 — Muslims surrender Granada to Ferdinand and Isabella.

△ King Ferdinand and Queen Isabella of Spain. Their marriage in 1492 united the two strong Christian kingdoms of Aragon and Castile.

△ Edward IV was the son of Richard, Duke of York. He took the English throne in 1461, after defeating the house of Lancaster at Towton, but was later ousted. He regained the throne again in 1471.

△ A Moorish nobleman and merchant. In 1492, the army of Ferdinand and Isabella forced the Moors to surrender Granada, the last Muslim region within the boundaries of Spain.

Italian city-states

Unlike Spain, Italy remained a divided country, split up into several states ruled by different powers. In the north were the wealthy city-states, such as Florence, Milan, and Urbino. The crest (right) belongs to the Sforza family, who ruled over Milan.

French expansion

France had beaten England, but it too faced rebellion. During the confusion of the long war, the French kings had lost much of their power to the nobles, but they had also built up a tough and well-trained standing army. When Louis XI came to the throne in 1461, he set out to bring his noblemen under control.

His chief enemy, Charles the Bold, died in battle in 1477, and after this, Louis was able to seize Burgundy, then most of southern France. The king unified much of the modern French state under a very strong monarchy.

A united Spain

In 1479, Ferdinand II became king of Aragon. His wife Isabella was already queen of Castile, so most of Spain came together under one pair of rulers. They wanted to establish the country as a Catholic stronghold. Non-Christians were driven from Spain with threats of imprisonment, torture, or death.

Ferdinand and Isabella also completed the great "reconquest" of Spain from Muslim control, which had begun over 400 years earlier. Within 20 years of the surrender of Granada, they had seized Navarre from France, and the country was ready to begin building its empire overseas.

△ The emblem of the House of York was a white rose; a red rose represented the House of Lancaster. The war between these two houses was known as the "Wars of the Roses."

> We read that we ought to forgive our enemies; but we do not read that we ought to forgive our friends.
> ## COSIMO DE' MEDICI (1389–1492)

Cosimo Medici was a member of the powerful Medici family in Florence.

The word "renaissance" means rebirth. We use it to describe the period from about 1400 onward, which saw a rebirth of human interest in the past, especially in the great works of the classical civilizations of Greece and Rome.

The Renaissance

Many of the classical works had been lost or forgotten for centuries. Artists, architects, and writers of the 1400s rediscovered them. They learned from ancient objects and texts and developed a fresh way of looking at the world. Some of the greatest poets and painters flourished in this new atmosphere of inspiration and creativity.

Conflict and war

The new ways of thinking also led to conflict. At the beginning of the 1500s, Europe was the center of the Christian world. But within 50 years the continent had been split in two by an argument over the Christian religion. This period of division was known as the Reformation. On one side was the established Catholic church of Rome, and on the other was the new Protestant faith. The split caused arguments, wars, and massacres which are still bitterly remembered today. And all the time the Muslim empire of the mighty Ottomans in the East was growing stronger and stronger.

144

The age of exploration

It was the Ottoman threat that pushed European sailors into finding new ways of reaching the riches of the Far East. Muslim power blocked the land routes, so traders were forced to travel by sea. In this way began an amazing age of exploration and discovery. Europeans reached America for the first time, while others crossed the Indian Ocean. The very first round-the-world voyage was completed in 1522 by one of the ships from Ferdinand Magellan's fleet, although Magellan himself did not live to witness the feat.

Wealth and power

The opening of the New World, America, and new trade routes brought great wealth to Europe, especially from China, India, and South America. By about 1600 Europe was the richest and most powerful region in the world. Countries such as Spain, the Netherlands, and Britain were beginning to take control of empires that would continue for many centuries to come.

The Renaissance began in Italy. Rome, the capital city, had been one of the main centers of the classical world. It was full of magnificent old buildings and other objects that inspired the "rebirth" of culture.

Renaissance Italy

Money was an important reason why the Renaissance started in Italy. The Italian city-states were home to many wealthy families, who were eager to pay for new paintings, sculpture, and architecture. Many of the great artists who were available to do the work lived in Italy. They made this one of the most stunningly creative periods in history.

Artists and patrons

One of the most powerful families was the Medici of Florence. The family spent huge sums on new buildings and on the work of master painters such as Raphael and Botticelli. In Milan, the Sforza family employed Leonardo da Vinci on many projects. The Este family of Ferrara paid for paintings by Mantegna and poetry by Ariosto. But the richest patron of all was the pope in Rome. A succession

AD
1100
1200
1300
1400
1500
1600
1700
1800

Giotto, revolutionary painter, at work in Padua. — *c.* 1305

Brunelleschi's dome added to Florence Cathedral. — 1436

Birth of Leonardo da Vinci near Florence. — 1452

Botticelli paints his Primavera ("Spring"). — *c.* 1478

Leonardo begins work on The Last Supper in Milan. — *c.* 1495

Michelangelo works on painting the Sistine Chapel ceiling in Rome. — 1509

Palestrina begins career as musical director and composer in Rome. — 1561

Palladio publishes his Four Books of Architecture. — 1570

△ St. Peter's Church in Rome, one of the world's largest Christian churches. The top of its huge dome, designed by Michelangelo, reaches more than 390 feet above the ground.

△ A view of modern Florence. Many of the city's finest buildings, such as the Medici Palace and Library, were paid for by the wealthy Medici family.

△ A close-up view of figures adorning the magnificent doors of the Baptistery, an eight-sided building on one of Florence's main piazzas.

△ A painting of Lorenzo de Medici. The Medicis made their money through banking in the Middle Ages. Their wealth gave them control of the city of Florence.

da Vinci

Leonardo da Vinci was one of the great Renaissance painters. His portrait of the *Mona Lisa* is known throughout the world. Da Vinci was also a great inventor, recording ideas on subjects ranging from anatomy to geology. This is his painting called the *Head of Leda.*

of popes lavished money on works of art for their palace at the Vatican. The most stupendous of these was Michelangelo's huge fresco on the ceiling of the Sistine Chapel, completed in 1511.

Painting and sculpture

For the first time since the classical period, artists felt free to show the beauty of the human body. They were helped by two things – the old Greek ideas of proportion and perspective, and the new research on how the body worked. A nude sculpture such as Michelangelo's *David* shows a deep knowledge of the action of muscles, sinews, and bones.

Almost all medieval art had depicted religious subjects. Renaissance artists began to paint other things, such as landscapes and scenes of gods and goddesses from mythology. They also painted portraits – of their patrons and of themselves – which expressed human emotions more openly than ever before.

New buildings

As a young man, Filippo Brunelleschi went to Rome and studied the huge dome of the ancient Pantheon temple. This inspired him to design another dome, which topped the city cathedral of Florence in 1436. Many people argued that his structure, built without any frame or supports, would collapse, but Brunelleschi proved them wrong.

The Italian Renaissance architect Andrea Palladio made his buildings perfectly balanced, decorating them with temple columns and roofs.

△ A column designed by Andrea Palladio, one of the great Renaissance architects. His buildings were designed using classical ideas.

In the early 15th century, the people of Europe knew very little of the wider world. They might have heard of the adventures of travelers such as Marco Polo, but very few Europeans had gone farther afield than the Mediterranean or the Black Sea.

Exploring the World

The Muslim empires made land travel difficult beyond this region, and their merchants kept tight control of the trade routes from the East. But all the most precious goods came from the East – silks and porcelain from China, valuable spices from the Moluccas and Sri Lanka, and gold and silver from central Asia. Could European traders travel there by another route?

The route east

The answer was yes – by sea. The first to look for a new way to the East were Portuguese sailors. In 1419, Prince Henry of Portugal, known as Henry the Navigator, began sending out a series of expeditions to find a sea route around Africa. But no one knew how big the African continent was. Each ship went a little farther along the coast, and it was not until 1488 that Bartholemew Diaz sailed around the southern cape and into the Indian Ocean.

Now the route lay open to India and the Far East. In 1498 another Portuguese captain, Vasco da Gama, crossed the Indian Ocean to reach the Indian port of Calicut. He returned with a priceless cargo of pepper, cinnamon, and other goods, and a direct trading link was forged between the countries of Portugal and India. In 1514 the first Portuguese vessel sailed as far east as China.

Prince Henry of Portugal begins project to find sea route round Africa.	1419
Bartholemew Diaz rounds Cape of Good Hope.	1488
Columbus crosses the Atlantic and lands on the Bahamas.	1492
World divided between Spain and France by Treaty of Tordesillas.	1494
Cabot sails from Bristol to discover Newfoundland.	1497
Vasco da Gama sails across Indian Ocean.	1498
Columbus explores coastline of Central America.	1502
Magellan begins expedition which will eventually sail around the world.	1519

△ Ferdinand Magellan's ships thread their way through a narrow channel (later named after him) in the far south of America. They crossed the Pacific to the Philippines. Only one ship returned home, having made the very first voyage round the world.

△ The Chinese commander Zheng-ho returned from his travels with many treasures and curiosities, including a giraffe. Chinese ships under his command visited India, Arabia, and East Africa.

Ancient maps

By the late 1400s European scholars agreed that the world was round. The Americas did not start to appear on maps of the world until the early 1500s.

The route west

Among those who saw Diaz return from his historic voyage was a young Genoese called Christopher Columbus. He longed to see the wonders of China and Japan, and he had a surprising plan. Instead of sailing eastwards, he wanted to sail westwards right round the world to reach the civilizations in the East.

The Portuguese king would not give Columbus money for this scheme. So he went to the Spanish king and queen, who eventually gave him three ships. In 1492 Columbus and his fleet set out across the Atlantic Ocean. When they found land, Columbus believed he was near Japan. In fact, he had reached the Bahamas. He did not know that between Europe and eastern Asia was another vast continent – North America.

Around the world

Many other Europeans soon followed Columbus across the Atlantic. The fiercest rivals over trade and exploration were Spain and Portugal. To settle the argument, the Pope in 1494 fixed an imaginary line around the world from the North Pole to the South Pole, dividing the Atlantic in half. Spain could have the western half (including most of America), and Portugal the eastern half.

I believe that this is a very great continent which until today has been unknown.

CHRISTOPHER COLUMBUS, ON REACHING THE CONTINENT OF NORTH AMERICA IN 1498

△ Early explorers navigated with the help of an instrument called an astrolabe. It was used to measure the angles of stars above the horizon.

During the Renaissance, explorers and traders found new worlds across the seas. At the same time artists found exciting new subjects and techniques, while scholars across Europe found new ways of studying human society.

Science and Technology

Scientists and inventors at this time were making important discoveries too. They were asking questions which would change our view of the earth – and the heavens – forever.

Printing

Throughout history, books had been rare and precious things, kept in the libraries of monasteries or wealthy houses. Each one had to be copied out by hand with pen and ink, so very few people had the chance to learn to read. The Chinese had developed a simple system of printing in the 11th century, but it was only in about 1450 that a German named Johannes Gutenberg built the first true printing press.

Using movable metal type, Gutenberg was able to make exact copies of books very cheaply. The first books he printed were the Bible and other religious works. Soon other printers started, and by 1500 they were producing many different sorts of literature, including poems and stories. For the first time, books were available to everyone.

Astronomy

In classical times, an astronomer named Ptolemy had said that the Earth was at the center of the Universe. It stayed still, while the sun and all the other heavenly bodies moved around it.

▷ Gutenberg built his press in Mainz, Germany. His metal-working skills may have come from his uncle, master of the local mint.

Gutenberg produces first printed work using movable type.	1454
First printing press set up in France.	1470
da Vinci designs flying machine with flapping wings.	c. 1503
Copernicus works on theory that Earth orbits the Sun (published 1543).	c. 1530
Vesalius publishes important work on the human body.	1543
Tycho Brahe begins his catalog of the stars.	1572
Invention of the telescope in the Netherlands.	1608
Galileo publishes his first account of observing the stars and planets.	1610

△ *Galileo Galilei was both an astronomer and a physicist. His observations about the heavens helped to confirm the ideas of Copernicus.*

△ *Galileo's telescopes were more powerful than any that had been used before. He was the first person to study the night sky through a telescope.*

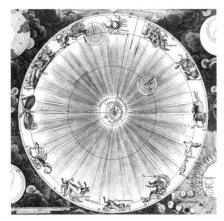

△ *Copernicus' view of the universe. He proposed that the sun, not the earth, lies at the center of the universe. He developed the idea in a book* On The Revolutions of the Heavenly Spheres.

da Vinci inventions

Throughout his life, Leonardo da Vinci drew many designs for flying machines. Among these was a kind of parachute and a helicopter with spinning blades. The first successful aircraft did not fly for another 400 years.

This theory became an important part of the Christian faith and of the way medieval people saw themselves. But in 1543 a new theory appeared which shocked and angered Church leaders.

According to the Polish astronomer Nicolaus Copernicus, it was the sun – not the earth – which was at the center of the Universe. The earth and other planets simply revolved around it. His idea was proved correct in the 1620s, when the Italian Galileo Galilei used an early telescope to observe the planet Jupiter. He could clearly see that there were other moons in orbit round Jupiter. Here were bodies which were not moving round the earth. This meant one thing: that the earth was not the center of the Universe.

Medicine

Doctors of the Renaissance made a much closer study of the human body than ever before to find out how it worked. They began to dissect (cut up) corpses, something which the Church had always considered sinful. The doctors described what they saw – organs, muscles, blood vessels, and bones. This helped them to discover new ways of treating injuries and disease.

Most of the important medical discoveries at this time were made in Italy and Spain. Girolamo Fracostoro showed that diseases are often spread from one person to another by infection. Miguel Serveto realized that blood is pumped through the lungs by arteries from the heart. Others found safer ways of treating wounds caused in battle, especially the increasing number from gunfire.

Flying machines

Not all the inventions actually worked. The great artist and engineer Leonardo da Vinci was determined to find a way of making people fly like the birds. His grandest idea was for an aircraft with flapping wings, which he dreamed up in about 1503. He organized a test flight but according to legend the machine crashed.

151

We know very little about the early history of Africa. There must have been great civilizations there, but very few of them developed writing or left any records.

Distant Empires

Some African civilizations built fine communities, such as the east coast port of Kilwa or the mysterious stone complex of Great Zimbabwe. After about AD 700, Muslims from the Near East began to take over many coastal regions and trade routes.

King of Mali

One of the wealthiest of the medieval African empires was Mali. Starting in 1240, its Islamic rulers built up a kingdom stretching for around 990 miles over West Africa. Much of the land was desert, but Mali grew rich from gold. Merchants brought gold there from mines in the south, and traded it for salt and other vital goods from the north.

By 1330 the king of Mali was the most powerful man in West Africa. His name was Mansa Musa, and he had amazed the outside world with a trip to Mecca (the holiest city of Islam). He had arrived there with thousands of followers and camel trains carrying gold and other gifts. Mali itself had gold coinage and city streets lined with copper statues.

The Songhai Empire

Later, an even bigger state ruled much of West Africa. In 1500 the Songhai Empire covered an area from the Atlantic coast across to the center of modern Nigeria. The people of the empire started as simple farmers or fishermen, but swiftly took control of the trade routes

Indian city of Delhi founded by Turks.	c.1206
Foundation of Muslim kingdom of Mali.	1240
Great Zimbabwe built in southern Africa.	c.1270
Mali Empire at its height.	c.1330
Ali of Songhai conquers Timbuktu.	1469
Songhai Empire at its height.	c.1500
Babur begins conquest of northern India.	1526
Akbar conquers Bihar and Bengal for Moghul Empire.	1576

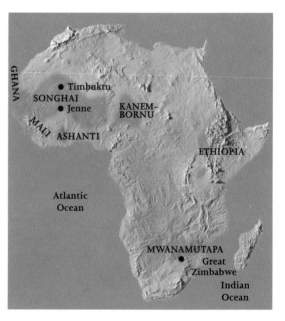

▷ The great inland empires of Africa, which were at their most influential between about 1100 and 1550.

▷ The tomb of Humayan, one of the founders of the Moghul Empire. Humayan was the son of Babur, and father of Akbar. He was ruler of the Empire from 1530–1556.

△ The young Akbar. In later life he was revered by European visitors as "The Great Moghul." He proved himself to be a brave warrior and a wise ruler.

across the Sahara. They exchanged products from Europe and Arabia for gold and other goods from the south. The armies of Muslim Songhai conquered the wealthy cities of Timbuktu and Jenne.

Empire of the Moghuls

Many different peoples had invaded India since the Dark Ages. Huns came from central Asia and Muslim armies from Arabia and Persia. Since 1206 the largest city, Delhi, had been the center of an Islamic state. In 1526 came the greatest conqueror so far – Babur, founder of the Moghul Empire.

The first emperor

Babur was born into a warlike family. He was a descendant of not only Genghis Khan but also the terrifying Timur Lang, who had ravaged India a century earlier. Babur invaded Afghanistan, then crossed the Indus and defeated the Sultan of Delhi at the battle of Pannipat. This gave him firm control over much of northern India.

Akbar, Babur's grandson, came to the throne in 1556, and reigned for nearly 50 years. He extended his dynasty's rule over much of India, uniting most of the north and conquering parts of the south.

Great Zimbabwe

A view showing what the Great Enclosure inside the city of Great Zimbabwe may have looked like. The buildings were made of stone, which is unusual. At that time most structures in Africa would have been built from clay.

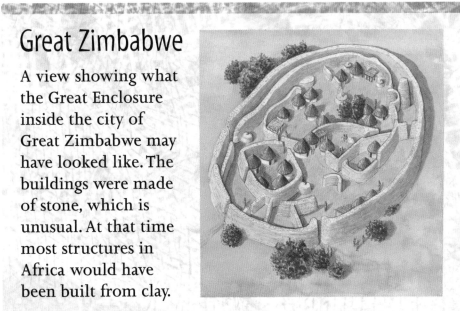

△ A figurine of an African chieftain. The civilizations of West Africa had a long artistic tradition of producing fine metalwork.

After Columbus's expedition of 1492, many Spaniards volunteered to sail out to the West Indies and South America. They thought they would make their fortunes from the gold and other treasures which lay waiting to be plundered.

The Conquest of the New World

At first the hopes of the Spanish adventurers were dashed. The Indians of the Caribbean islands and the American coast had little gold. They could not even be sold as slaves, because most of them died quickly of European diseases caught from the settlers.

Expedition inland

In 1519, a force of 650 Spanish troops sailed from Cuba to explore the Mexican interior. Led by Hernando Cortez, the expedition sailed to the Gulf coast and marched inland. They were now in the land of the Aztecs, a century-old empire extending from the Pacific to the Atlantic. The capital city was Tenochtitlan, with a population of over 100,000 – more than any Spanish city at that time.

The Aztec emperor, Montezuma, sent messengers to meet Cortez with gifts and to warn the Spaniards to turn back. But Cortez marched on, right into the middle of Tenochtitlan, and took the emperor hostage.

The end of the Aztecs

Montezuma had a huge and well-trained army, many times bigger than

△ The Spanish troops were hugely outnumbered when fighting the well-trained army of the Aztec emperor Montezuma. However, the invaders had the advantage of horses, metal armor and guns. Also, many Aztecs believed that the Spaniards were actually gods.

Cortez lands on Mexican coast.	1519
Cortez storms Tenochtitlan and defeats Aztecs.	1521
Pizarro conquers Inca Empire of Peru.	1532
De Soto lands on Florida coast.	1539
Spanish begin convoy system for safe transport of treasure across the Atlantic.	1540
Orellana completes first expedition across South America, down the Amazon.	1542
Huge find of silver at Potosi in Peru.	1549
Aguirre leads first expedition across the Amazon Basin.	1561

AD

△ In search of gold and silver, Francisco Pizarro went into Peru with a party of only 180 men — far smaller even than the force led by Cortez. The Spaniards' steel weapons and horses terrified the native peoples.

Treasure fleets

By 1550, Spain ruled most of Central and South America and the West Indies. Fleets of Spanish galleons carried gold and silver and plundered treasures across the Atlantic to Europe.

the Spanish force, but his enemies had more powerful weapons. The Spaniards were able to seize the palace and kill Montezuma. Cortez then managed to escape from the angry mob in Tenochtitlan. He gathered fresh troops and destroyed the city, forcing the Aztecs to surrender in 1521. He now controlled all Mexico, seizing its treasures and turning the Aztecs into slaves.

Pizarro in Peru

Soon, news reached the Spaniards in Central America of a much wealthier empire in the south. This belonged to the Incas of Peru. In 1532, Francisco Pizarro advanced into Peru with a small party of men. Pizarro copied one of the tactics used by Cortez. He swiftly kidnapped the Inca ruler Atahualpa, and demanded a massive ransom in return for his release. When the ransom was paid, Pizarro had Atahualpa murdered.

Pizarro went on to capture the capital, Cuzco, and the whole Inca Empire collapsed. Within a few years the Spanish conquerors, or "conquistadors," had overrun Peru, Bolivia, and Chile. For well over a century, Spanish treasure ships filled with gold and jewels taken from conquered peoples and silver from the rich mines at Potosi were carried back across the Atlantic to Spain, making it the richest country in Europe.

△ A steel helmet worn by the Spanish conquerors. It was held on by a leather strap beneath the chin. The thick metal ridge on top gave solid protection against hefty blows.

These great buildings rising from the water, all made of stone, seemed like a city made by a sorcerer.
ACCOUNT BY A SPANIARD ON FIRST SEEING THE CITY OF TENOCHTITLAN

Martin Luther was a Catholic monk from Germany. In 1510 he visited Rome, the home of the Catholic church, and was deeply shocked. He saw the Pope and his household living in great luxury, surrounded by costly paintings, sculpture, and music.

The Reformation

The Catholic church was bloated with wealth and power. Many of its priests were corrupt or just ignorant (some could not even read), and Luther believed that Christ's original teachings had been discarded.

Luther's revolution

In 1517, Luther went to Wittenberg Castle church and nailed a piece of paper to the door. On it was a list of 95 arguments against the sale of "indulgences" by priests – which promised pardon for sins in exchange for cash. Luther went on to attack other abuses of the Christian religion and stated that God judged people by the strength of their faith, not by how much money they gave to the church.

He begged the nobles of Germany to help him reform the old

AD

Luther nails his 95 theses at Wittenberg, Germany.	1517
Pope excommunicates Luther from the Roman Catholic church.	1520–1521
Protestant princes in Germany form the Schmalkaldic League.	1531
Henry VIII becomes head of the Church of England.	1534
King Christian makes Lutheranism the state religion of Denmark.	1536
Pope approves the Society of Jesuits to spearhead a "counter-Reformation."	1540
Calvin publishes his revolutionary ideas for church government.	1541
St. Bartholomew's Day massacre of Huguenots in France.	1572

△ Luther nailed his list of 95 arguments against the church's sale of indulgences to the door of Wittenberg Castle church in 1517. His ideas quickly spread across northern Europe.

△ King Henry VIII of England defied the Pope and declared himself head of the church. In 1532, he introduced laws to cut off England from Rome's power.

△ During the Reformation, the Bible became available for all to read, thanks to the new printing technology. Also, for the first time it was translated from Latin into local languages.

Monasteries

The ruins of Tintern Abbey in Wales. In 1536, Henry VIII ordered that monasteries such as Tintern be "dissolved," or closed down and ransacked.

religion. This alarmed the Pope, who sent an order, or "Bull," that declared Luther was a heretic and that ousted him from the church. Luther burned the Bull in public. He was now an outlaw.

Birth of Protestantism

A number of German princes met at Speyer in 1529, and protested against the Pope's treatment of Luther. From then, the movement became known as Protestantism. Catholics and Protestants formed rival leagues, thus splitting the Christian world in two. Meanwhile, the demand for religious reform was growing fast. Luther's ideas spread to the countries of Scandinavia by the early 1530s. In Switzerland, Huldreich Zwingli and John Calvin established their own new forms of the Protestant religion.

Reforming the church

Very soon Europe was divided in two. On one side were the strongly Catholic countries such as France, Spain, and the Italian states. On the other were newly Protestant countries such as England, Denmark, and the German states. In spite of this crisis, the Pope at first ignored all calls for reform.

The Reformation caused strains in Europe which quickly led to persecution and war. On a single day in 1572, more than 3,000 Huguenots (French Protestants) were massacred by mobs all over France. Catholic monarchs tried to force Protestant countries to return to the old faith and launched themselves into long wars. Philip II of Spain spent many years attempting to invade England and defeat the Protestant queen, Elizabeth I.

◁ A heretic is led to the stake to be burned to death. Many hundreds died in this way. They were not all Protestants, but had often been condemned for disagreeing with the Catholic church's teachings.

"God has not yet ordained that England shall perish." These were the words of Elizabeth I as her country faced invasion by Spain in 1588. But she could have said them many times during her long reign.

The Age of Elizabeth

When she had been crowned queen 30 years earlier, both Elizabeth and her throne were in great danger. The previous queen, her sister Mary, had tried to turn England back into a Catholic country again, causing rebellion and bloodshed.

Many powerful people did not believe that an even younger, and still unmarried woman was strong enough to rule any better.

A Protestant monarch

Elizabeth soon showed herself to be tough and decisive and chose intelligent advisers. In 1559 she pushed through laws which confirmed England as a Protestant nation, with priests ordered to use the new English Prayer Book. In 1572 she made an alliance with France to give England support against her many Catholic enemies.

Wisely, the queen refused to get married. Many kings and princes – both Catholic and Protestant – wooed her, but she stayed single. She knew that a foreign husband would make her unpopular with her subjects.

Elizabeth born in London, second daughter of Henry VIII.	1533
Elizabeth becomes queen upon the death of her sister Mary.	1558
Laws passed to establish the Protestant faith in England.	1559
Mary Queen of Scots takes refuge in England.	1568
The Pope excommunicates Elizabeth and declares she has no right to rule.	1570
Mary Queen of Scots executed.	1587
The defeat of the Spanish Armada.	1588
The Nine Years' War begins in Ireland against English rule.	1594
Death of Elizabeth and end of the Tudor dynasty.	1603

△ One of the most devastating weapons used against the Spanish were fireships, burning boats sent in among the fleet. Attacked by warships and scattered by a terrible storm, the Spanish Armada could only escape by heading to the north of Scotland. Only 60 ships reached home.

△ Elizabeth ended her reign as one of the best-loved and most successful of all English rulers. Her country was stronger and more peaceful than it had ever been.

Mary, Queen of Scots

Mary was not a good ruler. In 1568 she was forced to flee Scotland and find refuge in England. Here she soon became the center of many Catholic plots to overthrow her cousin Elizabeth, who kept her a prisoner.

Mary, Queen of Scots

Catholic leaders of Europe, especially Philip II of Spain, were eager to get rid of the Protestant Elizabeth. But who would take her throne? The ideal replacement was Elizabeth's cousin Mary Stuart. Mary was already a queen (of Scotland), and she was a Catholic. Better still, she had a son and heir, and Elizabeth had none. By 1587, Mary had become too big a threat to Elizabeth. She was tried for treason, found guilty, and beheaded.

The Spanish Armada

Philip of Spain had once hoped to return England to Catholicism by marrying Queen Elizabeth. She had refused him. Now, he decided to change England's religion by force. The execution of Mary Stuart gave him the perfect excuse. In 1588, Philip assembled a fleet of 130 ships and sent them to pick up soldiers from the Netherlands and invade England. The great Spanish "Armada" sailed across the English Channel, but never reached its goal.

The defeat of the Armada did not end the war with Spain – it dragged on for another 16 years, but there were no more big battles. Elizabeth also faced unrest in Ireland, which was still largely Catholic. Her armies could not defeat the rebels, who had to be starved into surrender.

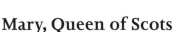

△ Elizabeth's signature on the death warrant of Mary Stuart. Elizabeth hesitated for days before signing it. She knew Mary's death would give her Catholic enemies an excuse to attack her.

"I know I have the body of a weak and feeble woman, but I have the heart and stomach of a king, and of a king of England too.

QUEEN ELIZABETH I, (1533–1603)

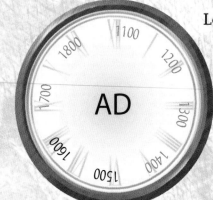

AD

London in about 1600 was dirty, plague-ridden, and overcrowded. Many people were poor and worked very hard and long hours, yet they still enjoyed themselves. They drank in the city's many public houses or watched cruel sports.

Plays and Poets

Best of all, Londoners liked to go to the playhouses. Here, after paying a penny, they could see a marvelous world, full of color and romance, with heroes, clowns, lovers, witches, and even pitched battles on the stage. More than 15,000 people flocked to see such plays every week.

The players

Being an actor was not very glamorous in early Elizabethan times. "Players" were thought to be tramps and troublemakers, who made their living by putting on plays in marketplaces, village greens, and inn yards. After a performance, they would pass around a hat for spectators to throw money in.

In 1572, a new law forced the players to organize themselves better. They had to have a patron, who supported them, and they had to pay for a special license. After this, several bands, or companies, of players built their own permanent theaters, where the audiences had to pay to enter.

William Shakespeare

One of the most famous of these companies was called The Lord Chamberlain's Men. Their success was largely due to the man who wrote many of their plays – William Shakespeare. He developed a new kind of verse drama, ranging from

William Shakespeare born in Stratford-upon-Avon, Warwickshire.	1564
The Red Lion, London's first modern theater, is opened.	1567
Byrd and Tallis publish a collection of choral settings.	1575
Hilliard paints his series of miniatures.	1580–1600
Shakespeare probably writes his earliest plays.	1589
Edmund Spenser begins his long poem, The Faerie Queene.	1590
First performance of Shakespeare's Hamlet.	1601
Death of William Shakespeare.	1616

▷ London's Globe Theatre. In Shakespeare's time, ordinary spectators watched from the ground where there were no seats. A seat in the covered galleries was more expensive.

▷ Many musical instruments in the Middle Ages were forerunners of those played today. The big fiddle became the modern violin. The shawm (far left) was an early version of the recorder.

comedies such as *Much Ado About Nothing* to bloody tragedies such as *Macbeth*. These explored the whole range of human feelings in language that any Elizabethan could easily understand. These emotions – love, hatred, jealousy, and ambition – make Shakespeare's plays as relevant and interesting today as they were 400 years ago.

The Globe Theatre

The Chamberlain's Men performed at the Globe, on the bank of the River Thames. Shakespeare described it as "this wooden O," and it was shaped as a hollow circle with a stage at one side. An Elizabethan playhouse was a noisy place. Actors had to make themselves heard above the talking, eating, and drinking of the audience, who would shout at the actors if they didn't like them.

Poets and painters

The period around 1600 saw a flowering of many other arts in Britain. Edmund Spenser wrote his epic poem in praise of Elizabeth I, *The Faerie Queene*. Among leading artists was Nicholas Hilliard, who painted delicate miniature portraits. Composers such as William Byrd and Thomas Tallis created rich choral music.

△ William Shakespeare was the greatest poet and playwright of the Elizabethan age. Before him, very few good plays had ever been written in the English language.

Don Quixote

An illustration from *Don Quixote*, a novel in two parts (1605 and 1615) by the Spanish writer Miguel de Cervantes. It tells the story of a landowner who, attracted by tales of knights of old, dresses up in armor and sets out to perform heroic deeds. The down-to-earth attitude of his trusty servant Sancho Panzo contrasts with Quixote's own idealism.

△ An inkwell and quill pen. The feather was trimmed before it was used, and the point sharpened with a knife was also used to scrape out mistakes.

AD

1100
1200
1300
1400
1500
1600
1700
1800

"There never has been and never will be a more dreadful happening," wrote a monk after the Turks captured Constantinople in 1453. But he was wrong. The Christian world was going to get many more shocks from the Ottoman invaders during the next 200 years.

Suleiman the Magnificent

Suleiman "the Magnificent" becomes Ottoman sultan.	1520
Hungarian king defeated at battle of Mohacz.	1526
Death of Suleiman.	1566
Turkish fleet defeated at battle of Lepanto.	1571
Sinan completes building of his masterpiece, the Selimye Mosque at Edirne.	1574
Turks regain Baghdad after losing it to the Persians.	1638
Turks join with Cossacks to invade Poland.	1672
The siege of Vienna. Turkish army routed by allied troops.	1683

Constantinople became the new center of the Ottoman empire, which continued to grow until it included large parts of southeastern Europe. The Ottomans seized Muslim lands too, conquering Syria in 1516 and Egypt a year later, taking control of the three holy cities of Islam – Medina, Mecca, and Jerusalem.

The Great Sultan
In 1520 the greatest of the Ottoman rulers came to the throne. His name was Suleiman, and he was soon to become known as "The Magnificent" because of the splendor of his court and the might of his armies. His capital Constantinople, renamed Istanbul, was the biggest city in the world.

Suleiman set out to expand his empire still farther. He captured cities as far apart as Belgrade, Baghdad, and Algiers, as well as Aden and the island of Rhodes. In 1526 he smashed the forces of the Hungarian king at the battle of Mohacz. Meanwhile his navy, led by the corsair Barbarossa, ruled the Mediterranean.

Patron and law-giver
Suleiman was not just a fine leader and warrior. He was also a poet and a scholar.

△ After the death of Suleiman the Turks continued to be victorious in battle, capturing the Christian island of Cyprus in 1571. But in the same year came a defeat at Lepanto (above) off the Greek coast, when 200 Turkish warships were sunk or captured by the Spanish and Italian fleets.

△ Suleiman I was a wise and noble emperor, but he quarreled with his sons and had two of them executed.

Islamic art

The empire brought Suleiman great wealth, which he used to hire the best artists and architects. Among them was Mirman Sinan, who designed at least 165 mosques and palaces.

Suleiman was also known as *al-Qanuni*, "the law-giver." He had complete control over the daily lives of his subjects and chose slaves from his own bodyguard to govern the provinces of the empire. He also reformed the legal system, so that land rents and taxes were collected properly.

Defeat at Lepanto

After Suleiman's death in 1566, the Ottoman Empire continued to grow. But the defeat at the battle of Lepanto in 1571 marked a long and slow decline in the Ottomans' power. Their later leaders were often weak or mad – Mehmed III had all 19 of his brothers put to death in 1595 so he would have no rivals! The huge empire had become difficult to govern, and there were mutinies in the army.

The final advance

Yet the Turks were still the greatest power in Europe and Asia. They even began a new program of conquest, invading Poland in 1672 and Austria in 1683.But this was as far as they got. The Ottoman army laid siege to the Austrian capital, Vienna, but could not capture it. After three months, they were attacked by an allied force and driven away. The once dreaded Turks were never a threat to Europe again.

△ Intricate detail from a Persian carpet shows birds, animals, and trees. Such subjects were rare, for the Islamic religion in the Middle East banned images of living things.

I who am Sultan of Sultans, the sovereign of sovereigns, ... the shadow of God on earth, the Sultan lord of the White Sea and of the Black Sea ...
EXTRACT FROM LETTER WRITTEN BY SULEIMAN

During the 1600s and 1700s, Western Europe became the center of world power. The strong nations, such as Britain, Spain, and France, took control of countries far overseas. They used trade to open up worldwide links.

Empires and Industry

These powerful European countries established bases on the African coast, in Southeast Asia, India, Australia, and South, Central, and North America. Some of these bases grew into colonies, and the collections of colonies gradually began to develop into large-scale empires.

Revolution in industry

These empires brought vast amounts of goods into Europe. At the same time, they were markets where European goods could be sold. This revolution in trade was part of another revolution – in industry. The newly discovered power of coal and steam, and the invention of new machines, helped to produce more iron that cost less, cotton cloth, and other valuable products. Factories started to replace cottage workshops, and peasants moved to the expanding cities to find work. Farmers developed ways of growing more food to feed the rapidly increasing populations of the cities and towns.

Strong leaders

This was also an age of mighty monarchs. Leaders such as Peter the Great of Russia and Frederick the Great of Prussia almost single-handedly turned disunited and backward countries into major world powers. Most glittering of all was Louis XIV of France, who became known as the "Sun King." Other kings failed miserably. The weaknesses of Charles I drove England to a bitter civil war and ended with his own execution.

Europe at war

In fact, the countries of Europe spent most of their time fighting each other during this period. In all of the 1600s, there were only four years of complete peace. Armies and navies grew bigger and more heavily armed, and battles in the 1700s sometimes involved hundreds of thousands of troops. But European armies did not always win. In 1783, Britain was forced to admit defeat and give freedom to her North American colonies. The United States of America was born.

The Spanish were the first Europeans to land large numbers of people on the American continent. They were also the first to conquer territory, seizing the empires of the Aztecs in Mexico and the Inca peoples in Peru.

New World Colonies

By about 1600 Spanish and Portuguese explorers had taken control of much of South and Central America. The huge expanse of North America still lay open and unknown. It contained no gold and silver, but there were vast resources of timber and valuable furs, and fertile land for growing crops.

1565 Spanish found city of St. Augustine, in Florida.

1585 First English attempt at settlement, on Roanoke Island.

1606 James I grants charter to establish colonies in Virginia.

1608 French build a fort at the site of Quebec.

1620 The Pilgrims found Plymouth Colony in New England.

1624 Dutch establish their first settlement at Manhattan, called New Netherland.

1633 First settlers in Massachusetts.

1643 The population of Virginia reaches 5,000.

The first colonies
Spain and France got an early foothold in the north. The French explorer Jacques Cartier reached the Gulf of the St. Lawrence River in 1534, and traveled to the site of modern Montreal. To the south, a small French colony was set up in Florida. Spanish settlers destroyed this in 1565 and created their own. The Spanish city of St. Augustine is the oldest in North America.

The English soon followed. In 1583 Humphrey Gilbert claimed Newfoundland in the name of Elizabeth I. In 1585 Walter Raleigh placed settlers on the island of Roanoke, off the Carolina coast. This was the first English settlement, but it only lasted for a year.

Virginia and Quebec
It was not until 1607 that about 100 English settlers landed on the

△ Many settlers lived along the New England coast, where there were plentiful supplies of timber to build their homes and to build ships. The early settlers built houses which were similar to those back in England, with thatched roofs and stone chimneys.

△ This painting by the American artist George H. Boughton shows a group of Pilgrims walking to church. The men are armed with muskets to protect the group from attack by local native peoples.

The Mayflower

A modern replica of the *Mayflower*, the ship in which the first Pilgrims set sail from England in 1620. They founded the Plymouth Colony in what is now Massachusetts.

American east coast and founded a sizeable colony. They called it Virginia (in honor of Elizabeth I, "The Virgin Queen"), and named the first city Jamestown (in honor of James I). Soon after, the explorer Champlain built a small fort at Quebec on the St. Lawrence River. This was the first French settlement in what became Canada.

Hard times

At first, life was a bitter struggle for the pioneer settlers. Crops failed, winters were harsh and there were disputes with the native peoples. Food was so scarce in Quebec that fresh supplies had to be brought from France.

Things got better slowly. The settlers began to grow a new and valuable crop for exporting to Europe – tobacco. They made treaties with the friendly local Indians, and supplied them with firearms to help defeat their enemies.

In 1620, a shipload of Puritans from England set up a second colony in New England. They are known as the Pilgrims. From here, they spread out to establish New Hampshire in 1623 and Connecticut in 1633.

△ In the colonies, girls would embroider samplers – squares of cloth decorated with words and patterns of needlework. They usually added their name and age, as well as the date.

> They may beginne their first plantation and seat of their first habitation at any place on the coaste of Virginia.
>
> ## EXTRACT FROM CHARTER GRANTED BY JAMES I
>
> *King James I of England granted a charter which allowed people from England to settle in the New World.*

AD

The bloody struggle between Catholics and Protestants in Europe lasted for more than a century. It was made up of a series of great "wars of religion," which involved countries as far apart as the Netherlands, Spain, Sweden, France, and England.

The Thirty Years' War

The last and biggest of these religious wars began where the Reformation itself had begun – in the bickering states of Germany. This messy conflict became known as the Thirty Years' War.

△ In 1618 Protestants invaded the royal palace in Prague. They seized a number of Catholic officials and threw them out of an upstairs window. This event became known as the "Defenestration of Prague."

The "defenestration" of Catholic officials in Prague.	1618
Bohemian Protestants defeated by Spain at White Mountain.	1620
Danish army invades northern Germany.	1625
Gustavus Adolphus of Sweden defeats Spanish at Breitenfeld.	1631
Swedish army destroyed at Nordlingen.	1634
France declares war on Habsburg Spain.	1635
French and Swedes invade Bavaria.	1646
Treaty of Westphalia ends the war in Germany.	1648

Out of the window

The war started in a dramatic way. Protestants in Bohemia (now part of the Czech Republic) were angry with their new king, Ferdinand. He was a member of the powerful Spanish Habsburg family and wanted to restore Bohemia to the Catholic faith. He closed Protestant schools and in 1618 ordered that Protestant churches in Prague be pulled down.

The Protestants banded together and threw some Catholic officials from an upstairs window in Prague Castle. The incident sparked off a civil war in Bohemia. In 1619 the rebels expelled Ferdinand and chose a new king, the Protestant Frederick.

The war spreads

Two days later, Ferdinand became the new Holy Roman

▷ The French army, under its leader Louis II, Prince of Condé, was victorious at the battle of Rocroi in 1643. The French troops destroyed the best of the Spanish infantry.

△ During the 1600s the magnificent Palace of Versailles was built outside Paris. It was the residence of the French royal family. The palace contains paintings and sculptures by artists from all over Europe.

emperor, with massive new powers. He immediately used these to take revenge on the Bohemians, defeating them at White Mountain in 1620. Frederick fled, and Catholicism was the state religion again.

Ferdinand's army pushed on into northern Germany, alarming other Protestant countries. Christian IV of Denmark organized a Protestant army and invaded Germany in 1625, but the Catholic forces were too strong and defeated him.

The turning point

The next to enter the war was King Gustavus Adolphus of Sweden, determined to protect his small country against Ferdinand. A small, well-trained army defeated the Spanish at Breitenfeld in 1631. A year later the Swedes won a second great victory at Lutzen. The Swedish army was eventually defeated in 1634. But now help came from a surprising ally – Catholic France. The French supported the Protestants because Cardinal Richelieu, France's most powerful man, wanted to stop the growth of Spanish control in Europe.

Richelieu declared war on Spain in 1635, attacking its territories in Spain and Italy. By 1648 the war was over. Spain's power in Europe was broken, and three decades of war left Germany in ruins.

Rembrandt

The master Dutch painter Rembrandt van Rijn was at work during the period of the Thirty Years' War. He produced a great number of works of art, including around 600 paintings and 100 or so self-portraits, such as the one seen here. By the late 1630s Rembrandt was Amsterdam's most fashionable portrait artist.

△ This matchlock musket gun is a typical weapon used by infantry soldiers during the Thirty Years' War. Its long and heavy barrel had to be supported on a forked rest.

In 1603, Britain had a new monarch – James I. He was the first of the Stuart kings, and ruled not only England and Wales, but also Scotland. James believed strongly that God had given kings their right to govern, and no one could question this authority.

Civil Wars in Britain

James' arrogant views and behavior made him very unpopular with his subjects. His son Charles I, who followed him to the throne in 1625, was even less popular. Soon Britain was split by civil wars.

Trouble with parliament

Charles wanted to rule without consulting parliament. In 1629 he dismissed parliament, and did not call another for 11 years. But he needed to raise taxes to pay for a bigger army – and he had to have parliament's agreement for this.

By 1640 Charles was facing rebellion. The Scots had invaded northern England, and the English army was weak and ill-equipped. Reluctantly, Charles summoned parliament and asked for permission to raise new taxes. A rebellion in Ireland in 1641 meant that Charles now needed an even bigger army, but members of parliament demanded that the king hand over the army command to them.

Charles I becomes king.	1625
English defeated by Scots in first "Bishops' War."	1639
Catholic rebellion in Ireland.	1641
Charles declares war on parliament.	1642
Roundhead victory at Marston Moor.	1644
New Model Army created. Royalist army smashed at Naseby.	1645
"Second" civil war.	1648
Execution of Charles I.	1649
Cromwell becomes Lord Protector.	1653
Restoration of the monarchy.	1660

△ A combined force of Scots and Roundheads defeated Charles and his Royalist forces at the battle of Marston Moor, in Yorkshire, in 1644.

▷ Charles I was brought to trial by the English parliament. He was found guilty of treason against his own subjects and beheaded outside Whitehall Palace, London on January 31, 1649.

War begins

Enraged by this, Charles tried to arrest five members of parliament for treason. The action made him hated all the more, and he was forced to flee London. By August 1642 he had declared war on the parliamentary supporters (known as "Roundheads"). He tried to retake London but his Royalists were beaten back at Turnham Green.

Defeat and execution

By 1644 the parliamentary side had the advantage, having gained a powerful ally in the Scots. To make sure of victory, they needed one more decisive battle. Inspired by Oliver Cromwell, the Roundheads crushed the Royalists at Naseby in 1645 and captured the king.

The Restoration

After the execution of Charles I in 1649, England had no King for the next 11 years (England became a Commonwealth). The new leader was Oliver Cromwell, who was appointed Lord Protector until his death in 1658. Two years later, Charles II (son of Charles I) was invited back from exile and crowned king. This event was known as the Restoration.

△ A Roundhead (left) and a Royalist soldier (right). Roundheads wore iron helmets and breastplates for protection.

Oliver Cromwell

After the execution of Charles I, Cromwell was made Lord Protector. He had been a very successful commander during the Civil War, and was a strong leader. However, he did not get along well with parliament. His son, Richard, took over as Lord Protector after Cromwell's death in 1658, but was forced to abdicate soon after, when Charles II, son of Charles I, was made king.

△ A Roundhead helmet. Oliver Cromwell reorganized the Roundhead forces into a professional force known as the "New Model Army."

AD

"If I have seen further," wrote Isaac Newton, "it is by standing on the shoulders of giants." Newton was the greatest scientist of his age, but he knew that his success was built on the work of great thinkers and researchers before him.

The New Science

The 1600s was a golden age for science, with astonishing advances in many areas from astronomy to medicine, and from biology to mathematics.

Student genius

In 1665, following a new outbreak of plague, universities were closed and the students sent home. Young Isaac Newton of Cambridge University used his long holiday to work out the ideas which were buzzing around in his head. First, he uncovered the secrets of light and color. He passed a beam of sunlight through an angled glass "prism." This split the white light into a rainbow band of colors. When he passed the rainbow through a second prism, it was mixed back into white light again. Next, Newton watched the way an apple fell to the

Huygens invents the first clock to be driven by a pendulum.	1657
Newton discovers the nature of white light by passing it through a prism.	1666
Newton builds his first reflecting (mirror) telescope.	1668
Japanese mathematician Seki Kowa solves simultaneous equations.	c. 1670
Malpighi confirms Harvey's theory about the circulation of the blood.	c. 1680
Van Leeuwenhoek invents the precision microscope.	1683
Newton publishes his Mathematical Principles.	1687
Fahrenheit invents the mercury thermometer.	1714

△ Isaac Newton at work in his study. Later, he expanded his theories about gravity to show how it is linked with movement.

172

△ The English scientist Robert Hooke used an early microscope such as this one to discover the existence of living cells in plants.

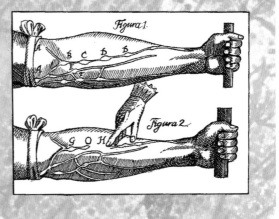

△ Edmond Halley correctly predicted that a comet which he had seen in 1683 would reappear in 1759. (This is now known as Halley's Comet, and it last appeared in 1986.)

ground. He realized that objects were pulled toward the earth by a force he named gravity.

Looking at the heavens

Newton became the first person to use a telescope to see the moons orbiting the planet Jupiter. He also used his theories about gravity to show why the planets orbit the sun. Edmond Halley was greatly influenced by his friend Newton's work. In 1676 he made a catalog of the stars which can be seen from the southern half of the world. He also studied the way objects such as comets move.

Microscopes and medicine

Other scientists were looking inward at the secrets of the human body. They were able to use a new instrument to help them – the two-lens microscope which had been invented in about 1590. During the 1670s, Italian physician Marcello Malpighi made a close study of the lungs, liver, and other organs. Dutchman Antonie van Leeuwenhoek made the most powerful microscope of the time, which could make objects appear up to 270 times bigger. He was the first to identify red corpuscles in blood.

I seem to have been only like a boy playing on the sea-shore … whilst the great ocean of truth lay all undiscovered before me.
SIR ISAAC NEWTON (1642–1727)

△ Newton used his discoveries about light to build a new kind of telescope. It used a reflecting mirror instead of glass lenses to magnify images.

In many ways, the stories of China and Japan in the 1600s look very similar. Both were united and peaceful under a strong military rule. Both were growing wealthier and more thickly populated.

China and Japan

China was the world's richest and most powerful country in the 1600s. It had a population of about 150 million – almost twice as big as that of Europe. Production of food in China (especially the country's all-important rice crop) rose rapidly during this period.

AD

Tokugawa clan takes control of Japan.	1603
All foreign traders banned from Japanese soil apart from the Dutch.	1641
Manchus conquer China, ending the Ming dynasty.	1644
Ching dynasty force all Chinese to wear a pigtail.	1645
K'ang-hsi founds porcelain factories in China.	1680
Manchus conquer Taiwan.	1683
Teaching of Christianity banned in China.	1716
Chinese troops invade Tibet.	1751

Triumph of the Ching
The Manchu people had invaded China from the northeast, completing their conquest in 1644. They placed on the throne a new dynasty, or family, of emperors called the Ching. Although the Manchu people were foreigners, they soon adopted traditional Chinese customs and culture.

The greatest of the early Ching emperors was K'ang-hsi, whose long reign lasted until 1722. His armies extended the Chinese Empire to include Taiwan, Tibet, Turkestan, and Outer Mongolia. K'ang-hsi was not just a clever general, he was also a wise and tolerant ruler. He encouraged foreign traders and Catholic scholars to visit China, and he traveled widely to see his subjects.

A declining empire
However, this prosperity could not last. During the 1700s, China's population grew at an even faster rate, reaching about 320 million by 1800. It was impossible to grow enough rice, and

▷ *A Japanese shogun. The shoguns disliked the influence of foreigners. They wanted to keep Japanese society as it had always been.*

▷ *A Dutch trading ship outside the port of Nagasaki. By 1641 only the Dutch were allowed to trade in Japanese ports, sending one ship each year to Nagasaki.*

△ *Dutch traders tend their allotment while confined by the shoguns to the island of Deshima in Nagasaki Bay.*

there were many food shortages. This led to riots and a full-scale rebellion in 1795, greatly weakening the power of the Ching.

Land of the shoguns

Japan was going along a very different path than China, slowly cutting itself off from the outside world. In 1603, clan leader Tokugawa Ieyasu at last defeated his rivals and established himself as shogun (military ruler) of the whole country. Law and order were enforced by the fierce warrior class called samurai.

Trade was booming by this time. Japan's most precious asset was silver, most of which went to China to pay for raw silk. This was turned into beautiful fabrics and garments and sold to foreign merchants. Spanish, Portuguese, Dutch, and British ships came to trade, bringing firearms and other goods in exchange for the silk.

Expelling the foreigners

The shoguns distrusted the Europeans, especially the Christian missionaries. During the 1630s, they expelled the Spanish and Portuguese traders and began to torture and execute the missionaries and their converts.

The tea trade

Dutch traders shipped tea from China to Europe for the first time in 1610. Tea drinking soon became popular, particularly in Britain. European ships queued outside China's ports to load up with tea and other goods. This engraving shows tea traders buying and selling tea for export.

▷ *A samurai sword. Following a ban on the use of guns, the only legal weapons were swords, bows and arrows, and spears. Only the samurai were allowed to carry them.*

Peter the Great was a giant figure, well over six feet tall, and full of violent energy. When he became tsar (emperor) of Russia in 1696, he was determined to use all his energy to make Russia a strong and modern state.

The Rise of Russia

After many years of civil war, invasion, and bloodshed, Russia had just begun a slow progress out of its backward and primitive past. Under the new tsar, this progress became far more rapid.

Learning from Europe

Peter spent two years touring western Europe to find out for himself how other countries were run. He visited England, Austria, Holland, and Germany, looking at factories, mills, and science laboratories. He even worked in a London shipyard and learned how to be a dentist! Back home in Russia, Peter put what he had learned into practice. He set up new high schools and urged the children of nobles to study abroad.

City in the swamp

Peter was also a great builder. He built new roads and canals, and introduced modern methods to mining and other industries. He ordered the building of a complete new capital city on marshy land near the Baltic coast. The city of St. Petersburg became one of the most beautiful cities in the world.

For decades, the Russian army had been weak and ill-equipped. Peter turned it into a modern force, with new weapons, able officers, and

At the age of nine, Peter becomes joint ruler with his brother.	1682
Peter becomes sole tsar of all Russia.	1696
Peter makes grand tour of western Europe.	1696–1698
Founding of new city of St. Petersburg.	1703
Major victory over Swedes at battle of Poltava.	1705
Death of Peter the Great.	1725
Murder of Peter III; Catherine becomes empress.	1762
Major rebellion of serfs and Cossacks is brutally put down.	1775
Death of Catherine the Great.	1796

△ Russian peasants had a harsh life. Even after Peter's reforms, they still used wooden plows and harrows, instead of iron ones and lived in huts made of timber and mud.

△ Peter the Great started the first Russian newspaper and opened the country's first museums. He reformed the system of government and brought the church under the state's control.

St. Petersburg

The beautiful city of St. Petersburg lies beside the river Neva. Its magnificent Winter Palace was the winter home of the tsars. As a result of working in the difficult marshy conditions, thousands of peasants died while building Peter the Great's new city.

rigorous training. He also used his knowledge of shipbuilding to create a powerful new Russian navy.

Rebellion

For the poor peasants, however, little had changed. These "serfs," who were virtually slaves, made up the vast majority of the Russian population. They lived and worked on the land, where the harsh conditions had barely altered since the Middle Ages. There were many uprisings by peasants and farmers, but the tsar's troops crushed them with great cruelty. After Peter's death in 1725, rivals fought to take his place. In 1762 the reigning tsar, Peter III, was battered to death with a footstool.

Empress of Russia

Russia's next strong ruler was Catherine the Great, wife of the ill-fated Peter III. She plotted his death and succeeded him to the throne. Catherine built more schools and hospitals and abolished capital punishment (except for treason). She made the serfs' lives harder by forcing more work and military service on them, and by tightening their landlords' control over them.

△ Religious paintings that are considered to be sacred by the church in Russia are known as icons. Peter the Great reduced the church's power considerably, as well as the amount of land it owned.

I shall be an autocrat: that's my trade. And the good Lord will forgive me: that's his.
EMPRESS CATHERINE THE GREAT (1729–1796)

In 1700, more than 90 percent of Europe's population lived in the countryside. Most people were peasants working on the land. They grew their own food, using tools and farming methods which had changed very little since medieval times.

The Farming Revolution

At this time Europe's population was about to rise rapidly. By 1800 the number of people in Europe soared from 120 million to over 180 million. Farmers found ways to grow much bigger quantities of crops, and there was enough food to feed many more people.

Jethro Tull invents the seed drill.	1701
Viscount Townshend develops his system of four-course crop rotation.	1730
Robert Bakewell begins his improved livestock breeding.	1745
New wave of land enclosures in Britain.	1760
Thomas Coke begins program of improving farmland on his estate.	1776
Robert Ransome invents the "self-sharpening" metal plow.	1785
John Deere makes the first all-steel plow.	1837
Fergus McCormick develops his mechanical reaper.	1839

Enclosing the land

Many villages still used the old system of strip farming, where fields were divided into strips and shared among the farmers for growing crops. Rougher land was left as "common" pasture for grazing. Many animals had to be slaughtered every winter because there was too little feed for them.

One way of improving the quality of food was to enclose the common land with hedges and ditches. This stopped animals from wandering and gave better drainage. It allowed wealthy farmers to buy up land and build bigger, more carefully managed farms. But enclosure also took away common land from poorer people.

Rotating crops

The medieval system of growing crops was wasteful. A field was sown with winter corn one year, spring corn the second, and left fallow, or unplanted, the third year so that it could regain fertility. By about 1650, Dutch farmers had developed a more efficient way of "rotating" their crops.

△ In the four-course crop rotation, wheat was grown in the first year and turnips in the second. Sheep or cattle ate the turnips, providing valuable manure. Barley was sown in the third year, then grass or clover.

turnips

barley

clover

△ Tobacco plants in flower. Farmers in North America began to grow tobacco as a commercial crop in the early 1600s. The first tobacco farms were in Virginia, where the climate and soil were just right.

Tull's seed drill

Since farming began, famers had scattered seed by hand. Jethro Tull's seed drill put the seed directly into the soil in neat rows. This allowed farmers to hoe out weeds between the rows.

Instead of leaving a field fallow, they made it fertile more quickly by spreading manure or growing clover and grasses to improve the soil. In the 1730s, farmers such as Charles Townshend of England began using a four-part system of planting crops in rotation.

Better breeding

The four-course rotation of crops meant that many more animals could be fed through the winter, instead of being killed. Farmers could fatten them up with hay and grain, as well as roots such as swedes and turnips. By keeping them in enclosed fields, the farmers had better control over the animals' health. This opened the way for the animals to be improved by careful breeding. Pioneers such as the Englishman Robert Bakewell did this by selecting the best animals from their herds and breeding them together.

New machines

Scattering seed by hand was wasteful, and a lot of seed was eaten by birds. In about 1701 Jethro Tull invented a machine for sowing seeds more efficiently. In 1785 Robert Ransome devised the first completely cast-iron plow, which stayed sharp.

wheat

△ As a result of improved breeding techniques, farmers were able to produce sheep which gave better wool. They also had short legs and barrel-like bodies for more meat.

Our farmers round, well pleased with constant gain,
Like other farmers, flourish and complain.

THE PARISH REGISTER, GEORGE CRABBE (1754–1832)

Crabbe was an English poet who wrote about working class life.

The beginning of the 18th century saw the fading of the old European powers, such as Spain and the Holy Roman Empire. It also saw the end of wars over religion. Instead, three new strong nations were emerging – France, Britain, and Prussia.

War and Rebellion

United under powerful leaders, the new nations struggled for control of large parts of the continent of Europe. This struggle even spilled over into North America and India and led to several long-running wars.

The Sun King

Louis XIV had come to the throne of France at the age of five in 1643. During his adult life he had built up a strong army and navy and extended French power. He had also inspired a golden age of culture in France.

King Charles II of Spain was just the opposite – weak and sickly. When he died without heirs in 1700 he left his throne to Louis XIV's grandson. Louis grandly declared that France and Spain were united. Alarmed at this, England, Prussia, the Netherlands, and other states formed an alliance against the French. In a long and bitter war, they repeatedly defeated the French. When peace came in 1713, Louis' grandson remained king of Spain, but France and Spain stayed separate.

Great Britain united

The Act of Union in 1707 joined together England, Wales and Scotland. Many Scots hated being ruled from London, and eagerly

△ At the heart of Louis XIV's reign was a glamorous court, based around his splendid palace at Versailles. Louis chose the sun as his emblem, and was known as the "Sun King."

▷ English troops shattered the Jacobite rebels, led by Bonnie Prince Charlie, at the battle of Culloden in 1746. Prince Charlie had to flee to France. After this, the Act of Union was safe.

△ Bonnie Prince Charlie's proper name was Charles Edward Stuart. The grandson of James II, he was the last member of the Stuart family to try and claim the throne of England.

supported any attack on the English. James Stuart, the son of James II who had been forced from the English throne in 1688, tried to seize the British crown several times with French support. His followers (called Jacobites) found a more glamorous leader in his son Charles. Bonnie Prince Charlie led the Jacobite army to victory over the English in 1745 but was defeated at the battle of Culloden. the following year.

Frederick the Great

Frederick II of Prussia was a clever and cultured man with interests ranging from music to philosophy. He encouraged agriculture and industry and freed the serfs on the royal estates. His main interest was war and Prussia's growing strength. He invaded Silesia (part of the Austrian Empire) in 1740 and later added parts of Poland.

Angry at Frederick's aggressive tactics, Austria formed an alliance with Russia and France to force him out of Silesia. Frederick invaded Saxony in 1756, marking the start of the Seven Years' War. He then defeated both the French and Austrian armies. In 1758, the British joined Frederick in further battles against their old enemy, France, but Britain's real aim was to extend her empire overseas.

Voltaire

Voltaire was a French philosopher and writer, with a keen sense of justice. He wrote more than 50 plays as well as philosophical stories and poems. As a young man, he was condemned for criticizing the government and spent 11 months in the notorious Bastille prison in Paris.

△ A French sword. In 1758 French troops lost to the joint forces of Prussia and Britain. By the end of the Seven Years' War, Britain had taken France's colonies in India and America.

The world was speeding up. During the 1700s, populations began to grow, especially in Europe and North America. These extra people needed more food, more homes and more jobs.

Industrial Revolution

At the same time, industry was expanding at an amazing rate, thanks to the development of new machines, new methods of making things and new sources of power. The result was a dramatic change in the way people lived and worked. We call this change the Industrial Revolution.

King cotton

The growing demand for cheap cotton cloth transformed the spinning and weaving industry. For centuries, these had been slow processes performed by hand. Now a series of inventions in Britain made them much faster. The "flying shuttle" of the 1730s doubled the speed of weaving. The "spinning jenny" and the "mule" produced spun thread much more quickly and inexpensively. The one big obstacle to the expansion of the cotton industry was removed by Eli Whitney's invention of the cotton gin in 1793. It made the process of cleaning cotton 50 times faster!

Coal and iron

Coal became increasingly important as the fuel for ovens and forges. Coal mines were dug deeper as demand grew, leading to greater dangers of floods, collapse, and gas explosions. Inventions such as Newcomen's

△ The ironworks at Coalbrookdale in Shropshire, England. it was here, in 1709, that ironmaster Abraham Darby discovered that coal could be turned into coke by baking it. With this, he was able to make better quality iron in his furnaces. The iron was needed to make the newly invented industrial machines.

AD

Abraham Darby uses coke to smelt iron. — 1709

Thomas Newcomen builds the first practical steam pump. — 1712

John Kay invents the flying shuttle. — 1733

James Hargreaves develops his "spinning jenny." — 1764

Improved steam engine built by James Watt. — 1769

Eli Whitney invents the cotton gin. — 1793

Alessandro Volta assembles the first electric cell. — 1800

Friedrich Krupp opens his ironworks in Essen, Germany. — 1810

Michael Faraday discovers how to produce an electric current with magnets. — 1831

△ Benjamin Franklin was an American statesman as well as a scientist. Franklin proved that lightning and electricity are the same thing by flying a kite in a storm. He was struck by lightning and was lucky to survive.

Cotton Gin

Raw cotton, grown mainly in the United States, was very difficult and slow to clean. Whitney's cotton gin was a simple machine which brushed out the troublesome seeds from the cotton fibers.

steam pump (to remove water) and Davy's safety lamp eased these problems. Abraham Darby's discovery that coal could be turned into coke led to the production of coke-smelted iron. The improved iron could be used to make everything from ploughs and bridges to steam engines and drilling machines.

Steam power

The old sources of power – water, horses, and wind – still drove the new machines. They were soon replaced by a new, less expensive kind of power which never tired – steam. One coal – powered steam engine could do the work of hundreds of horses.

In 1712 Thomas Newcomen devised the first efficient steam pump. James Watt's improved steam engine, built in 1769, could turn wheels. Now steam power could be harnessed to work spinning machines and looms, as well as giant hammers and the bellows for blast furnaces.

Factory life

Machines in factories created millions of new jobs, so many people began to leave the countryside to work in the towns. Houses and factories had to be built for them. By 1850, over 60 percent of Britons lived in towns. Factory workers led hard lives, often working 14 hours a day, six days a week.

△ Davy's safety lamp warned miners of gas leaks underground. Inventions such as this only encouraged coal miners to go into farther and more dangerous depths.

> In every cry of every Man/ In every Infant's cry of fear,/ In every voice, in every ban,/ The mind forg'd manacles I hear.
>
> ## from "LONDON," WILLIAM BLAKE (1757–1827)
>
> *Blake wrote several poems about the effects of the Industrial Revolution.*

Britain had started her collection of overseas colonies in the reign of Elizabeth I. By 1602, both England and the Netherlands had founded an "East India Company" on the Indian coast to trade with the Far East.

Britain's Colonies

The first settlements in North America took root and flourished in early Stuart times. In 1661, Britain gained her first African foothold, seizing James Island on the Gambia River. By the middle of the 1700s, these scattered colonies had begun to grow into a powerful and profitable empire.

Ruling the waves

In 1623, Dutch settlers murdered ten English merchants on the island of Amboina in the China Seas. After this, relations grew worse between the two countries. A series of wars began in 1652, only ending in 1868 when the Dutch king, William III, took the British throne.

Over the next 50 years the British navy became bigger and stronger still. With faster and better-armed warships which could sail much closer to the wind, it defeated most other national fleets. By the 1750s British vessels "ruled the waves," making passage easier for merchant ships trading with the developing colonies.

1732	The new colony of Georgia is founded in North America.
1739	Collapse of the Moghul Empire in India.
1744	War breaks out between Britain and France in North America.
1757	Victory at Plassey secures British control of northern India.
1753	French advance south into Ohio.
1759	French surrender Quebec to the British.
1763	Britain gains control of Canada and most land east of the Mississippi.
1807	Abolition of the slave trade in Britain.
1821	George IV crowned King.

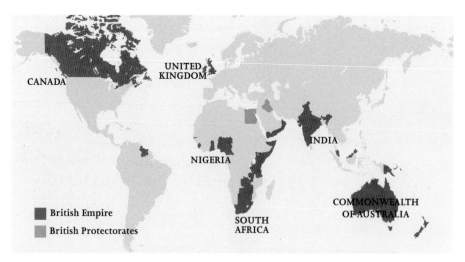

△ By the mid-1700s Britain's empire was very large. By 1763 Britain had won most of France's territory in North America. This shows the extent of the empire in 1821.

△ During the 1600s, British ships transported some 75,000 African slaves to Britain and the Americas. The slaves usually traveled in such terrible conditions that many died on the voyage.

△ St Edward's Crown is the official crown of the British king or queen. The crown was regarded as a symbol of the British empire, and India was sometimes called the "jewel" in Britain's crown.

▷ Fur trappers in North America. By 1740 the number of British colonists in North America was approaching one million. Furs and other valuable goods from the colonies, such as tobacco, timber, and grain, were sold throughout Europe.

General Wolfe

British general James Wolfe brought French power in North America to an end. Wolfe's troops attacked and seized Quebec, the most important town in French Canada, in 1759. Wolfe himself died before the battle of Quebec ended.

The slave trade

One of the most valuable cargoes was slaves, who were captured in Africa and carried across the Atlantic to work in the New World. Although started by Spanish and Portuguese settlers in America, the slave trade was controlled by British merchants from around 1600. By the end of the 1700s Britain had transported a staggering total of 2.5 million slaves. Slave labor played a huge part in the increase in sugar, tobacco, rice, and cotton growing in America, allowing many British traders to become very wealthy.

Control of India

The most successful of the trading posts set up on the Indian coast were run by the English East India Company and their close rivals, the French. India became a vital staging post on the trade route to China. By the 1720s, however, India had become an unstable country without a central ruler. The Europeans began to fight each other for power in the north. Under Robert Clive, the British won an important series of battles against French and Indian forces.

By the 1760s, explorers had traveled far enough to give map makers a rough idea of the shape of the world. But one enormous mystery remained – the Pacific Ocean. No one knew how big it was or how many islands it contained.

Discovering Australia

Many believed that there must be a large continent somewhere in the southern seas, waiting to be discovered. Seamen such as Abel Tasman and William Dampier had reached the coasts of Australia and New Zealand but had thought they were just small islands. Few wanted to venture farther. The southern Pacific is a dangerous place, with typhoons and swirling currents.

Cook and the *Endeavour*
In 1768, the British government sent an expedition to find the mysterious southern continent. Its leader was James Cook, and his ship was a small but tough vessel called *Endeavour*. After visiting the island of Tahiti, Cook sailed southward, then west until he sighted an unknown land. It turned out to be New Zealand.

Landfall in Australia
The *Endeavour* sailed on, searching for the east coast of Australia. Previous explorers had spotted Tasmania and the rocky western shore, but no European had yet landed on the east side. At last, Cook reached the coast of what he knew to be Australia.

△ *Cook's first meeting with the Maori people of New Zealand took place in 1769. With great care, Cook made a voyage lasting six months around both the North and South islands of New Zealand. Charting the coastline as he sailed, Cook soon realized that he had not found a vast continent.*

Willem Jancz is the first European to sight the Australian coast.	1606
Abel Tasman gains first sight of the island named after him – Tasmania.	1642
James Cook charts the coast of New Zealand's North and South islands.	1769
Cook explores and lands on Australia's east coast.	1770
Britain establishes first convict colony at Botany Bay.	1788
Traders and whale hunters begin regular visits to New Zealand waters.	c. 1790
Flinders sails right round Australia, proving it to be a single huge island.	1801–1803
Western Australia claimed for Britain by Charles Fremantle.	1829

△ In 1776, Cook set sail to find a sea passage from the Pacific around the north of America to the Atlantic. Ice blocked his way. He was the first European to reach Hawaii, where he was killed in 1779.

Scientific work

On board the *Endeavour* was a group of scientists whose task was to record the animals and plants they saw on the voyage. The name of Botany Bay was chosen because of the unusual plants the scientists saw on its shores.

He followed it northward until he found a suitable place to land. He called this Botany Bay.

Later voyages

A year later, in 1772, Cook set out again from England for the Pacific. Although Australia seemed big, it was not big enough to be the new continent. This time, Cook had to explore all of the southern ocean. His great voyage took him as far as the pack ice inside the Antarctic Circle and around the globe. It proved that there was no vast continent in the south.

Convicts and settlers

James Cook had opened up the Pacific region to later explorers and settlers. He had also claimed Australia as a British possession. His government decided to use this seemingly wild and empty land as a punishment colony for criminals. The first shiploads of convicts and their guards landed at Botany Bay in 1788.

More convicts and settlers arrived in the early 1800s, forcing the native Aboriginals to leave large areas of their tribal lands. Many fell victim to European diseases. It was the same in New Zealand, where the Maoris were helpless against Western firearms and germs.

> [My aim was] not only to go farther than anyone had done before but as far as possible for man to go.
> CAPTAIN JAMES COOK (1728–1779)

△ *A Maori headdress. When Cook first arrived in New Zealand, the Maori population was about 100,000 strong. The Maoris were skilled hunters, sailors, and woodworkers.*

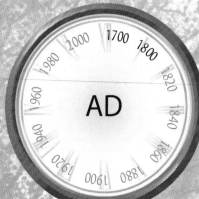

AD

The Seven Years' War saw the end of French power in North America. By 1763, more than two million British colonists were living there. Now they wanted to be able to govern themselves. Britain, however, had different ideas about her colonies, because they were an important market for trade.

American Revolution

Britain imposes *Stamp Act* on the colonies.	1765
Many taxes removed but not the tax on tea.	1770
Boston Tea Party sparks rebellion throughout Massachusetts.	1773
First battles at Concord and Lexington lead to war.	1775
The American Declaration of Independence.	1776
American victory at Saratoga.	1777
France enters the war on the American side.	1778
Cornwallis surrenders at Yorktown.	1781
Treaty of Versailles grants independence to the United States.	1783

A large British army and naval fleet was still stationed to protect North America. The British government was concerned about who was going to pay for these forces. The answer was the colonists themselves – through new and increased taxes.

Protest and rebellion

The British government imposed several new taxes, on things as different as official paper and molasses. The Americans had never been taxed before and protested loudly. Some of the taxes were removed, but import duties on luxury goods such as tea were increased.

The Americans had no one to put their case democratically to the parliament in London, so they took direct action. At the famous

△ The American victory over British forces at Saratoga in 1777 was a turning point in the war. Surrounded on all sides and outnumbered, the British were forced to surrender.

▷ In 1773, a band of colonists seized three British ships in Boston harbor and dumped their cargo of tea overboard. This incident became known as the "Boston Tea Party." It enraged the British government, who sent troops to put Massachusetts under military rule.

"Boston Tea Party" the colonists dumped the cargo of tea from three British ships into Boston harbor.

War begins

By 1775, the whole colony was in a state of rebellion. The British commander learned that Americans were stockpiling ammunition at the village of Concord, and they sent soldiers to destroy it. The resulting battle, and another at nearby Lexington, marked the opening of America's struggle for freedom.

The war went badly for Britain from the start. A force was sent to cut off New England from the other colonies in 1777, but it was defeated at the battle of Saratoga. In 1778, the Americans gained new allies when the French declared war on Britain and sent troops and ships across the Atlantic, attacking settlements in the West Indies.

△ In 1775, George Washington was elected as commander-in-chief of the colonists' army. To many Americans at that time, he became a leading symbol of their fight for independence.

Surrender at Yorktown

In 1780, British troops, led by Lord Cornwallis, captured the town of Charleston and defeated the colonists at Camden. Once again the British forces were cut off, and in October 1781, Cornwallis was forced to surrender at Yorktown. The war was over.

Declaration of Independence

On July 4, 1776, representatives of the 13 colonies signed the Declaration of Independence. This broke off all political connections with Britain, abandoned loyalty to the British monarchy, and created the United States of America. Thomas Jefferson, one of the lawyers who helped to draw up the declaration, later became president of the United States.

△ The American flag, which later became known as the Stars and Stripes, was first flown at the battle of Bennington in 1777. The 13 red and white stripes, and the 13 stars, stood for the 13 original colonies that signed the Declaration of Independence. The modern American flag has 50 stars, one for each state.

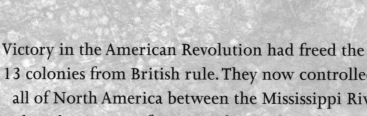

Victory in the American Revolution had freed the 13 colonies from British rule. They now controlled all of North America between the Mississippi River and the Atlantic, apart from British Canada and Spanish Florida. Their next task was to organize themselves into a nation.

The Birth of the U.S.

In 1787, American leaders (the "Founding Fathers") wrote a constitution for the United States, which became the basis of all the country's laws. They also set up a government and chose George Washington to be their very first president.

The Founding Fathers write the Constitution.	1787
George Washington becomes the first president.	1789
The Louisiana Purchase.	1803
Tecumseh leads Creek Indians against the white settlers in southern USA.	1813
The Indian Removal Act is passed.	1830
US war against Mexico to secure Texas and Oregon.	1846–1848
Gold Rush to California begins.	1848
War against the Sioux tribes of the Plains.	1854–1890
War against the Apache in the far south.	1861–1900

The Louisiana Purchase
Weakened by war, Spain had given up its hold in North America. The French took over a large area of territory called Louisiana, stretching from west of the Mississippi across to the Rocky Mountains. But France also had a European war to cope with, and in 1803, France sold Louisiana to the United States government. The Louisiana Purchase doubled the size of the country.

Into the west
By 1820, the United States had grown even larger. It took over the Red River Basin from Britain and gained possession of Florida from Spain. Already settlers were pouring westward into the new territory, founding communities by the Mississippi, then spreading beyond it into Missouri and Texas. Thousands of settlers cleared land in order to build farms and houses. They were followed by a steady stream of traders, manufacturers, doctors, and teachers, and soon the first frontier towns were forming.

△ In 1803, an exploration party set out to discover what the northwest territory was like. Led by Meriwether Lewis and William Clark, the party crossed the Rockies to the Pacific coast and brought back important news about the region.

△ *The Native Americans stood little chance against the powerful firearms and huge numbers of the settlers. They were defeated in a series of bitter wars during the 1700s.*

Thomas Jefferson

Thomas Jefferson was the third president of the United States. A serious political thinker, he wrote the Declaration of Independence. His handbook of rules for the US Senate is still in use today.

War with Mexico

Many Americans believed that the United States should govern all of North America. But large areas, including most of Oregon and Texas, were still under the control of Mexico. As white settlers pushed into these territories, there was bound to be trouble.

By 1836, the settlers had taken over most of eastern Texas and declared it an independent country. The United States government took over the region in 1845 and a year later moved into Oregon. The war against a weak Mexican army was short and one-sided. In 1848, the Mexicans gave in and signed a peace treaty, granting the United States the land stretching from the Gulf of Mexico to the Pacific coast. This almost doubled the country's size once again.

Native Americans

As the settlers flooded west, they invaded the ancient tribal lands of the Native Americans. Alarmed at losing their hunting grounds, the Native Americans began to fight the newcomers. In 1830, the government allowed troops to move the tribes to empty land beyond the Mississippi. From about 1850 to 1890, the tribes who lived on the Great Plains were gradually conquered or wiped out. Survivors were confined to "reservations" on land that the settlers did not want.

"'Tis our true policy to steer clear of permanent Alliances, with any portion of the foreign world. There can be no greater error than to expect favours from nation to nation.
GEORGE WASHINGTON'S FAREWELL ADDRESS, 1796

△ *As new lands opened up, railroads were built to carry settlers and supplies to the west more quickly. The Union Pacific Railroad, linking the east and west coasts, opened in 1869.*

In 1789, the people of France overthrew their monarchy in the name of liberty and equality. This was the start of the French Revolution. The events of the revolution eventually sparked off a whole series of wars in Europe that lasted until 1815, when the French emperor, Napoleon Bonaparte, was finally defeated and sent into exile.

Power and Rights

Liberty was also the cry in South America, as colonies under the control of Spain and Portugal began to demand their independence. The main leaders in the fight for independence were the Venezuelan, Simon Bolívar, and the Argentine, José de San Martín. By 1830, the countries of South America were free of foreign rule.

In Europe, too, there were battles for independence. The *Risorgimento* is the name given to the movement for Italian unification. The kingdom of Italy was formed in 1861, and Rome became the capital of the newly united country ten years later. In that same year, the first *kaiser* (emperor) of a united Germany was crowned.

Trade wars

The 1800s was a time of European power, when many nations began to establish new overseas empires. In Britain, and later in France, Russia, and Germany, the Industrial Revolution encouraged the search for new sources of inexpensive raw materials and new markets for manufactured goods. Britain expanded its control in India, and white exploration began to open up the continent of Africa to European exploitation. In the Far East, Britain and the U.S. forced both China and Japan to open their markets to foreign trade.

Slave wars

In the U.S. conflict over the issue of slavery led to a bitter civil war between the northern and southern states. Slavery was finally abolished, but at the end of the war, much of the South lay in ruins. The country expanded westward, as pioneer families continued to try their luck on farms in California, Oregon, and on the Great Plains. As white settlers moved into these areas, the Native Americans were forced off lands that had been their home for generations.

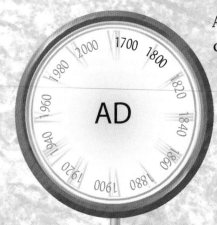

AD

At the end of the Seven Years' War, France lost its colonies in America and India to Britain. In retaliation, French troops fought alongside American colonists in the American War of Independence. The cost of these wars left France virtually bankrupt.

Revolution in France

Harvests fail in France.	1788
Estates-General meet in May. Declaration of Rights of Man and of the Citizen.	1789
Crowds attack Bastille Prison in Paris (July 14). French Revolution begins.	1789
Royal family tries unsuccessfully to escape.	1791
France goes to war against Austria and Prussia. France is declared a republic.	1792
Louis XVI is executed on the guillotine. "Reign of Terror" starts.	1793
"Reign of Terror" ends with execution of Robespierre.	1794
Napoleon seizes control of government.	1799

To try to raise money, the French king, Louis XVI, proposed an increase in taxes. However, most of the country's richest people – the clergy (known as the First Estate) and the noblemen (the Second Estate) – did not pay tax. So the burden of taxes fell on the ordinary people – the peasants and middle classes (known as the Third Estate).

A population boom meant that there was too little food for too many people. The noblemen and clergy refused to change the law on taxes, so the king called a meeting of all three states – the Estates-General.

Events of 1789

The Estates-General met at the Palace of Versailles in May 1789. The meeting coincided with unrest in France, as harvests in 1788 had failed and many people were facing starvation. Still, the first two estates refused to let the Third Estate have a say in governing the country. The Third Estate formed a national assembly and vowed not to disperse until government was reformed in France. Louis appeared to give in – at the same time gathering troops to break up the assembly.

△ On July 14, 1789, a mob attacked the royal prison in Paris, the Bastille. Although only a few prisoners were released, this event marked the end of royal power in France and the beginning of the Revolution. Bastille Day is still celebrated as a national holiday in France each year on July 14.

△ Queen Marie Antoinette, wife of Louis XVI. Her forceful personality enabled her to influence the weak-minded king. Although beautiful, Marie Antoinette was unpopular with ordinary French people because of her extravagant spending.

The guillotine

A French doctor, a member of France's National Assembly, suggested the use of the guillotine as an instrument of execution. He recommended it as a quick and painless way to behead people.

As rumors multiplied and food supplies worsened, panic began to spread. When a Paris mob stormed the Bastille prison in Paris in July, the power of the monarchy was seriously weakened, and the Revolution had begun. In August, the National Assembly issued a Declaration of the Rights of Man, stating that all citizens were free and equal and had the right to resist oppression.

The French Republic

Louis XVI remained opposed to the National Assembly's reforms, refusing to share power with the new government. In 1792, France went to war against Austria and Prussia. The revolutionaries accused the king and his aristocratic friends of helping the enemy, and in August, the king and his family were imprisoned. In September, the monarchy was abolished, and France was declared a republic.

Louis XVI was tried for betraying his country and beheaded. This period was known as the "Reign of Terror," when thousands of people suspected of plotting against the government were killed. In these troubled times, French armies continued to repel their enemies, due partly to a military leader named Napoleon Bonaparte. In 1799, he seized power from the government – the revolution had ended.

Liberté
Egalité
Fraternité

△ The new French Republic adopted as its official slogan the words "Liberté, Egalité, Fraternité" [which means liberty, equality, fraternity (brotherhood)].

Any law which violates the indefensible rights of man is essentially unjust and tyrannical; it is not a law at all.

MAXIMILIEN ROBESPIERRE, 24 APRIL, 1793

Robespierre was one of the leaders of the Revolution.

After years of political dispute and unrest, the French people welcomed Napoleon as their new leader in 1799. Not only was Napoleon a brilliant general, he also proved himself to be a skillful administrator. He reorganized the administration of France, dividing the country into regions called departments.

The Napoleonic Wars

Napoleon ordered the reorganization of French law into codes. The *Code Napoléon* still forms the basis for part of French law today. In 1804, the French people voted for Napoleon to be emperor of France. He crowned himself emperor at Notre Dame Cathedral at the end of that year.

To war

Although Europe was at peace briefly in 1802, Napoleon's thoughts soon turned to extending French control and building an empire. To raise money, he sold a large area of land in North America, called Louisiana, to the Americans. In 1803, France and Britain went to war again. Napoleon wanted to land an army in Britain, so he needed to control the seas. But in 1805, a British fleet under Lord Nelson defeated the combined French and Spanish fleets at the battle of Trafalgar. This defeat ended Napoleon's hopes of invading Britain.

AD

Treaty of Amiens brings peace between France and Britain.	1802
Napoleon sells Louisiana territory to United States to raise money for war.	1803
Britain and France go to war once again.	1803
Napoleon crowns himself emperor.	1804
British destroy French and Spanish fleets at battle of Trafalgar.	1805
Napoleon's army wins at Ulm and Austerlitz.	1805
Start of Peninsular War in Spain and Portugal.	1808
French troops are defeated by bitter Russian winter.	1812
Napoleon exiled in Elba. He returns to be defeated at Waterloo.	1815

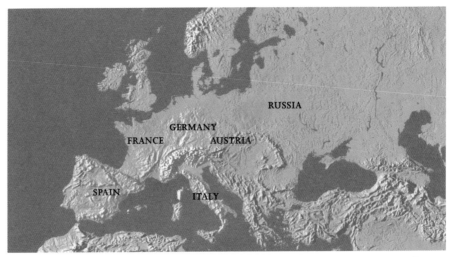

△ The French Empire under Napoleon. After abandoning attempts to increase French influence in North America, Napoleon's attention turned to expanding his empire in Europe.

> The combined armies of Britain, Austria, Prussia, and Russia defeated Napoleon's army at the battle of Waterloo in 1815. It was to be Napoleon's last battle. The French had more soldiers and better artillery but they were still soundly beaten.

△ Napoleon is considered to be a great military genius and one of the greatest commanders in history. Yet he was also described as an "enemy and disturber of the peace of the world."

In 1805, Russia, Austria, and Sweden joined Britain in a coalition against France. But Napoleon's massive armies won major victories at battles such as Ulm (against the Austrians) and Austerlitz (against the Russians). In 1806, Napoleon decided to blockade the transport of British goods. Any ship that entered a French-controlled port after calling at a British port was seized by the French authorities. However, this policy disrupted trade across Europe and made Napoleon very unpopular. Neither was it very successful, as Britain continued to expand trade with its overseas colonies.

End of the empire

By 1812, Napoleon had created a French empire that covered almost all of Europe. However, after a disastrous campaign in Russia, Napoleon's empire began to crumble. In April 1814, Napoleon was forced to abdicate. He went into exile in Elba, an island off the coast of Italy, only to return with fresh troops the following year to make another bid for power. Napoleon's final defeat came at the battle of Waterloo in June 1815. He was sent into exile on the island of St. Helena in the South Atlantic Ocean, where he died in 1821.

Josephine

Napoleon's first wife was Josephine, the daughter of a planter from the French West Indies. She was both intelligent and beautiful, but she and Napoleon had no children. They divorced, and Napoleon had one son with his second wife, Marie Louise.

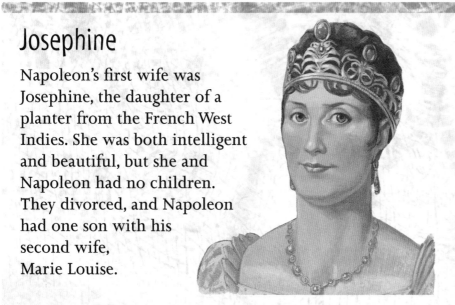

△ Napoleon's distinctive hat. Napoleon was a great military strategist, who seemed instinctively to know the best time to attack during a battle. But his campaign in Russia during the winter of 1812 was disastrous, ending without victory and with the death or capture of about 500,000 French soldiers.

AD

In the early 1800s, colonies in South America under the control of Spain and Portugal began to demand their independence. The main leaders in the struggle against Spanish rule were the Venezuelan, Simon Bolívar, and the Argentine, José de San Martín.

Struggles in South America

Venezuela declares independence.	1811
José de San Martín leads fight for *Argentine* independence from Spain.	1812
Argentina becomes independent.	1816
Chile becomes independent from Spain after battle of Chacabuco.	1818
Bolívar leads troops to victory against Spanish at battle of Boyacá.	1819
San Martín leads army into Peru.	1820
San Martín proclaims independence of Peru.	1821
Venezuela becomes truly independent after battle of Carabobo.	1821
Bolivia named after Simon Bolívar.	1825

Bolívar was born into a wealthy family and was sent to Europe to complete his education. It was in Rome in 1804 that Bolívar made a vow to liberate his country. Taking advantage of the weakening of Spanish authority caused by the Napoleonic Wars, Venezuela declared its independence from Spain in 1811. But the Spaniards retained control of the country, and it took another ten years of fighting before Venezuela became truly free from colonial rule.

Simon Bolívar

The turning point came in 1819 when Bolívar and his small army surprised the Spanish in the colony of New Granada (present-day Colombia). He mounted an attack on them at the battle of Boyacá. After this resounding victory, Bolívar set up the Republic of Gran Colombia.

▷ The struggles for independence in South America began in the early 1800s. One by one, the countries freed themselves from foreign rule. The dates shown are when each country gained its independence.

198

▷ Caracas is the capital city of Venezuela and is the birthplace of Simon Bolívar. The revolutionary leader made a triumphant entrance into the city in June 1821 after the battle of Carabobo.

△ *Simon Bolívar was known as el Libertador (the Liberator). He was a great general and military leader who was inspired by the ideal that all people should be equal and free.*

It included the present-day countries of Colombia, Venezuela, and Ecuador. In 1821, Bolívar finally took control of the Venezuelan capital, Caracas, after the battle of Carabobo.

José de San Martín

In the southern part of the continent, a similar process was happening under the leadership of San Martín. He was an army officer who had fought in the Spanish army against French invaders in the Napoleonic Wars. But in 1811, San Martín decided to return home and join the fight for independence. Argentina declared its independence in 1812. San Martín then joined forces with a freedom fighter from Chile, Bernardo O'Higgins. Together, they led a force across the Andes Mountains and surprised the Spanish at the battle of Chacabuco. Chilean independence followed in 1818.

Only Peru remained under Spanish rule. In 1820, San Martín led an army into Peru, and in the following year, he proclaimed independence. But a small stronghold of Spanish troops remained. In 1822, San Martín requested assistance from Bolívar, and it was left to Bolívar's armies to liberate the last regions in South America from Spanish rule. Bolivia was named in Bolívar's honor in 1825.

José de San Martín

San Martín is one of the greatest heroes of modern Argentina. After joining forces with Bernardo O'Higgins and defeating the Spanish at Chacabuco in 1817, San Martín went on to win another victory – at Maipú in northern Chile – the following year.

△ *The fighting in South America ended about 300 years of colonial rule by five nations in Europe — Portugal, Spain, Britain, Holland, and France.*

The Crimean War was fought in the Crimean Peninsula (in present-day Ukraine) between Russia and the allied armies of Britain, France, the Ottoman Empire (Turkey), and Sardinia-Piedmont. The war was a result of religious conflicts between Russia and the Ottoman Empire.

Conflict in Europe

Russia invades Turkish provinces. Turkey declares war on Russia.	1853
British and French forces land in the Crimea.	1854
Battles of Alma (September), Balaklava (October), Inkerman (November).	1854
Treaty of Paris ends Crimean War.	1856
Guiseppe Garibaldi and army of "red shirts" start revolt in Sicily.	1860
Victor-Emmanuel II becomes king of Italy.	1861
Franco-Prussian War ends with crowning of Wilhelm as emperor of Germany.	1870– 1871
Rome captured and made capital of unified Italy.	1871

The governments of Britain and France were particularly concerned about Russia's intentions to expand its territories. In 1853, Russia invaded Turkish provinces on the River Danube and declared war on the Ottoman Empire.

When Russian ships destroyed part of the Turkish fleet, Britain and France declared war on Russia. In order to avoid the threat of Austria joining the alliance against it, Russia withdrew from the Danube provinces in the summer of 1854. Austria then occupied these provinces.

British and French forces landed on the Crimea in 1854. The aim was to launch a swift attack on the Russian fortress of Sevastopol. Instead, the campaign to take the fortress turned from a swift and decisive victory into a year-long siege in which many thousands of soldiers on both sides lost their lives. Eventually, Russia finally agreed to sign a peace treaty in March 1856.

The unification of Italy
The Treaty of Paris that brought the Crimean War to an end did little to bring stability to Europe. The leader

△ In 1860, Guiseppe Garibaldi, having returned from exile, led his army of "red shirts" in a revolt that started on the island of Sicily. Having conquered the Kingdom of the Two Sicilies, Garibaldi and his army of 1,000 volunteeers then went on to take the city of Naples.

△ Paris in 1848, the so-called "year of revolutions" when unrest and rebellion broke out in many European countries. In Paris, people took to the streets to demand a new republic as well as votes for all males. Government soldiers shot and killed some of the rioters.

Florence Nightingale

Florence Nightingale was an English nurse who organized the care of wounded British soldiers in the Crimea. In 1854, she sailed to the Crimea with 38 nurses. She introduced many reforms and raised nursing standards.

of Sardinia-Piedmont, Count Cavour, used the meetings at Paris to demand unification for Italy. At that time, Italy was made up of many separate states, most controlled by Austria. Sardinia-Piedmont was the only independent state.

The movement for independence, known as the Risorgimento, started in the 1820s and 1830s. In 1858, Sardinia-Piedmont allied itself with France and drove out the Austrians from much of northern Italy. The successful revolt by Guiseppe Garibaldi and his "red shirts" led eventually to the unification of all of Italy. Italy was declared a kingdom under King Victor-Emmanuel II in 1861. Rome was captured and made the capital of a unified Italy in 1871.

The unification of Germany

After the Napoleonic Wars, Germany's many small states were joined to form the German Confederation. Of the 39 states in the Confederation, Austria, and Prussia were the most powerful. In 1862, King Wilhelm of Prussia appointed Otto von Bismarck as his prime minister. Bismarck masterminded three wars which allowed Prussia to extend German territory, seize control from Austria, and take the region of Alsace-Lorraine from France. In 1871, Wilhelm was crowned the first *kaiser* (emperor) of a united Germany.

"Anyone who wants to carry on the war ... come with me. I can't offer you either honors or wages; I offer you hunger, thirst, forced marches, battles and death.
GUISEPPE GARIBALDI, 1882

△ Florence Nightingale was known as the "Lady with the Lamp" because of the light she carried at night. She would walk through the hospital corridors, checking on her patients.

Throughout history, travel had been a problem. Roads were poor, often muddy and full of holes (one traveler actually drowned in a pothole in 17th-century England). Transport depended on muscle power – people on two legs or horses and mules on four.

AD

1600 1700 1800 1820 1840 1860 1880 1900 1920 1940 1960 1980

Travel and Transport

Heavy goods could go more swiftly by sea, but there were always the dangers of storms and pirates. The Industrial Revolution, which began in Europe in the early 1700s, saw dramatic improvements in travel and the carrying of cargo.

Better roads

In Britain, private roads called turnpikes were built in the 1750s, and travelers had to pay tolls to use them. But these soon became rutted and in need of repair. In about 1810, a Scottish engineer called John Macadam developed a new type of hard-wearing road surface that drained easily. It consisted of a thick layer of stones covered with gravel and rubble. Another Scot, Thomas Telford, built roads with a foundation of large flat stones, helping to make travel smoother and faster.

By river and canal

People had always used rivers for carrying freight. Pulling a barge, a horse could haul a load 30 times heavier than the one it could haul by road. As industry expanded, greater loads of heavy goods such as coal

Canal du Midi completed in France.	1681
First major canal built in England – the Grand Trunk Canal.	1777
Trevithick builds steam locomotive Catch-me-who-can.	1804
Fulton tests first successful steamboat.	1807
Macadam develops new type of road surface.	1810
Erie Canal opens.	1825
Brunel begins building the Great Western Railway.	1835
Atlantic steamship Great Western launched.	1837
Union Pacific Railway links east and west coasts of U.S.	1869

▷ Scottish engineer Thomas Telford was most famous for building bridges. From 1792, he designed over 1,200 bridges for roads and railways, such as the Menai Bridge, shown here.

▷ A painting of the Erie Canal in the northeast United States. Its first section was completed in 1820. The canal allowed ships to travel from the Atlantic Ocean to the Great Lakes.

△ American Robert Fulton built the first successful steamboat, the Clermont, in 1807. It operated passenger services on the Hudson River. Soon paddlesteamers were at work on rivers and channels across the U.S. and Europe.

and iron had to be taken across country. Rivers did not always go in the right direction, so canals were dug instead. The first modern canal system opened in France in 1681 and was later copied in Britain and the U.S. By about 1800, there were nearly 4,400 miles of canal in Britain.

Steam power

Steam power was the driving force of the Industrial Revolution. But early steam engines were too heavy to move themselves around. It was only in 1804 that the Englishman Richard Trevithick built a steam engine which could move itself along iron rails. His idea was developed by George Stephenson, whose locomotive *Rocket* was used to pull trains from 1829. For the first time, people could travel faster than a galloping horse. Trains could also carry large cargoes of raw materials to industrial centers and food to the growing towns.

Steam was also being used to power ships. In 1807, Robert Fulton built the first financially successful steamboat. Then, in 1837, English engineer Isambard Kingdom Brunel launched the *Great Western*, the first all-steam ship to carry passengers across the Atlantic.

Washington

Brunel's massive ship the *Great Eastern* had screw propellers as well as paddlewheels. The success of the *Great Eastern* inspired ship builders in Europe and the U.S. to invest in steam powered ships. The USS *Washington* is one such example.

△ A paddlewheel from Brunel's Great Eastern, launched in 1843. The iron-built vessel was the model for today's ocean-going ships.

The American Civil War (1861–1865) was fought between the northern (Union) states and the southern (Confederate) states. The differences between the two arose mainly from the question of slavery.

The American Civil War

The economy of the southern states was based on large plantations growing tobacco and cotton, using slave labor. The economy of the northern states was based on smaller farms and manufacturing. Many people in the North were appalled by the continued use of slave labor in the U.S.

Slave labor

Around 4 million slaves worked in the southern states, accounting for almost one-third of the south's population. The northern states wanted to ensure that slavery would be banned in any new states admitted to the Union. By the 1850s, many had begun to call for the complete abolition of slavery. The southern states threatened to leave the Union if this abolition was imposed on them.

Abraham Lincoln becomes president. Southern states withdraw from the Union.	1860
Six southern states form the Confederacy.	1861
First battle of the American Civil War at Fort Sumter.	1861
First battle between iron-clad ships the Virginia and Monitor.	1862
Emancipation Proclamation. Battle of Gettysburg.	1863
Union armies destroy large portion of southern states.	1864
Civil War ends. Abolition of slavery becomes law in the 13th Amendment.	1865

△ The battle over Fort Sumter in Charleston Harbor, South Carolina, marked the beginning of the American Civil War. Confederate soldiers fired on the Union troops garrisoned there.

△ *Robert E. Lee, commander of the Confederate forces, was a clever general and a skilled military planner.*

Union and Confederate states

The United States was split into two halves by the Civil War. In the north were the states of the Union; in the south were the 11 states that broke away and formed the Confederacy. The war killed more Americans than any other war.

Union states

Confederate states

Union states containing Confederate supporters

△ *Abraham Lincoln was assassinated by a Confederate sympathizer in 1865, five days after the surrender of General Lee and the Confederate forces.*

President Lincoln

In 1860, Abraham Lincoln was elected president of the United States. He was against slavery, and his election convinced the leaders of the southern states that the only choice they had was to leave the Union. South Carolina was the first state to secede (leave) in 1860, soon followed by Mississippi, Florida, Alabama, Georgia, and Louisiana. These states formed the Confederate States of America in 1861. The northern states were determined to preserve the Union, if necessary by force. The first shots were fired at Fort Sumter in South Carolina on April 12, 1861.

A bloody war

Large armies were quickly raised on both sides, and thousands of black soldiers became Union troops. The Confederate armies were commanded by General Robert E. Lee; the Union commander was General Ulysses S. Grant. At first, the Confederate armies were victorious, but a turning-point came at the battle of Gettysburg in 1863, after which Union armies pushed the southerners back into Virginia. In the same year, President Lincoln abolished slavery throughout the United States – a measure that became law in 1865.

In 1864, Union armies destroyed large areas of the South in a final effort to break the will of the Confederate states. When the war finally came to an end in 1865, slavery had been abolished and the Union preserved. But thousands of people had died, many from disease, and large areas of the United States lay in ruins.

△ *Black slaves working on a cotton plantation in the South. Southerners argued that they needed the slaves to keep the South's economy going.*

△ *The Confederates' battle flag. It had 13 stars – 11 for the states of the Confederacy and one each for Kentucky and Missouri, which did not secede.*

For 700 years, Japan was under the rule of the Japanese military leaders known as shoguns. The shoguns had been careful to control European influence in Japan. In the 1600s, Christian missionaries were banned from the country and, after 1639, only Dutch ships were allowed into Japanese waters to trade.

Emergence of Japan

In the 19th century, the United States and several European countries forced Japan to open up to world trade. In 1853, American warships sailed into Edo Bay under the command of Commodore Matthew Perry. Perry delivered a letter requesting trade and diplomatic relations with Japan. He returned the following year for an answer, and the shogun had little choice but to sign a trade treaty with the United States. This was soon followed by treaties with Britain, France, the Netherlands, and Russia.

The Meiji restoration

The 1860s was a time of uncertainty and political unrest in Japan. Finally, in 1868, the situation became so serious that Emperor Mutsuhito took control from the last shogun. Mutsuhito became known as the Meiji emperor, and this event is called the "Meiji restoration." Under the emperor's authority, Japan embarked on

▷ During the period of Meiji rule, education was introduced for all Japanese people. The Meiji emperor also gave farmers ownership of their land and changed Japan's army and navy into modern military forces.

American warships sail into Edo Bay under command of Commodore Matthew Perry.	1853
Trade agreements signed between Japan and U.S.	1854
More trade agreements between Japan, U.S., Britain, the Netherlands, Russia.	1858
"Meiji restoration" — return of imperial rule.	1868
Iwakura mission tours Europe and North America.	1872
Chinese-Japanese war. Taiwan becomes a Japanese province.	1894–1895
War between Japan and Russia.	1904–1905
Korea becomes a Japanese territory.	1910
End of Meiji era.	1912

AD

▷ The modern city of Tokyo, the capital and largest city in Japan. Emperor Mutsuhito moved Japan's capital in 1868 from Kyoto to Edo, then renamed the city Tokyo.

△ Commodore Perry and his fleet of warships sailed into Edo Bay on July 8, 1853. He handed over the United States' demands for setting up trade and diplomatic relations with Japan.

a program of modernization. In 1872, a group of Japanese politicians went on a tour of Europe and North America to learn more about industry, education, and ways of life in the West.

As a result, factories were built in Japan, and the country began to change from an agricultural to an industrialized nation. A railway network was constructed, the Bank of Japan opened, and new education systems were put in place. The unfair treaties that had been signed in 1858 were renegotiated in the 1890s, with better terms for Japan.

Japan at war

Japan also built up its armed forces and went to war to acquire colonies of its own. In 1895, Taiwan became a Japanese province following a war with China. In 1904, Japan captured Port Arthur, destroyed a Russian fleet, and declared war on Russia. The Japanese won many land and sea battles during the Russo-Japanese war, which ended when both sides signed a peace treaty the following year. In 1910, Korea became a Japanese territory.

By the time the Meiji era came to an end in 1912, with the death of Emperor Meiji, Japan was already established as a world power.

War for Korea

During the Meiji period, Japan wanted to extend its territories. In 1894-5 its forces crushed the Chinese navy and gained control of Taiwan. Here you can see a Chinese ship sinking during the battle of Yalu in 1894.

△ Under Meiji rule, Japan's industrialization was accelerated, using Western technology. This included the establishment of a national railway system.

During the 1700s, the slave trade brought misery to thousands of Africans, who were transported across the Atlantic Ocean and forced to work as slaves on plantations in the Americas. This trade also brought huge wealth to those who ran it – the shipbuilders, shipowners, merchants, and traders.

The Scramble for Africa

Many people began to condemn the slave trade and to call for it to be abolished. The slave trade came to an end in the British Empire in 1807, and slavery was finally abolished within the empire in 1833. Slavery continued elsewhere, however. It did not come to an end in the United States until after the American Civil War in 1865. It continued in Brazil until 1889.

Into Africa

In 1822, Liberia was founded on the coast of West Africa by freed slaves. Many of these slaves came from the United States. There were others that came from slave ships that were captured by the British navy after the abolition of the slave trade.

British slave trade abolished.	1807
Liberia founded on coast of West Africa as a country for freed slaves.	1822
Abolition of slavery in British Empire.	1833
King Leopold II of Belgium lays claim to Congo region.	1880
Britain takes control of Egypt and Suez Canal.	1882
Conference in Berlin divides Africa among European countries.	1884
Italians take control of Eritrea.	1890
French take control of Mali.	1893

▷ In the late 1880s, the continent of Africa, with the exception of Ethiopia and Liberia, was divided up between the European nations of Belgium, Britain, France, Germany, Italy, Portugal, and Spain.

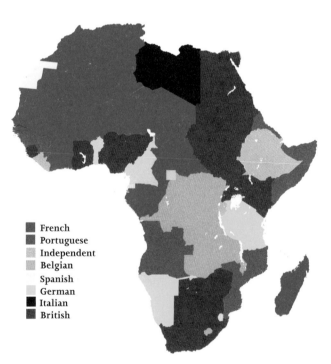

■ French
■ Portuguese
Independent
Belgian
Spanish
German
■ Italian
■ British

△ The anti-slavery movement was strongest in Britain and the United States. After the abolition of slavery, many abolitionist speakers, shown here, joined the struggle to gain equal rights for black people.

David Livingstone

Livingstone first went to Africa in 1841 to join a Christian missionary station in Bechuanaland (modern Botswana). In 1853, he set out on the first of three great expeditions, walking from Africa's west coast across to the Indian Ocean in the east.

△ While slavery was abolished throughout the British Empire, it continued in the US. Some slaves worked as servants in the homes of their owners. They often enjoyed better living conditions and more privileges.

Elsewhere in Africa, European adventurers were beginning to explore the interior of the continent. Although Europeans had established trading bases around the African coastline, very little was known about the empires and people of Africa. In 1788, an association was formed in London to encourage British exploration and trade in Africa. In the 1800s, the Industrial Revolution had resulted in increasing European interest in Africa as a source of cheap raw materials and as a market for manufactured goods.

Many British explorers set out to explore Africa along its rivers. They included Mungo Park, Richard Burton, and John Speke. Probably the most famous of all the expeditions was led by David Livingstone, who set out to look for the source of the River Nile. After being out of contact for almost three years, Livingstone was "found" by the American journalist Henry Stanley. Stanley went on to organize expeditions along the Congo River on behalf of the king of Belgium, who wanted to establish an overseas empire.

Dividing Africa

In the late 1800s, other European countries also began to lay claim to large areas of Africa. In 1884, a conference was held by the European nations in Berlin, Germany, to decide how Africa should be divided between them. No African representatives were present at the conference. By 1914, the only two countries on the African continent that still remained independent were Liberia and Ethiopia.

△ This is a typical colonists' hat. Colonists argued over each other's claims to the colonies. Yet colonial rule lasted for fewer than 100 years in most countries.

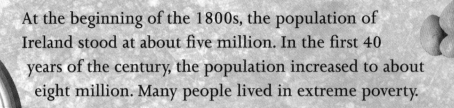

At the beginning of the 1800s, the population of Ireland stood at about five million. In the first 40 years of the century, the population increased to about eight million. Many people lived in extreme poverty.

Famine in Ireland

In 1845, a fungus affected the vital potato crop in southern England. It soon spread to Ireland, and in an unusually cold and wet year, the fungus quickly swept across the entire country.

Famine strikes

With the failure of the potato crop, people began to die in the thousands either from hunger or disease. In 1845, British Prime Minister Sir Robert Peel organized relief for the poorest people, so they could afford to buy inexpensive corn imported from the United States. It helped to prevent many people from starving to death. But when Peel resigned, the new government did little to assist the people of Ireland, limiting its help to building extra workhouses and opening up soup kitchens.

Potato crop fails in southern England. Fungus spreads to Ireland.	1845
Famine in Ireland kills about one million people. Many thousands emigrate.	1845–1849
Fenian Brotherhood formed in U.S.	1858
Home Rule movement founded by Isaac Butt.	1870
Charles Parnell becomes leader of Home Rule movement.	1878
First Home Rule Bill is defeated. Gladstone forced to resign.	1886
Second Home Rule Bill defeated by the House of Lords.	1893

△ Poor Irish people relied on potatoes as their main source of food. Between 1845 and 1849, an estimated one million people in Ireland died, either from starvation or disease.

△ Irish politician Charles Parnell addresses an audience in support of Home Rule. He became leader of the Home Rule Party in the British parliament and fought tirelessly for his beliefs. Parnell was even imprisoned by the British for a time.

▷ Irish emigrants wait to board a ship taking them to the United States. They were often forced to endure appalling conditions during the long voyage. One in nine emigrants from Cork, in Ireland, died before they reached their destination.

The famine came to an end after 1849, when the potato crop only partially failed. By then, the population of Ireland had been reduced to just over six million by famine and emigration.

Emigration

Many thousands of Irish people decided that their only escape from the great hunger caused by the famine was emigration. Over half a million people emigrated across the Atlantic to the United States between 1845 and 1849.

Many Irish people felt great bitterness towards the British government once the famine was over. This led to the founding of organizations, such as the Fenian Brotherhood in the U.S., which were prepared to fight for the establishment of an Irish republic, completely separate from Britain.

Home Rule

In 1870, a movement calling for Home Rule was founded in Ireland. Supporters of Home Rule wanted a separate parliament to deal with Irish affairs in Dublin. Although the British government was forced to introduce many reforms, two bills to introduce Home Rule were defeated in parliament in the 1880s and 1890s.

William Gladstone

Gladstone was prime minster of Britain four times during the reign of Queen Victoria. He believed that the Irish should run their own affairs and was a strong supporter of Home Rule. But he failed to get his Home Rule Bill approved by parliament.

△ When Ireland's potato crop failed, people dug up their crops only to find them rotting in the ground. Others picked what looked like sound potatoes, but they simply went rotten later on.

When Queen Victoria came to the throne in 1837, Great Britain was one of the wealthiest and most powerful countries in the world. Much of Britain's wealth came from its colonies, which provided sources of inexpensive raw materials and markets for British manufactured goods.

The British Empire

Britain began to acquire its overseas colonies during the 1600s. Although it lost the colonies in America in 1783, British influence continued to be extended in other parts of the world.

Britain takes control of Cape Colony in southern Africa.	1806
Start of reign of Queen Victoria.	1837
Revolt against British in India ends in terrible bloodshed.	1857–1858
End of rule of East India Company. British government takes control.	1858
Suez Canal is opened.	1869
Queen Victoria becomes empress of India.	1877
First Boer War ends with British defeat.	1880–1881
Second Boer War – Boers are forced to surrender.	1889–1902

Captain James Cook claimed parts of Australia and New Zealand in the 1770s. The first convicts were sent to Australia in 1788 because Britain was using the new land as a prison colony. In 1801, the Act of Union made Ireland part of the United Kingdom of Great Britain and Ireland. At the end of the Napoleonic Wars, Britain kept control of some of the colonies it had seized during the fighting.

India

The British set up their first trading post in India in 1612 and by the end of the 1600s had bases at Madras, Bombay, and Calcutta. These trading stations were run by the East India Company. In 1757, there was an uprising against the British in Calcutta but they eventually emerged victorious. This date marks the beginning of the British Empire in India.

The British gradually extended their power across India and trade flourished. One of the exports to India was cotton

△ Resentment to British rule boiled over in 1857, when Indian troops mutinied and marched on Delhi. The rebellion spread quickly across India, and thousands died in the fighting.

212

△ *During Queen Victoria's long reign, lasting 63 years, Britain's empire expanded greatly. At its largest, the British Empire accounted for one-fourth of the world's population.*

Suez Canal

Although Britain had played no part in building the Suez Canal in Egypt, it benefited greatly when the canal opened in 1869. The new 118-mile-long waterway shortened the route from Britain to India by around 6,000 miles.

cloth, produced inexpensively in British factories. However, local Indian producers could not compete with the British cloth and many went out of business.

In 1857, Indian soldiers mutinied against British control. By the following year, the rebellion had been put down and the British had regained control. But the East India Company's rule came to an end in 1858, and the British government took over running India. Queen Victoria was crowned empress of India in 1877.

The Boers

In southern Africa, Cape Colony came under British rule in 1806. However, the area was already home to the Boers – descendants of Dutch settlers. To escape British control, thousands of Boers undertook a journey northward in the 1830s, known as the "Great Trek." They founded two Boer states: the Orange Free State and the Transvaal. When the British tried to increase their power in southern Africa, the two sides went to war. The first Boer War (1880–1881) ended with a British defeat.

In 1886, major gold deposits were discovered in Witwatersrand in the Transvaal. Britain feared the growing power and wealth of the Boer states, and war broke out again in 1899. The Boers were finally forced to surrender in 1902.

Move [the statue of] Queen Anne? Most certainly not! Why it might some day be suggested that *my* statue should be moved, which I should much dislike.
QUEEN VICTORIA, 1887

△ *Traditional Zulu spears and shield. In the 1820s, the Zulus were the most powerful nation in southern Africa, but in 1879, they were defeated by the British.*

The early settlement of North America by Europeans was along the east coast. However, the Appalachian Mountains formed a natural barrier, initially preventing expansion farther west. In 1783, after the American Revolution, the United States took control of land west of the Appalachian Mountains as far as the Mississippi River, and pioneers began to settle in the area.

Pioneers in the U.S.

Following the purchase of Louisiana from France in 1803, President Jefferson had sent out an expedition to find out more about his new territories. The expedition leaders, Meriwether Lewis and William Clark, were the first of the many explorers and traders who started to travel westward, opening up routes called trails.

The Oregon and California trails

The first pioneers to go west were lured by tales of rich farmland on the far side of the Rocky Mountains. From the 1840s onward, large

President Jefferson makes Louisiana Purchase, almost doubling size of the U.S.	1803
Journey of Lewis and Clark to the west.	1804–1805
Start of great migration westward on California and Oregon trails.	1840s
Southern Oregon given to U.S. by Britain.	1846
Mexican War fought between U.S. and Mexico ends with victory for U.S.	1846–1848
Mormons begin their settlement of Utah.	1847
Gold discovered in California, setting off Gold Rush.	1848
U.S. government begins policy of "concentration" for Native Americans.	1851

△ The bolder pioneers made their way westward in long trains of covered wagons. They crossed the vast expanse of treeless plains to the Rocky Mountains, drawn by stories of fertile farmland and abundant forests.

△ As the news of the discovery of gold spread, people from all over the world poured into California. However, very few actually made their fortunes.

Custer's last stand

At the battle of the Little Bighorn in June 1876, Lieutenant Colonel George Custer and his unit of around 200 soldiers were killed by Sioux and Cheyenne Indians. The battle became known as "Custer's last stand."

△ By 1835, around 100 miles of railway track were in operation in the United States. The U.S. government had granted over 200 railroad charters.

△ Cowboys would drive huge herds of cattle across the plains on long trail drives. They took the cattle from the ranches in the west to railway stations to be shipped to the towns of the east.

numbers of people made the hazardous journey westward. Many traveled across the continent along the 1,990 mile Oregon Trail. It started in Independence, Missouri, and ended in the Columbia River region of Oregon. An alternative trail, the California Trail, followed the same route until it branched southward west of the Rocky Mountains, ending in the Sacramento Valley.

The pioneers traveled in wagons known as "prairie schooners" because their white canvas tops looked like sails. Settlers moved along the trail in groups for safety and for companionship, and there could be up to 100 wagons in a single wagon train. Although the greatest fear for pioneers was attack from Native Americans, the major killer was actually disease, and many pioneers died on the trails.

The gold rush

In 1848, James Marshall discovered gold in the America River at Sutter's Mill in California. Gold seekers began to come from all over the world, traveling by ship to San Francisco. Others walked across the American continent. Many died before they even reached California.

Native Americans on the move

As more people settled in the West, Native American ways of life were destroyed. In 1860, there were at least two million buffalo, on which the Native Americans relied, roaming across the Great Plains. White hunters began to destroy the large herds, and within 25 years, the number of buffalo had dropped drastically to about 2,000. Many Native Americans fought for their land and traditions, but they were usually no match for the well-equipped soldiers of the American government.

AD

During the 1800s and the beginning of the 1900s, many important discoveries were made in a wide range of scientific fields – from evolution to electricity, and from medicine to communications

Science and Technology

Pioneering work was done by people such as Charles Darwin, Thomas A. Edison, Alexander Graham Bell, and Guglielmo Marconi, changing the way people thought and lived in many parts of the world.

Steam power

The importance of steam power was already well established by the early 1800s, but it was not until 1829 that the British engineer George Stephenson built the first practical steam locomotive, the *Rocket*. The opening of the Liverpool to Manchester railway in northwest England in the following year marked the beginning of the railway age.

Steam was also used to power ships. The first regular transatlantic steam-powered service began in 1838 by the steamship *Sirius*. It had side wheels to push it through the water. The next major development in sea travel was the development of the screw propeller. The *Great Britain*, built by Isambard Kingdom Brunel, was the first propeller-driven ship to cross the Atlantic, in 1845.

Scientific expeditions

Of the scientific expeditions undertaken during the 1800s, one of the most famous was the voyage made by Charles Darwin on the HMS *Beagle*.

Steamship Clermont makes first trip on the Hudson River	1807
British engineer George Stephenson builds steam locomotive Rocket.	1829
Darwin's voyage on the Beagle.	1831– 1836
Steamship Sirius starts first regular transatlantic steam-powered service.	1838
Great Britain is first propeller-driven ship to cross the Atlantic.	1845
Publication of Darwin's The Origin of Species.	1859
Great Eastern lays first successful underwater telegraph line across Atlantic.	1866
Alexander Graham Bell develops first telephone.	1876
Guglielmo Marconi develops wireless telegraphy.	1895

△ From the observations made on his 37,000 mile journey on board the Beagle, Darwin began to piece together his theory of evolution. It caused a storm of controversy when it was first published, although many people came to accept it.

Samuel Morse

In 1840, the American inventor Samuel F. B. Morse launched a code based on dots, dashes, and spaces. Known as the Morse code, it speeded up the sending of messages through the telegraph.

△ *One of the first electric street lamps. American Thomas Edison invented the first working electric lamp in 1879. In the late 1800s, electric lamps began to replace gas ones.*

From 1831 to 1836, the naval survey ship sailed around the world. Darwin collected plant and animal specimens for scientific institutions in Britain. From his observations he, developed his theory of evolution, published in 1859. It stated that all living things evolved from ancestors by a process of natural selection.

Communications

The first truly rapid system for communicating between one place and another was the electric telegraph, which sent messages along wires. Soon most major cities were linked by telegraph, and in 1866, the first successful underwater telegraph line was laid across the Atlantic Ocean by the *Great Eastern*.

In 1876, a Scottish inventor, Alexander Graham Bell, made the first telephone. For the first time it was possible to transmit the human voice along a wire link. The next major breakthrough in communications was to send information without wires. In 1895, an Italian inventor, Guglielmo Marconi, developed wireless telegraphy, which made use of invisible radio waves to carry information. In 1906, a Canadian, Reginald A. Fessenden, made the first broadcast, transmitting speech and music to his astonished listeners.

"We must, however, acknowledge, as it seems to me, that man with all his noble qualities, . . . still bears in his bodily frame the indelible stamp of his lowly origin.
CHARLES DARWIN (1809–1882)

△ *A new kind of bicycle called the penny farthing appeared in the 1860s. It had a very large front wheel and a smaller back wheel.*

The Manchus (from Manchuria) ruled China for more than 250 years, from 1644 until 1912. This time is known as the Qing dynasty.

Rebellion in China

In the early part of Manchu reign, China was peaceful and prosperous. The population increased, and new, improved crops were introduced. Trade flourished, and China exported large amounts of tea and silk to countries in Europe. However, like rulers before them, the Manchus were careful to restrict imports from Europe. Foreign traders were allowed to do business in only one Chinese port, Guangzhou, and they had to pay for Chinese goods only in silver or gold.

The Opium Wars

In the early 1800s, British merchants began to trade opium illegally from India to China. Despite the fact that the addictive dangers of opium were well known, the British government backed the merchants. They wanted to force China to accept more open trade.

The first Opium War broke out in 1839, ending with the Treaty of Nanjing in 1842. Under the terms of this treaty, Hong Kong became a British colony and more Chinese ports were opened up to European trade. A second Opium War (1856–1860) extended the trading rights of European nations in China.

First Opium War fought between China and Britain.	1839– 1842
Taiping Rebellion against Qing dynasty ends in terrible bloodshed.	1851– 1864
Second Opium War ends with more trading rights for Britain.	1856– 1860
War between China and Japan results in loss of Taiwan to Japan.	1894– 1895
Boxer Rebellion. Attacks on westerners and Chinese Christians.	1900
Revolution in China.	1911
End of the Qing dynasty.	1912

△ *The Boxers were one of a number of Chinese secret societies strongly opposed to the spreading influence of Western and Christian ideas in China.*

▷ Under the Qing dynasty, Guangzhou was the only Chinese port that Western ships could use. Traders were strictly controlled and were only allowed access to a small area of the port.

△ The first Opium War began when Chinese officials seized 20,000 chests of opium in Guangzhou. It lasted from 1839 until a treaty was signed in 1842.

Uprising and rebellion

By the end of the 1700s, China's population was growing so fast that food production could not keep up. There was widespread corruption and any attempts to modernize were met with opposition from bureacrats and officials. There was a series of rebellions against Manchu rule in the 1800s, which helped to weaken the Qing dynasty. The Taiping Rebellion lasted for 14 years, and thousands of people died in these uprisings. In 1894–1895, China fought a war against Japan which resulted in the loss of the territory of Taiwan.

After the treaties that ended the Opium Wars, Western ideas began to spread in China. Some Chinese people opposed Western influences, and in 1900, the Boxer Rebellion broke out. Many Europeans were killed, but a combined European army eventually put down the rebellion.

After 1900, revolutionary groups began to oppose the Manchu rulers. The Manchus started to reform the government – but it was too late. In October 1911, there was a revolution and the last emperor was forced to abdicate. China had become a republic.

Hong Kong

The skyline of modern Hong Kong. The island of Hong Kong came under British control in 1842, and Britain later gained part of the nearby Kowloon Peninsula. Control of Hong Kong passed back to the Chinese government in 1997.

△ Under Manchu rule, all Chinese males had to follow the tradition of wearing their hair in a pigtail. It was seen as a sign of loyalty to the Qing dynasty.

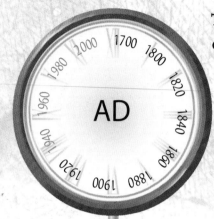

The women's movement had its roots in the late 1700s and early 1800s. Changes such as the American and French revolutions promoted ideas of "equality" and "liberty," yet women were not permitted to vote, and most had limited access to education.

The Women's Movement

In 1792, a British writer named Mary Wollstonecraft published *A Vindication of the Rights of Women*, setting out her belief in equal rights for men and women. This idea took hold during the 1800s, and many women began to campaign for reform.

Reform in the U.S.

The campaign for women's rights in the United States developed from the fight against slavery. The first Women's Rights Convention was held in Seneca Falls, New York, in 1848, organized by Lucretia Mott and Elizabeth Cady Stanton. Stanton declared that "all men and women are created equal" and called for reform in the laws concerning suffrage (the right to vote), marriage, and ownership of property. Stanton later teamed up with another reformer called Susan B. Anthony, and they traveled all over North America giving lectures and speaking at rallies in support of women's rights.

In 1890, Wyoming became the first state to grant women the right to vote. But it was to be another 30 years, not until 1920, before women's suffrage was extended to all the states.

△ Emmeline Pankhurst, founder of the WSPU, is arrested. She died a month after British women gained equal voting rights.

Mary Wollstonecraft's A Vindication of the Rights of Women.	1792
First Women's Rights Convention held in Seneca Falls, New York.	1848
Wyoming becomes first US state to grant women the right to vote.	1890
New Zealand is first country in the world to allow women to vote in elections.	1893
In Britain, Emmeline Pankhurst founds the WSPU.	1903
Suffragette Emily Davison throws herself beneath the king's horse at a race.	1913
Women over 30 given the vote in Britain.	1918
All women over 21 given the vote in Britain.	1928

△ The suffragettes engaged in many different forms of protest, from interrupting public meetings by shouting slogans to chaining themselves to railings outside the residence of the British prime minister.

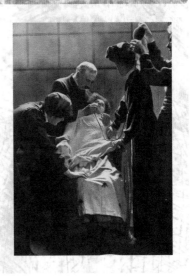

In prison

In Britain, the suffragette campaigners often went on hunger strikes when imprisoned for their actions. The authorities did not want the suffragettes to die and arouse public sympathy, so they fed the women by force.

Suffragettes

In 1893, New Zealand became the first country in the world to allow women to vote in national elections. Australia followed suit in 1903 and Finland in 1906. In other parts of the world, however, women were engaged in a bitter and often violent battle for the right to vote. In Britain, Emmeline Pankhurst founded the Women's Social and Political Union (WSPU) in 1903. The WSPU believed in actions rather than words, and many of its members, known as suffragettes, were arrested and imprisoned. In 1913, a suffragette called Emily Davison was killed when she threw herself beneath the king's horse at a race. Women over 30 were finally given the vote in 1918, after World War I. The right to vote was extended to all women over the age of 21 in 1928.

Just as in Britain, World War I was a turning-point in many countries for the women's movement. During the war, women had filled the places of the men who had gone off to fight, working in industries such as munitions factories, on farms as laborers, and in the mines. After the end of the war, equal voting rights were introduced in Canada (1918), Austria, Czechoslovakia, Germany, and Poland (1919), and in 1920 in Hungary and the United States.

△ During wartime women were brought in to fill the jobs of those men that had gone to fight. These posters emphasized the important role women had to play.

> " The divine right of husbands, like the divine right of kings, may, it is hoped, in this enlightened age, be contested without danger.
>
> ## MARY WOLLSTONECRAFT (1759–1797)
>
> *Wollstonecraft's book* A Vindication of the Rights of Women, *which she wrote in 1792, called for equal rights for women.* "

AD

The events of the Industrial Revolution brought great changes to towns and cities in Britain, and then across Europe and North America. British cities such as Birmingham, Manchester, Leeds, and Liverpool became important industrial centers, and their populations expanded rapidly.

Urban Development

First law concerning public health passed in England.	1848
Much of Paris redesigned and rebuilt.	1851–1870
Invention of Bessemer process makes use of steel in construction.	1856
First skyscraper, Home Insurance Building in Chicago, completed.	1885
Construction of Eiffel Tower for Paris Exhibition.	1889
Empire State Building constructed in New York City.	1931

People needed to live close to their workplace, so large numbers of houses were built to accommodate this new class of industrial worker. The speed with which many towns and cities expanded led to problems with overcrowded, dirty, and unsanitary housing.

Slum conditions

Many workers were forced to live in slum conditions. Worse, the new factories created pollution that often contaminated both water supplies and the air. Early industrial cities were disease-ridden places with very high death rates. Cholera, in particular, killed both rich and poor, and it claimed more than 140,000 people in Britain in four epidemics from 1831 to 1866. It was not until the mid-1800s in Britain that measures began to be taken to improve sanitation and health, for example by installing proper sewerage systems.

The increase in city populations was dramatic during the 1800s. London's

▷ The new factories in Britain's industrial cities and towns created pollution, often contaminating water supplies and the surrounding air. This pollution, and the poor housing conditions, led to the spread of disease.

△ The families of many workers lived in appalling slum conditions in the cities, often without clean water and proper sewage facilities.

Skyscrapers

Land prices in American cities were so high that people began to build upward. The first "skyscraper," the ten-story Home Insurance Building in Chicago, was completed in 1885.

population jumped from just under one million at the beginning of the century to over two million in 1840. Chicago increased in population from about 4,000 in 1840 to over one million people only 50 years later.

Ideal cities

Some people were appalled by the conditions in industrial cities. Writers such as Charles Dickens exposed the desperation of the poor in London in many of his novels. Some reformers tried to show how workers could, and should, be treated. One such reformer was a British industrialist named Robert Owen. He drew up plans for an "ideal city," showing how the houses, factories, shops, and other buildings should be arranged. Sadly, his plans were not taken seriously by the authorities.

Improvements

Improvements came as governments realized that more control was needed over the design and position of buildings in cities. Public services such as clean water supplies, sewage, gas and electric lighting, and public transport were also put in place.

In some places, parts of the old city were swept away to be replaced by radical new designs. This happened in Paris, where much of the medieval center was replaced by the ambitious plans of Baron Haussmann. Haussmann opened up 60 miles of new streets in the center of Paris, creating some of the spacious avenues for which Paris is still famous.

In cities such as New York and Chicago, the first skyscrapers appeared, built around a framework of strong, light steel.

△ Life in the industrial centers revolved around the mines, mills, and factories where people worked.

The opening years of the 20th century saw rivalry growing between the nations of Europe. Countries such as Britain and France controlled vast colonies overseas – in Africa and Southeast Asia – giving them both power and wealth.

Revolutions and Wars

Germany, which had become a united country in 1871, wanted to expand its territory and began to build up its military power. As countries became increasingly suspicious of each other, they entered into alliances – promising to help each other in the event of attack. In 1882, Germany, Austria-Hungary, and Italy formed the Triple Alliance. In 1904, Britain announced its friendly relations with France, and in 1907, they were joined by Russia to form the Triple Entente. It was these tensions and suspicions that led to the outbreak of World War I in 1914.

Conflict and unrest

In Russia, many years of strikes and protests came to a head in 1905, when workers went to the palace of the tsar, Nicholas II, in St. Petersburg to ask for reforms. Troops fired on the unarmed crowd, sparking a revolution which was put down by the government. A series

of disastrous campaigns in World War I, rising unemployment, and constant food shortages led to the successful overthrow of the tsar's regime in 1917 and the installation of a new communist government in Russia.

In Ireland, the issue of Home Rule, the Irish governing themselves, was the cause of violent protest, which finally erupted into civil war in 1921. An uneasy peace was negotiated in 1923, but the Irish problem was to continue throughout the century.

The Great Depression

A disastrous stock market crash in 1929 in the United States left many people penniless overnight. The effects of the Wall Street Crash were felt all over the world. Many countries in Europe were hard hit because they had borrowed money from the U.S. at the end of World War I. Throughout the 1930s, unemployment soared and trade slumped in a period known as the Great Depression.

In Germany and Italy, Fascist governments swept to power in the 1920s and 1930s. The Fascist leaders Benito Mussolini and Adolf Hitler promised to make their countries strong and successful once more. In 1939, after a bitter civil war, Spain also had a Fascist government. In the same year, Germany invaded Poland, marking the beginning of World War II.

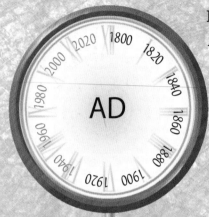

AD

In 1801, the grandson of Catherine the Great, Alexander I, became tsar (emperor) of Russia. Alexander had grand plans to introduce reform to his vast country, for example a program of building schools and the founding of new universities.

Revolution in Russia

Alexander I, becomes tsar of Russia.	1801
Russian army defeated by French at battle of Austerlitz.	1805
French retreat from Moscow.	1812
Nicholas I becomes tsar. Decembrist revolt.	1825
Crimean War.	1853–1856
Alexander II begins series of reforms.	1855
Serfs given freedom.	1861
Alexander II killed by terrorist bomb. His son Alexander III succeeds.	1881
Nicholas II becomes last tsar.	1894
Revolution put down by government troops.	1905
Russian Revolution.	1917

In 1805, the armies of the French emperor, Napoleon Bonaparte defeated a combined Russian and Austrian force at the battle of Austerlitz in Moravia. In 1812, French armies invaded Russia and advanced as far as Moscow. The French found the city deserted, and soon afterward, it was almost completely destroyed by fire.

Reform and modernization

At the end of the Napoleonic Wars, Russia emerged as a major European power. During the reign of Nicholas I, Russian armies helped to quell revolutions in Poland and Hungary, and gained territory for Russia around the Black Sea. But during the Crimean War, Russia was humiliated by its defeat at the hands of a combined French and British force.

Nicholas I remained deeply opposed to any change. He died in 1855 and was succeeded by his son, Alexander II. Shocked by the outcome of the Crimean War, the new tsar was determined to modernize Russia. He oversaw a massive program of reform, including railway building and the reorganization of local government and the legal system. Probably his most important action

△ In November 1917, armed workers, soldiers, and sailors, led by the Bolshevik revolutionaries, took up positions in the city of Petrograd (St. Petersburg). They stormed the Winter Palace, the headquarters of Russia's provisional government, and seized power.

△ Nicholas II and his family. Imprisoned by the Bolsheviks in 1917, they were most likely shot the following year.

V. I. Lenin

Lenin was one of the leaders of the failed rebellion in 1905. He was forced into exile but returned to Russia in 1917 when the tsar was overthrown. He led the Bolsheviks to victory in the revolution of 1917.

was to abolish serfdom. In 1861, serfs were given their freedom and land was distributed between them.

The Russian Revolution

The last tsar, Nicholas II, ruled from 1894 until his abdication in 1917. In the early years of his reign, there was increasing discontent among ordinary Russians. Many people, including the Bolshevik leader Vladimir Illyich (V. I.) Lenin, followed the teachings of Karl Marx, the founder of communism. In 1905, this discontent boiled over when troops fired on thousands of striking workers outside the tsar's Winter Palace in St. Petersburg. The rebellion was quickly put down, but hundreds of workers were killed and wounded.

During World War I, Russia was allied with France and Great Britain. The Russian armies suffered defeats on the Eastern Front, and the Russian economy began to collapse. In early 1917, riots broke out again – and this time the troops supported the rioters. Nicholas II abdicated, and a provisional government was put in place. Later in 1917, the Bolsheviks seized power and formed a new government with Lenin at its head. The events of 1917 are known as the Russian Revolution.

Communism is Soviet power plus the electrification of the whole country.
VLADIMIR ILLYICH LENIN, DECEMBER 1920

△ The red flag of the Bolshevik revolutionaries. Later, the symbols of a hammer and a sickle (to represent workers and peasants) and a star were added to create the official Communist Party flag.

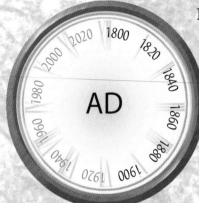

In April 1770, Captain James Cook had sailed along the east coast of Australia. He and his crew had landed at a place they called "Botany Bay" and claimed the land for Britain, naming the region New South Wales.

Colonies in Australia

Eighteen years later, in 1788, the first ships full of settlers arrived from Britain. These settlers were all convicts, transported from Britain for their various crimes. Under the command of Captain Arthur Phillip, the convicts were set to work founding a penal colony in Botany Bay.

Convicts and settlers

As more convicts arrived, the colony grew. When a convict's sentence was over, or if a convict was pardoned, he or she became free and was known as an "emancipist." Many emancipists stayed in the colony and made new lives for themselves. From the 1830s onward, an increasing number of free settlers also began to arrive in New South Wales, attracted by promises of grants of land. By the early 1850s, four new Australian colonies had been established: Western Australia, South Australia, Victoria, and Tasmania. The transportation of convicts ended in the 1840s and 1850s.

The Aborigines

The arrival of European settlers had a devastating effect on the original inhabitants of Australia, the Aborigines. The Europeans introduced diseases unknown to the Aborigines, to which they had no natural resistance. Many Aborigines were killed by outbreaks of diseases such as smallpox. As the number of colonists increased, forcing the Aborigines

First Fleet arrives in Botany Bay.	1788
Van Diemen's Land (Tasmania) settled.	1801
Assisted migration scheme introduced. Free settlers start to arrive in Australia.	1831
Gold discovered in Australia triggering a gold rush.	1851
Bush ranging comes to an end with execution of Ned Kelly.	1880
Economic depression in Australia.	1890
Commonwealth of Australia proclaimed (January 1).	1901

△ A set of modern Australian stamps commemorates the arrival of the First Fleet in Botany Bay in January 1788. The fleet consisted of 11 ships of convicts, army officers, and soldiers.

△ *About 300,000 Aborigines were living in Australia when the settlers first arrived from Europe. They were divided into about 500 tribal groups.*

△ *This carved club (left) and parry stick (right) are traditional Aboriginal weapons. The Aborigines' wooden clubs and spears were no match for the guns of the European settlers.*

Gold mining

Gold was discovered in New South Wales and Victoria in 1851. The find immediately attracted thousands of gold seekers from European countries and from China. Although a few prospectors grew rich, many found nothing and, unable to pay their passage home, settled in Australia.

off their traditional lands, conflict often broke out between the two sides. Thousands of Aborigines died in the fighting.

European exploration of the Australian continent continued in the 1800s. In 1840–1841, Edward Eyre became the first European to cross the Nullarbor Plain in south Australia. In 1861–1862 John Stuart made a successful journey northward across the Simpson Desert.

A new nation

By the 1880s, there were seven independent colonies in Australia. The introduction of the telegraph and construction of the railways improved links between the colonies, and a new movement started to join the colonies together in a federation. On January 1, 1901, the Commonwealth of Australia was created. Edmund Barton became the first prime minister of the new federal government. At that time, many people in Australia believed that only white people should be allowed into their new country. A "White Australia" policy was introduced to prevent Asian immigration into Australia. This policy was to last for more than 70 years.

At the beginning of World War I, both Australia and New Zealand sent troops to join the fighting. The Australia and New Zealand Army Corps – the Anzacs – took part in the disastrous campaign in Gallipoli, Turkey, establishing a brave fighting reputation. Many Anzac troops also fought in the trenches along the Western Front.

◁ *Convicts were to be transported to Australia and confined in prison ships like this one, until the late 1860s. Around 160,000 convicts were sent to Australia over an 80 year period.*

229

As the 19th century drew to a close, there was an increase in rivalry between the different nations of Europe. They competed against each other for control of colonies, and for industrial and military power.

World War I Begins

In 1882, Germany, Austria-Hungary and Italy (known as the Central Powers) formed an alliance, called the Triple Alliance, promising to protect each other in the event of an attack. In 1904, Britain joined with France in a similar alliance. They were joined by Russia in 1907 to form the Triple Entente.

Events in Sarajevo

Europe was finally plunged into war by the action of an assassin in the Bosnian city of Sarajevo in 1914. Since 1908, Bosnia had been part of the Austro-Hungarian Empire, but many people in Bosnia were Serbs, who wanted to be part of neighboring Serbia.

In June 1914, the heir to the Austro-Hungarian throne, Archduke Franz Ferdinand, and his wife Sophie made a tour of Bosnia. As they drove through the streets of Sarajevo, a Serbian assassin shot them both dead. In retaliation, Austria-Hungary, backed by Germany, declared war on Serbia.

Soon all the major European powers were drawn into the conflict. Russia, backed by France, supported Serbia. Then Germany invaded neutral Belgium and attacked France, drawing Britain into the conflict.

Germany, Austria-Hungary, and Italy form Triple Alliance.	1882
Germany develops naval force to rival Britain's navy.	1898
Britain and France agree Entente Cordiale.	1904
Russia joins Britain and France to form Triple Entente.	1907
Austria-Hungary adds Bosnia and Herzegovina to its empire.	1908
June: Archduke Ferdinand shot in Sarajevo.	1914
July: Austria-Hungary declares war on Serbia.	1914
August: Austria-Hungary invades Russia. Germany invades Belgium and France.	1914
September: German advance halted by Allies.	1914

△ German soldiers in trenches along the Western Front. During the four years of the war, many thousands of soldiers were to die in the trenches as they battled to gain a few yards, or miles, of ground. On the command of their officers, soldiers would climb "over the top" and run across "no man's land" while firing at the soldiers in the enemy trenches.

△ *A British soldier from World War I. Typically, soldiers would spend a week or more in a front-line trench before going back to their dugout in a support trench.*

Shooting in Sarajevo

The assassination of Archduke Ferdinand and his wife took place shortly after this photograph was taken. As they drove around Sarajevo, the assassin leapt onto the car and fired two shots.

The Western and Eastern fronts

The war was fought in two main areas in Europe, known as the Western Front and the Eastern Front. In September 1914, the Allies (France and Britain) managed to halt the German advance toward Paris at the first battle of the Marne. But after this crucial victory, the Germans and the Allies reached a kind of stalemate in which neither side could make any ground. Their troops dug themselves into zigzag lines of defensive trenches, which eventually stretched from the English Channel almost to Switzerland. This was known as the Western Front.

The Eastern Front ran along the borders between Russia and its Central Power enemies of Germany and Austria-Hungary. Despite having a huge army, the Russians were badly equipped, and they suffered heavy defeats at the battles of Tannenberg and the Masurian Lakes in 1914. However, further south Russian forces had more success against the Austro-Hungarian forces in Galicia, gaining territory that was subsequently lost again in 1915. After the Russian Revolution in 1917, the new government withdrew Russia from the war.

If I should die, think only this of me;
That there's some corner of a foreign field
That is for ever England.
THE SOLDIER, RUPERT BROOKE

Brooke was a poet who was killed in 1915. He was 28 when he died.

△ *A World War I gas mask. After the Germans used poisonous gas for the first time in April 1915, masks became an essential part of every soldier's kit.*

Before the war, Germany had built up its navy to match the strength of the British navy. However, the battle of Jutland in 1916 was the only major sea battle between the two navies during World War I, and Britain managed to maintain control of the seas throughout the war.

The Great War

1915 Allies land in Gallipoli. Italy declares war on Austria-Hungary.

1916 February: battle of Verdun. May: sea battle of Jutland. July: battle of the Somme.

1917 April: U.S. declares war on Germany. June: U.S. troops arrive in France.

1917 Battle of Passchendaele. Revolution in Russia. End of fighting on Eastern Front.

1918 President Woodrow gives "14 Points" for peace. Last battles on Western Front.

1918 Germans sign armistice on November 11.

1919 Paris Peace Conference.

From the start of the Great War, the name by which World War I was first known, British warships blockaded German ports. In this way Britain's navy prevented supplies from reaching Germany, causing severe shortages of food and other goods. The Germans retaliated with their submarines, called U-boats. After 1915, U-boats attacked both warships and merchant shipping carrying supplies to Britain.

In May 1915, a German torpedo hit a British passenger ship called the *Lusitania*. The ship was carrying nearly 2,000 passengers, including many Americans. The sinking of the *Lusitania* was one of the factors that eventually drew the United States into the war.

△ The surprise torpedo attack of the Lusitania took place off the Irish coast. The U-boats fired powerful torpedoes which exploded when they struck a ship traveling on the surface.

△ The battle of the Somme took place in northern France in 1916. It lasted for about five months, during which time over one million soldiers were killed.

△ Poppies were in bloom on many of the French battlefields of World War I. Today, artificial poppies are sold in Europe and the U.S. to raise money for war veterans.

△ Battles between enemy aircraft were known as "dogfights." The Germans' invention of a machine gun that fired rounds between the plane's propeller blades made this combat more dangerous.

Peace treaty

The Allies and Germany signed the Treaty of Versailles on June 28, 1919 in Paris. The date was the fifth anniversary of the shooting of Archduke Ferdinand in Sarajevo.

War on other fronts

During 1915 and 1916 the war spread to other regions. Italy entered the war on the side of the Allies in 1915, and Italian troops fought Austro-Hungarian forces in the Alpine regions along the border between the two countries.

In April 1915, the Allies attacked Turkey (which had joined the Central Powers in 1914) with the aim of capturing its capital, Constantinople. Allied troops, including many soldiers from Australia and New Zealand, were sent to the Gallipoli Peninsula on the coast of the Dardanelles. However, the attack was a failure and the Allies were forced to withdraw. Allied troops also fought Turkish forces in the Middle East, in a successful attempt to keep control of the vital supply link of the Suez Canal.

The end

On the Western Front, the deadlock continued. Battles such as the Somme offensive in 1916, and Passchendaele in 1917, achieved little and caused the deaths of thousands of soldiers. However, in April 1917 the U.S. joined World War I, boosting the Allies with new supplies of troops. Although Germany launched a fresh attack on the Western Front in 1918, by late September it was clear that the Central Powers were defeated.

The Paris Peace Conference

On November 9, Kaiser Wilhelm II, the German ruler, was forced to abdicate. On November 11, 1918 an armistice, or peace agreement, was signed and the war was over. At the Paris Peace Conference, held in 1919, Germany was held responsible for the war and forced to pay large amounts of reparations (compensation) to its former enemies.

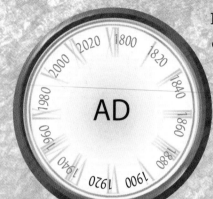

AD

During World War I, the issue of Home Rule continued to cause conflict in Ireland. The third Home Rule Bill had been passed by the British parliament in 1914, but the outbreak of war in the same year delayed the start of Home Rule.

Home Rule in Ireland

Third Home Rule bill passed by British parliament but held up by outbreak of war.	1914
Easter Rebellion in Dublin.	1916
Sinn Fein declares itself in favor of an Irish republic.	1917
Sinn Fein sets up Irish parliament, Dáil Eirann. Fighting breaks out.	1919
British parliament passes Government of Ireland Act, dividing country into two.	1920
Truce stops fighting. Anglo-Irish Treaty splits Sinn Fein.	1921
Civil war breaks out between supporters of treaty and those against it.	1922
Republicans, led by de Valera, accept Anglo-Irish Treaty.	1923

Many people in Ireland supported Home Rule because they believed that Ireland should have its own parliament in Dublin and control its own affairs. These nationalists were mostly Irish Catholics in the south of the country. They formed various organizations, including the political party Sinn Fein and the armed force of the Irish Volunteers.

Irish Protestants, however, were bitterly opposed to Home Rule. They were in the majority in the northern province of Ulster, and believed that they would be treated unfairly by a Dublin parliament. They formed the Ulster Volunteer Force to protect themselves if Home Rule was introduced.

The Easter Rising

When war broke out in 1914, most Irish Volunteers supported Britain in its fight against the Central Powers. But a breakaway group formed the Irish Republican Brotherhood (later known as the IRA). On Easter Monday 1916, protestors belonging to this and other nationalist movements seized buildings in Dublin and proclaimed Ireland a republic. British troops bombarded the rebels for a week until they surrendered.

△ The rebellion of Easter Monday 1916 became known as the Easter Rising. Many Irish people were unhappy about the heavy-handed tactics of the British soldiers, and the rebels soon became public heroes.

△ The British prime minister, David Lloyd George, met five representatives from the Dáil in London in 1921. Under his proposal, Northern Ireland would stay under British control but the Irish Free State would become a British dominion.

Michael Collins

Michael Collins was one of the leaders of the Irish Republican Army (IRA) who supported the 1922 Anglo-Irish Treaty. The peace treaty split the IRA in two. The bitter civil war between opponents and supporters of the treaty continued until a ceasefire was accepted in 1923.

Fifteen of the republican leaders were executed for their part in the uprising. One of the leaders, Eamon de Valera, was sentenced to death and then later reprieved.

The Anglo-Irish Treaty

In 1917, the political party Sinn Fein backed forming an Irish republic. The next year, the party won 73 seats in the general election. Sinn Fein's MPs formed their own parliament, the Dáil Eirann, in Dublin and in 1919 declared Ireland a republic. There followed three years of bitter fighting between the IRA and the Royal Irish Constabulary, backed by British troops known as "black and tans" because of the color of their uniforms.

In July 1921, a truce was declared and the fighting stopped. Lloyd George, Britain's prime minister, proposed that the country should be divided into Northern Ireland, made up of six counties of the northeast, and the Irish Free State, made up of the 26 counties of the south. The Dáil approved the Anglo-Irish Treaty in 1921. Fighting broke out between Republicans wanting a united, independent Ireland, and the Free Staters who supported the treaty. It ended in 1923 when de Valera's Republicans accepted the treaty.

> Before Irish Home Rule is conceded by the Imperial Parliament, England ... will have to be convinced of its justice and equity.
> ### LORD ROSEBERY, HOUSE OF LORDS, MARCH 1894

Rosebery favored social reform. He was Prime Minister from 1894–1895.

△ Ireland's flag was first used in the 1800s. Its green color stands for the Roman Catholic population, the white is for unity and the orange color stands for the Protestant people of Ulster.

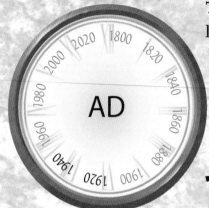

The end of World War I left devastation across large areas of Europe. Many countries were in economic chaos too. Germany was struggling to pay reparations to its former enemies. Countries such as France and Britain had borrowed large amounts of money to pay for the war effort, mostly from banks in the United States.

The Great Depression

The Great Depression started in 1929 in the United States, and continued for about ten years. It was a time of high unemployment and great poverty. Although the Depression began in the U.S., it quickly became a worldwide phenomenon that affected millions of people.

The Wall Street Crash

In the late 1920s, the price of shares on the New York Stock Exchange increased rapidly. More and more people bought stocks and shares in the hope of selling them again when their price had gone up – therefore making a large profit. When prices dropped in October 1929, people rushed to sell their stocks and shares before it was too late, but prices fell even further. This event is known as the Wall Street Crash. Thousands of

Panic selling of shares leads to the Wall Street Crash.	1929
Share prices continue to fall for following three years.	1930s
Drought and dust storms devastate the Midwest and southwest regions of the U.S.	1930s
Franklin D. Roosevelt becomes president and sets up the "New Deal."	1932
Outbreak of war brings an end to the Depression.	1939
John Steinbeck's The Grapes of Wrath tells about migrant families.	1939
Full employment returns in the United States.	1941

△ In October 1929 prices on New York's Stock Exchange began to collapse. This is the Stock Exchange at the time, with brokers spilling out onto the streets of the city.

△ In 1932 Franklin D. Roosevelt was elected president. His "New Deal" aimed to create jobs and to protect people's savings by regulating banks more closely.

△ During the worst years of the Depression, many people were forced to rely on charity and government hand outs for their most basic needs.

people lost all their money, many businesses and banks shut down and unemployment soared.

The situation in the U.S. was made worse by severe droughts in the 1930s in the Midwest states. Thousands of farm workers were ruined. Many made the long and difficult journey to look for work on farms in California. Thousands died from disease and hunger.

Depression in Europe

The economic collapse in the United States had a drastic effect on countries around the world. Banks in the U.S. withdrew funds from overseas and demanded the repayment of loans, triggering the closure of many European banks. Many European countries tried to protect their own trade by raising taxes on imports, but this encouraged a worldwide slump in international trade. Both Great Britain and Germany were very badly affected by the Great Depression. In Germany, Adolf Hitler rose to power in the 1930s, promising the suffering German people to make their country proud and strong once again.

A New Deal

In 1933, President Franklin D. Roosevelt introduced a program to help the needy, to create jobs, and to help struggling farmers. It was known as the "New Deal." But it was the onset of war that finally ended the Great Depression in both the U.S. and Europe. As countries such as Britain and Germany prepared for the possibility of war, the production of munitions and armaments soared, creating many jobs. And with the outbreak of war in 1939, orders flooded into factories on both sides of the Atlantic Ocean.

△ Wall Street lies at the heart of New York's business and banking district. Many banks have offices in the narrow street. The name "Wall Street" is a worldwide symbol for financial business.

Jarrow march

In 1935, a group of 200 unemployed workers from Britain's northern industrial cities marched from Jarrow to London to draw attention to their plight.

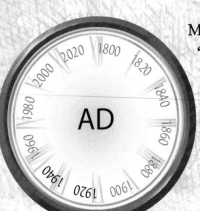

Many people hoped that World War I was the "war to end all wars." But the settlements drawn up in 1919 provided the starting-point for a whole new set of problems. In addition, the misery and suffering brought by the Great Depression during the 1920s and 1930s led to political changes in many countries.

The Dictators

1922 Benito Mussolini marches to Rome.

1925 Mussolini becomes dictator of Italy, known as il Duce.

1932 Sir Oswald Mosley sets up British Union of Fascists.

1933 Nazis come to power in Germany, led by Adolf Hitler.

1934 "Night of the Long Knives" in Germany as Hitler eliminates his rivals.

1936–1939 Spanish Civil War.

1938 Germany annexes Austria and the Sudetenland.

1939 General Franco becomes dictator of Spain.

In Europe, all these factors led to the growth of the Fascist movement. The word "Fascism" comes from *fasces*, meaning a bundle of branches. It was the symbol of authority in ancient Rome. Fascism promised strong leadership and to restore the national economy and pride. This was a very powerful message in the years of the Great Depression, and many people in Europe supported the various Fascist parties.

Fascism in Italy

Italy was the first country to have a Fascist ruler. In 1922, Benito Mussolini marched to Rome and demanded that the Italian king, Victor Emmanuel III, make him prime minister. By 1925 Mussolini had become a dictator, known as il Duce (the Leader). The Fascists seized control of all aspects of Italian life,

▷ Oswald Mosley set up the British Union of Fascists after a visit to Italy in 1932. At public meetings his supporters, known as "the Blackshirts," often behaved very violently.

238

△ The Italian Fascist leader Benito Mussolini was a great friend and ally of Germany's Adolf Hitler. Italy joined forces with Hitler in World War II.

△ Adolf Hitler was known as der Führer (the Leader). He believed that Germany needed strong leadership to solve its problems, which he blamed on communists and Jews. He put himself in charge of all Germany's armed forces.

Propaganda posters

The Spanish government produced anti-Fascist propaganda posters like this during the civil war. They urged the people to oppose the Fascist leaders.

such as newspapers, industry and education, and ensured that anyone who disagreed with Fascist points of view was imprisoned or murdered. Mussolini continued to rule until he was overthrown during World War II, in 1943.

General Franco

In Spain, a bitter civil war broke out in 1936. Supported by the Fascist *Falangé* group, the army rose against the Spanish government. The rebels, known as Nationalists, were led by General Francisco Franco. People who fought to save the government were known as Republicans. This war attracted much interest, as Fascist countries such as Germany and Italy supported the Nationalists. The Republicans were backed by the Soviet Union, and many people from other European countries went to Spain to fight for the Republican cause. The Nationalist forces eventually seized power in 1939, and General Franco became dictator of Spain, ruling until his death in 1975.

The Nazis

In the early 1930s, the Nazi party rose to power in Germany, led by Adolf Hitler. Humiliated by the terms of the peace treaties at the end of World War I, and suffering the effects of the Great Depression, the German people responded to Hitler's promises of national recovery. Hitler became chancellor of Germany in 1933, and began removing all opposition to the Nazi party. He set up a secret police force, banned opposing political parties, and started to persecute minority groups in the German population, such as gypsies and Jews. He also planned to take back land lost at the end of World War I. These actions led to the outbreak of World War II.

239

In March 1939, the German leader Adolf Hitler threatened to invade Poland. Hitler had already shown the seriousness of his intentions by taking over Austria (in 1938) and Czechoslovakia (in 1939).

World War II

Both Great Britain and France gave guarantees to help Poland if it was attacked. So when Hitler invaded Poland on September 1, 1939 Britain and France were forced to declare war on Germany.

September: Hitler invades Poland.	1939
September: Britain and France declare war on Germany.	1939
USSR invades Poland.	1939
April–May: Germany occupies Denmark, Norway, Belgium, the Netherlands.	1940
Germany occupies France. June: Allies evacuate troops from Dunkerque.	1940
June: French sign armistice with Germany. July: Battle of Britain starts.	1940
Italians invade Egypt. Allies fight to prevent Axis control of Suez Canal.	1940
Hitler sends General Erwin Rommel to North Africa.	1941
Germany invades USSR. December: Japanese attack on Pearl Harbor.	1941

Under Hitler's leadership, Germany had been well prepared for war. During 1939 and 1940, German troops scored victories in Poland, Denmark, Norway, Belgium, the Netherlands, and France. Before the war started, Hitler had signed a "non-aggression pact" with the Soviet Union, both sides promising not to attack the other. As German troops swept across Europe, Soviet troops attacked Estonia, Latvia, Lithuania, and Finland.

The Battle of Britain

The Allied forces of Britain and France became trapped by the rapid German invasion. The majority of the British army was saved in 1940 by a desperate evacuation from the French port of Dunkerque. In June 1940, the French signed a truce with Germany and Britain stood alone against the German military machine.

Italy joined the war, siding with the Germans, in June 1940, and Hitler made plans to invade Britain. However, first he needed to gain control of the skies. The Battle of

△ Allied troops wait on a beach at Dunkerque, in northern France, in June 1940. A rescue fleet of naval ships, fishing boats, yachts, and ferries sailed across the English Channel from England to carry them back to safety. In all, the evacuation rescued more than 300,000 soldiers, who had become trapped by the German army.

△ *Winston Churchill was Britain's wartime leader from May 1940 until just before the war ended. Here he is seen making his famous "V for victory" sign.*

Battle of Britain

The Battle of Britain was the world's first major air battle. The British fighter planes were able to shoot down many of the long-range German bomber aircraft, shown here.

Britain began in July 1940 between the German airforce, the Luftwaffe, and Britain's Royal Air Force (RAF). The Luftwaffe bombed RAF bases, as well as British towns and cities. The nightly air raids that took place in the autumn and winter of 1940–1941 are known as the Blitz. However, by May 1941 the RAF had gained the upper hand, and Hitler gave up the attempt to bomb Britain into submission although air raids continued throughout the war.

Pearl Harbor

Meanwhile, the fighting spread beyond Europe. In Africa, Italian troops invaded Egypt, threatening the Suez Canal. The canal was a vital link to the oilfields of the Middle East, so Allied troops were sent to defend Egypt. Germany also made a surprise attack on the Soviet Union, going back on the promises made in the non-aggression pact. The German invasion, in June 1941, took the Russian leader Stalin by surprise.

In December 1941 there was another surprise attack, this time by the Japanese airforce on the U.S. navy base at Pearl Harbor in Hawaii. Although the attack crippled the U.S. Navy in the Pacific Ocean, it also drew the U.S. into the war. The United States and the Allies declared war on Japan on December 8, 1941. Japan joined Germany and Italy to form the Axis alliance.

"…we shall fight on the seas and oceans, we shall fight with growing confidence …in the air, we shall defend our island, whatever the cost may be …
WINSTON CHURCHILL, JUNE 4, 1940

△ *A standard World War II helmet. About 17 million soldiers, from both the Allies and the Axis countries, were killed during the war.*

After the attack at Pearl Harbor in 1941, World War II became a truly global war. In Africa, the Allies succeeded in defeating the Italians, only to be pushed back once again by Axis troops under the command of Hitler's General Rommel.

A Global War

The turning point came at the battle of el-Alamein in October 1942, when Allied forces, under Lieutenant-General Montgomery, forced the Axis troops to retreat. The Axis forces eventually surrendered in North Africa in May 1943.

War in the Pacific

After Pearl Harbor, Japanese forces quickly took control of much of Southeast Asia, including Singapore, Burma (Myanmar), and the Philippines. The Japanese then advanced across the Pacific toward Australia and the Hawaiian Islands. From 1942 to 1945 the Allies continued to drive the Japanese out of their newly captured territories.

April: Doolittle Raid on Tokyo, Japan. *May: battle of Coral Sea.*	1942
June: Midway Island. *August: Guadalcanal.* *October: battle of el-Alamein.*	1942
February: siege of Stalingrad ends with Axis surrender.	1943
May: Axis forces surrender in North Africa.	1943
July: battle of Kursk. *September: Allied troops land in Italy.*	1943
June: D-Day invasion along Normandy coast, northern France.	1943
June: battle of the Philippine Sea. *December: battle of the Bulge.*	1944
May 7: German surrender. *May 8: Victory in Europe.* *September: Japanese surrender.*	1945

△ *On the morning of June 6, 1944, thousands of Allied troops went ashore along the coast of Normandy in northern France in what became known as the D-Day landings.*

▷ *Japan's surprise attack on Pearl Harbor, on December 7, 1941, brought the Americans into the war. During the summer of 1942, U.S. forces successfully halted the Japanese advance at the battles of Midway Island, Guadalcanal and Coral Sea.*

△ *Charles de Gaulle was the leader of the French troops, known as the Free French, who had escaped occupied France. After the war he became one of France's most powerful presidents ever.*

The Soviet Union

By November 1941 German troops had advanced almost as far as Moscow. The bitter Russian winter and the Soviet army combined to drive them back. The German forces advanced into Soviet territory again, reaching the city of Stalingrad (now Volgograd). The Soviet army finally defeated the Germans in a fierce battle in the city.

The end of the war

In June 1944, Allied leaders decided that it was time to attack Germany itself. Under the overall command of General Eisenhower, Allied troops landed in Normandy and advanced across France. Meanwhile, Soviet troops moved across eastern Europe.

In April 1945, as Soviet troops surrounded Berlin, Hitler committed suicide. The German surrender came on May 7, and the Allies declared May 8 V-E (Victory in Europe) day. However, in the Far East the war was not over. President Harry S. Truman, decided to use a secret weapon developed by British and American scientists – the atomic bomb. On August 6th and 9th, 1945, two atomic bombs were dropped on the Japanese cities of Hiroshima and Nagasaki. The Japanese surrendered on September 2.

The Holocaust

In places such as Belsen and Auschwitz, the Nazis had set up concentration camps, where millions of Jews were imprisoned and murdered. An estimated six million Jews died in these camps in World War II, an event known as the Holocaust.

△ *By 1945 many Allied cities, as well as the country's factories and railways, were in complete ruins as a result of the German bombing campaign.*

Technological advances in the machines and weapons of war were rapid during the 20th century. During World War I, inventions included the tank and the fighter aircraft. At sea, one of the major advances in military marine technology happened before the war, with the building of the battleship *Dreadnought*.

New War Technology

During World War II, the Germans used a new type of warfare, known as *Blitzkrieg* (lightning war). In the United States, scientists developed the atomic bomb, which was used to bring the war against Japan to its catastrophic end.

Trench warfare and tanks

By the end of 1914, the Allies and the Germans had reached a stalemate on the Western Front. Both sides dug defensive trenches to protect their troops. The trenches of the opposing sides were separated by a desolate and deserted strip called "no man's land."

From 1914 to 1918, both sides attacked the other's trenches with little success. Thousands of men were killed in these pointless offensives. Tanks were developed to move across rough ground and through the barbed wire that protected trenches, while giving the soldiers inside some protection.

War in the air

At the beginning of World War I, aircraft were used for reconnaissance, to collect information about enemy positions and movements. Enemy aircraft began to exchange gunfire in the air, and soon machine guns were mounted onto aircraft. Flying "aces" such as the German

△ The line of trenches dug by the forces of the Allies and the Central Powers in World War I eventually ran from the English Channel almost to Switzerland. The nearest trench to the enemy was known as the "front line," but complex trench systems extended many miles back from this.

Britain launches new type of battleship called Dreadnought.	1906
Trench warfare claims thousands of lives in World War I.	1914–1918
Tanks used effectively for first time at battle of Cambrai.	1917
World War II involves much of the world in a global war.	1939–1945
German troops use blitzkrieg tactics to invade Allied countries.	1940
U.S. sets up secret nuclear research project.	1942
First atomic bomb exploded in New Mexico.	1945
Atomic bombs dropped on Hiroshima and Nagasaki in Japan.	1945

△ Both the British and the French armies experimented with tanks during World War I. These armored vehicles were first used to effect at the battle of Cambrai in 1917.

Atomic bombs

The first atomic bomb was exploded in an experiment in New Mexico, in July 1945. A month later, atomic bombs were used to end the war. The bombs dropped on Japan killed about 130,000 people. Many more suffered radiation and burn injuries.

Red Baron, Erich von Richthoffen, fought daring one-to-one air battles in the skies.

Aircraft played a vital role in World War II. The German airforce, the *Luftwaffe*, tried to bomb Britain into submission in 1940. But in the Battle of Britain the British RAF finally gained control of the skies. The German *Luftwaffe* also dropped bombs immediately before overwhelming tank and infantry attacks on the ground.

War at sea

Although the battle of Jutland was the only major sea battle of World War I, control of the seas was vital. The Germans made very effective use of submarines, known as U-boats, to launch torpedo attacks on enemy shipping.

By World War II, massive ships called aircraft carriers could transport air power across the seas. The Japanese attack on Pearl Harbor in 1941 destroyed many U.S. battleships, but the U.S. Navy played a decisive part in the many Pacific battles of the war. The Atlantic Ocean was also a war zone, with German U-boats attacking ships to try to prevent supplies reaching Britain. However, the convoy system, in which ships traveled in groups protected by warships, helped to reduce the number of ships lost to U-boat attacks.

Men marched asleep. Many had lost their boots
But limped on, blood-shod. All went lame; all blind;
Drunk with fatigue; ...
DULCE ET DECORUM EST, WILFRED OWEN

Owen fought in World War I and wrote poems about his experiences.

△ The introduction of machine guns made World War I more deadly than earlier wars. From the trenches, machine guns easily wiped out large numbers of attacking soldiers.

World War II came to an end in 1945 after the Allies dropped two atomic bombs on the Japanese cities of Hiroshima and Nagasaki. To try to prevent such a conflict happening again, the victorious Allies set up the United Nations, an international peacekeeping organization.

Global Politics

At the end of the war, the Union of Soviet Socialist Republics (USSR) and the United States emerged as the world's two "superpowers." Differences between the USSR and its communist allies, including China, on the one hand, and the U.S. and other non-communist countries on the other, soon led to the start of the "Cold War." Although neither superpower fought the other directly, both sides began to build up large supplies of nuclear weapons.

Communism

After World War II, the USSR moved quickly to extend communist power in Eastern Europe. By 1948 there were communist governments in Albania, Bulgaria, Czechoslovakia, Hungary, Poland, Romania, and

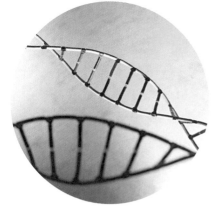

Yugoslavia. However, in the 1960s there was a major split in the communist world when China and the USSR ceased friendly relations. In China, Mao Zedong returned to power in 1966, launching the Cultural Revolution which lasted until his death in 1976. In the USSR, dissatisfaction with the communist system led to reforms in the 1980s and the eventual collapse of communism in Eastern Europe in 1989 and 1990. The USSR itself finally broke up into independent republics in 1991.

Independence

Another major change in the years after World War II was the break up of the colonial empires held by European nations. The independence of India in 1947 marked the beginning of this process. However, independence was often achieved with bloodshed. In India, the partition (division) of the country led to violence between Hindus and Muslims. In Africa, there were violent clashes in many places, and independence sometimes resulted in civil war. In South Africa, the white minority government enforced a racist policy called apartheid (meaning separateness), which tried to keep black and white people apart.

Into the 21st century

Many people's lives have been transformed by the communications revolution in the 21st century. Radio, television, and the Internet have made the world a smaller place, with people communicating more easily and quickly than ever before. Many people now realize that some of the major challenges of the 21st century cannot be faced by countries separately. Environmental matters such as pollution and climate change affect people all over the planet, and countries need to work together to find solutions. Global awareness is one of the main challenges facing the world in the 21st century.

AD

After the revolution of 1911, the last Chinese emperor, the six-year-old Pu Yi, gave up his throne. The revolutionaries named Sun Yat-sen as temporary leader of the new republic, but in 1912 a soldier named Yuan Shikai became president.

Communist China

Yuan quickly tried to seize more power, attempting to make himself emperor, but he died in 1916. Meanwhile, Sun Yat-sen had become leader of the Chinese National People's Party (also known as the Kuomintang), with support from many warlords (military leaders) in the south of China.

Last Chinese emperor gives up throne.	1911
Chinese Communist Party founded.	1921
Nationalist government established in China.	1928
Communists set up a rival government in the south.	1931
Mao Zedong leads "Long March."	1934–1935
War with Japan.	1937–1945
Nationalists flee to Taiwan. Mao Zedong proclaims the birth of the People's Republic of China.	1949
Period of "Five-Year Plan."	1953–1957
Start of the "Great Leap Forward."	1958
Mao launches Cultural Revolution.	1966
Death of Mao.	1976

For some years the Nationalist Party worked closely with Chinese communists, aided by the USSR who wanted to promote communism in China and help the revolution. The Communist Party attracted many students, including a young Mao Zedong. Mao and other students did much to spread communism among the rural poor of China.

Sun Yat-sen died in 1925, and the nationalists' new leader was Chiang Kai-Shek. A military leader, he led a campaign to defeat rebellious warlords in the north. He also crushed communist power in the cities, establishing a nationalist government in 1928.

The Long March

In 1931, the communists set up a rival government in the south. Chiang Kai-Shek sent his armies to crush the communists once and for all. The communists were forced to flee and

▷ A crowd gathers during the Long March of 1934–1935. About 100,000 communists made the difficult 6,000-mile journey northwards.

△ A poster from modern China. Wall posters have been used to provide information for many years. This one tries to encourage people to adopt a modern attitude.

△ Millions of Chinese would read the ideas of Mao printed in what became known as Mao's "Little Red Book."

Mao Zedong

During the Cultural Revolution, Mao and his supporters accused many people of failing to follow communist ideals. Students and young people formed groups of "Red Guards" in support of Mao.

moved north on a journey, known as the "Long March," led by Mao Zedong. Pursued by nationalist soldiers, thousands of marchers died.

War with Japan

The nationalist government also had to cope with constant threats from Japan, and in 1937 the Japanese invaded China. In World War II, China fought with the Allies against Japan. After the end of the war, and Japan's defeat, in 1945, China again descended into civil war. Aided by popular support, the communists gradually gained the upper hand. In 1949, Chiang Kai-shek and his supporters fled to Taiwan, and Mao proclaimed China the People's Republic of China.

China under Mao

After years of civil war, much of China was in ruins. Mao Zedong set about reforming the country according to communist ideals. Land was seized from landowners and divided up among the peasants. In Mao's "Five-Year Plan" (1953–1957) new roads and railways were built, industry was boosted, and health and education were improved. However, the main challenge was to produce enough food to feed China's huge population. The "Great Leap Forward," which started in 1958, was a second plan to improve agricultural and industrial output. But the plan failed and Mao retired in 1959.

In the early years of the People's Republic, China was supported by the USSR. However, China became increasingly critical of the USSR, particularly of its relations with the West, and the two countries ceased friendly relations in the 1960s. In 1966, Mao Zedong came back to power in China, launching the Cultural Revolution to promote communist ideals. Many teachers were forced to go and work on the land, and schools and universities closed down. Thousands of people were killed or sent into exile for criticizing Mao or questioning his policies. The Cultural Revolution eventually came to an end in 1976, when Mao died.

At the end of World War I in 1918, many people were determined that there should never again be such terrible slaughter and bloodshed. An international association called the League of Nations was formed by the leading nations involved in the war.

The United Nations

The League of Nations aimed to maintain peace between countries. However, although US president Woodrow Wilson was a driving force behind the League's formation, he was unable to persuade Congress to join it. In the years to come this proved to be a serious weakness.

Founding the United Nations

The League began to fall apart in the 1930s when several member states challenged its authority. After the outbreak of war in 1939 the League of Nations ceased to exist, but there were moves to establish a new organization to replace it. In 1941 President Franklin D. Roosevelt, and the British prime minister, Winston Churchill, signed the Atlantic Charter. It pledged to respect people's rights to choose their government, to

First UN conference held in San Francisco. UN Charter signed.	1945
UN approves plan to set up Jewish state of Israel.	1947
UN approves Universal Declaration of Human Rights.	1948
UN negotiates between U.S. and USSR during Cuban missile crisis.	1962
UN arranges ceasefire to end Six-Day War in Middle East.	1967
UN arranges ceasefire between Iran and Iraq.	1988
UN sends peacekeeping force to Croatia.	1992
UN peacekeeping troops sent to Bosnia.	1993

△ An aid worker in an African feeding station. The UN's World Food Program gives emergency food aid and other kinds of assistance to help developing countries.

250

> Representatives from 26 countries signed a document known as the "Declaration of United Nations" on January 1, 1942. An additional 21 countries later signed the same declaration. It was the first time the term "United Nations" had been used.

maintain peace, and to live without fear or want, as well as promoted disarmament and economic prosperity.

In 1944, representatives from the Unitrd States, the USSR, China, and Great Britain attended a series of meetings in the U.S. They drew up the basis for an international peacekeeping organization. The first conference of the United Nations (UN) was held in San Francisco in 1945, and the UN Charter was signed in October of that year.

The aims of the UN

Peace and security are the most important aims of the UN. Since 1945, the UN has helped to negotiate peace deals and has provided peacekeeping forces. The Cold War between the United States and the USSR caused many tensions in the UN, but since the break up of the Soviet Union, cooperation between member countries has increased.

△ An Ethiopian soldier of one of the UN's many peacekeeping forces. In recent years the UN has sent its peacekeeping forces into trouble spots such as southern Lebanon, Bosnia, Rwanda and East Timor.

As well as working for peace, the UN also has many other branches, called agencies, that deal with worldwide problems. Some of these agencies provide aid for people in need, such as refugees. Others are concerned with health matters, living and working conditions, and human rights.

The General Assembly

Delegates from the UN's member countries meet in the Auditorium of the General Assembly Building in New York. The General Assembly chooses the members of the UN's other main bodies, and decides how much money each member country should contribute to UN funds. It also controls the amount of money given to each UN organization.

△ The official flag of the United Nations consists of a map of the world circled by two olive branches. Olive branches are a symbol of peace.

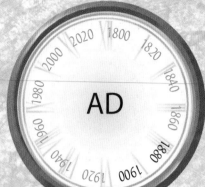

AD

During the 1800s, India became Britain's most important colonial territory. India provided Britain with cheap raw materials, particularly cotton, for its developing industries, as well as a large market for Britain's manufactured goods.

India's Independence

Many Indian citizens wanted independence from British rule and a chance to build up industry and wealth in India itself. In 1885, the Indian National Congress was founded. At first this political party worked for moderate reform, but after 1917 it became more extreme, campaigning for home rule.

During World War I, many Indian troops fought bravely in Europe for the Allies. In return, Indian citizens expected more participation in their own government. The first Government of India Act in 1919 made some reforms, but British officials kept most of the power. Protest meetings were held throughout India. In Amritsar, British troops fired on a crowd protesting against the reforms. Over 350 people were killed and at least 1,000 injured.

Amritsar and after

The Amritsar massacre inspired many Indian citizens to step up the fight for independence. In 1920, a lawyer named Mohandas Gandhi became leader of the Indian National Congress. He started a campaign of non-violent disobedience against British rule. It included the refusal to pay taxes and to attend British courts and schools.

In the early 1920s Gandhi organized a boycott of British manufactured goods in

△ Many of the demonstrations by Indian people seeking independence ended in violence. The British soldiers were often ruthless in their treatment of the demonstrators.

Indian National Congress founded.	1885
Mohandas Gandhi becomes leader of Indian National Congress.	1920
Gandhi launches campaign of non-violence against British.	1920
Gandhi leads "Salt March."	1930
World War II.	1939–1945
Gandhi imprisoned by the British.	1942
Two regions in northeast and northwest India become Muslim state of Pakistan.	1947
India becomes independent.	1947
Hindu assassin murders Gandhi.	1948

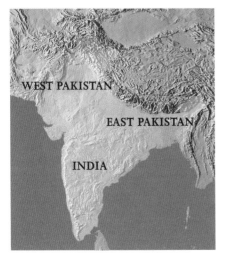

Gandhi

Mohandas Gandhi was known as Mahatma Gandhi (*mahatma* means "great soul"). In 1930 he led the famous "Salt March" to the coast in protest at a law forcing people to buy heavily taxed salt. Gandhi was assassinated in 1948, at the end of India's long struggle for independence.

△ India gained her independence from Britain on August 15, 1947. The previous day, two regions in northeast and northwest India had become the Muslim state of Pakistan.

India. Gandhi himself was imprisoned several times, where he continued his policy of non-cooperation by going on a hunger strike.

Partition and independence

By the end of World War II, it was clear that Britain could no longer ignore the demands of Indian nationalists. Negotiations were complicated by the demands of Muslims in India. Although the majority of India's population were Hindu, there were also a large number of Muslims. The leader of the Muslim League, Mohammed Ali Jinnah, demanded the creation of a separate state, called Pakistan, in regions of India where Muslims were in the majority.

Violence broke out between Hindus and Muslims, and Indians and British leaders eventually agreed to partition (divide) India into the two states of Hindu India and Muslim Pakistan. After partition took place in August 1947, millions of Hindus and Muslims fled from their homes, yet the violence continued. As people tried to move to their new homes hundreds of thousands of people were killed.

The first prime minister of independent India was Jawaharlal Nehru. Mohammed Ali Jinnah became the first governor-general of Pakistan.

Oh, East is East, and West is West, and never the twain shall meet, Till Earth and Sky stand presently at God's great Judgment Seat ...
THE BALLAD OF EAST AND WEST, RUDYARD KIPLING

Kipling was an English poet and writer who was born in Bombay, India.

△ In the center of India's flag is an ancient symbol of a wheel. It is known as the Dharma Chakra, which means the "Wheel of Law."

By the early 20th century, Jewish people lived all over the world, particularly in European countries, the United States and Russia. In the late 1800s, some Jews had established a movement known as Zionism.

The Middle East

The Zionists called for Jews to return to the area around Jerusalem, which they considered their spiritual homeland. Since Jerusalem was part of the Turkish (Ottoman) Empire, the area was inhabited largely by Arabs. As more Jews arrived in the area of Palestine, tension grew between the Arab inhabitants and Jewish immigrants.

In 1917, the British government issued the Balfour Declaration, offering support for a Jewish homeland in Palestine. At the end of the war the Turkish Empire was broken up, and the League of Nations gave Britain a mandate (authority) to rule Palestine. Jewish immigration increased rapidly in the 1930s as thousands of Jews fled Nazi persecution in Europe.

The creation of Israel

At the end of World War II, the demand for a Jewish state in Palestine grew. In 1947, the United Nations took over responsibility for Palestine, dividing it into an Arab state and a Jewish state. The Jews agreed to this

Founding of the state of Israel. Arab League declares war.	1948
End of first Arab-Israeli war.	1949
Egypt takes over control of Suez Canal. Second Arab-Israeli war.	1956
Palestinian Liberation Organization (PLO) is founded.	1964
Six-Day War ends in victory for Israel.	1967
Yom Kippur War.	1973
Israel and Egypt sign peace agreements at Camp David.	1978
Israel and PLO sign agreement to work to end differences.	1993

△ Civil war between Christians and Muslims broke out in Lebanon in 1975. Fighting continued during the late 1970s and 1980s, causing extensive damage in the city of Beirut.

▷ *Arab refugees from the Six-Day War between Israel and its Arab neighbors, which took place in May 1967. As a result of the war, Israel gained control of large areas of land in the Sinai Peninsula as well as the city of Jerusalem and Syria's Golan Heights.*

△ *Israel has borders with Lebanon and Syria, Jordan, and Egypt. In 1967 Israel occupied the territories of the Gaza Strip and the West Bank, home to over one million Palestinian Arabs, and the Sinai Peninsula.*

plan, but the Arabs did not. The state of Israel came into being on May 14, 1948. It was immediately attacked by Arab armies from Egypt, Syria, Lebanon, Iraq, and Transjordan (Jordan) – known collectively as the Arab League. By 1949, Israel had defeated the Arab League and added land to its own territory.

War in the Middle East

The Jewish immigrants who flocked to Israel needed land in the new state, so the Palestinian Arabs were pushed into smaller areas. Some fled to live as refugees in neighboring Arab states. Others demanded a separate state of their own. This led to the founding of the Palestinian Liberation Organization (PLO) in the 1960s.

Relations between Israel and its Arab neighbors continued to be extremely difficult. In the Six-Day War, Israel destroyed much of the Arab air forces and gained extra territories. Israel also gained the upper hand in the Yom Kippur War in 1973.

In 1993, Israel and the PLO recognized each other, and the first steps were taken toward Palestinian self-rule. The negotiations continue into the 21st century, although tensions between Israelis and Arabs continue to disrupt the peace process.

The United States and the Middle East

Since 1979, a number of peace treaties between Israel and its Arab neighbors have been signed, mostly under the watchful eye of the United States. President Bill Clinton (left) played a key role in the negotiations that led to the Oslo Accords, which were signed by the Israeli prime minster Yitzhak Rabin and PLO leader Yasir Arafat. They laid out the terms of a peace settlement between Israel and the PLO.

△ *The Damascus Gate, one of several historic gates leading into the old city of Jerusalem. Since the Six-Day War of 1967 both East Jerusalem and West Jerusalem have been under Israeli control. The city is a sacred place for Jews, Muslims, and Christians alike.*

255

After World War II, European nations found themselves coming under increasing pressure to dismantle their colonial empires. In some places independence was achieved peacefully. In others, the move to independence was marked by violence and bloodshed.

New Nations

The independence of India marked the start of the break up of the British Empire. In 1948 Ceylon (present-day Sri Lanka) and Burma (Myanmar) became independent. In Africa, the first British colony to achieve independence was the Gold Coast, which became Ghana in March 1957.

The Commonwealth

After independence many former British colonies became members of the Commonwealth of Nations. This is an association of states that maintain friendly links and cooperation with each other. They accept the

Ceylon (present-day Sri Lanka) and Burma (Myanmar) independent.	1948
Ghana is first African British colony to become independent.	1957
Start of war in Vietnam (lasted until 1976).	1957
Algeria becomes independent from France.	1962
Kenya becomes independent from Britain.	1963
Rhodesia (present-day Zimbabwe) declares independence from Britain.	1965
Angola and Mozambique independent from Portugal.	1975
End of apartheid in South Africa.	1991
Nelson Mandela becomes first black president of South Africa.	1994

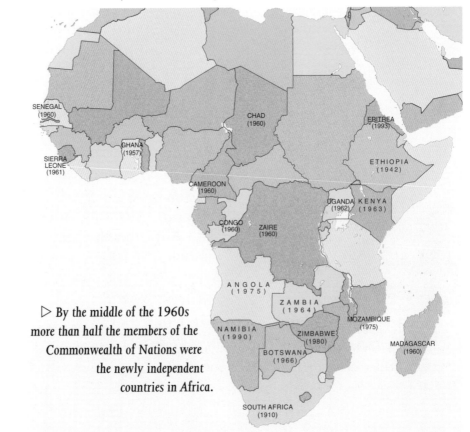

▷ By the middle of the 1960s more than half the members of the Commonwealth of Nations were the newly independent countries in Africa.

△ Kwame Nkrumah became prime minister of the Gold Coast in 1952 and led the country to its independence, as Ghana, in 1957. He was president of Ghana from 1960 to 1966.

△ South Africa's policy of apartheid involved separating black and white people in public places such as parks, beaches, cinemas, and sports stadiums.

△ The flag of the Commonwealth of Nations, which includes Britain and more than 50 independent nations that were at one time British colonies.

Vietnam War

The Vietnam War between North and South Vietnam lasted from 1957 until 1976. In 1965 the United States was drawn into the war to support South Vietnam. This is a statue of remembrance in Washington D.C.

British monarch as the symbolic head of the Commonwealth. It now consists of more than 50 independent nations.

Conflict in Africa

Although the process of independence was orderly and peaceful in many British colonies, in some places there was conflict. This happened particularly in places where there were white settlers, who were often unwilling to give up or share power. In Kenya, this situation led to guerrilla warfare between British forces and a group called the Mau Mau. After years of violence, Kenya finally became independent in 1963. In British Central Africa, the white minority seized power and declared its independence in 1965, as Rhodesia. Years of struggle resulted in victory for the black majority in 1980, and the country's name was changed to Zimbabwe.

In South Africa, the white government adopted a racist policy called "apartheid" (separateness), which denied black people the right to vote and segregated (divided) them from white people in housing, public places, transport, and schools. This policy came to an end in 1991, and Nelson Mandela was elected as the first black president of South Africa in 1994.

The French Empire

The dismantling of the French Empire led to conflict in many areas. This was because the French saw their colonies as part of "Greater France" and were unwilling to let them go completely. There were also many French settlers in places such as Algeria, where independence was granted in 1962 after fighting that claimed over 250,000 lives. In Southeast Asia, the French fought the Indochina War against the Communist Vietminh. The outcome was French defeat in 1954, and the division of Vietnam into two nations.

After World War II, the United States and the USSR emerged as the two main powers in the world — known as "superpowers." Although they had fought together to defeat Nazi Germany, differences between the two superpowers soon led to the start of the "Cold War."

The Cold War

AD

2020 1800 1820 1840 1860 1880 1900 1920 1940 1960 1980 2000

Blockade of Berlin and Berlin airlift.	1948–1949
NATO founded.	1949
Korean War. North Korea is backed by the Soviets, South Korea by the U.S.	1950–1953
Warsaw Pact founded among countries of Eastern Europe.	1955
Split between USSR and China.	1960
Berlin Wall constructed.	1961
The Cuban missile crisis.	1962
USA becomes involved in Vietnam War, defending South Vietnam against invasion from the communist north.	1964

The Cold War was a political war between the USSR and its communist allies, and the U.S. and other non-communist countries. It did not involve fighting, although there was a threat of military action on several occasions.

The Iron Curtain

After the end of World War II, the Soviet leader Joseph Stalin quickly placed communist governments in the eastern European countries that Soviet troops had liberated from the Germans. The British prime minister, Winston Churchill, claimed that an "iron curtain" fell across Europe as the USSR tightened its control of eastern Europe. The Soviets wanted to protect themselves against any future threat from Germany, and to spread communism. By 1948, there were communist governments in Albania, Bulgaria, Czechoslovakia, Hungary, Poland, Romania, and Yugolsavia.

The Berlin airlift

At the end of World War II, Germany itself was divided into four zones, controlled by the United States, France, Great Britain, and the USSR. The capital of Germany, Berlin, lay within the Soviet zone, but was itself divided. In 1948, the United States,

△ During the blockade of the German capital Berlin by Soviet forces in 1948–1949, aircraft flew essential supplies to the people trapped inside the city for 11 months. This operation became known as the Berlin airlift.

△ In 1945 the three Allied leaders – Winston Churchill, Franklin D. Roosevelt, and Joseph Stalin – met at Yalta to discuss the problems facing postwar Europe.

J. F. Kennedy

John Fitzgerald Kennedy was president from 1961 until he was assassinated in 1963. During his presidency the Berlin Wall was built, dividing the city in two and stopping East Germans escaping communist rule.

France, and Great Britain (the Western Allies) joined their zones to form the German Federal Republic (West Germany). The USSR replied by blockading the parts of Berlin controlled by the Western Allies. In May 1949 the USSR ended the blockade, and the Soviet-controlled part of Germany became the German Democratic Republic (East Germany).

The Cuban crisis

In 1949, the Western Allies formed the North Atlantic Treaty Organization (NATO) for defense against the communist presence in Europe. In the same year, the USSR exploded its first atomic bomb. With both superpowers holding nuclear weapons, fear and mistrust between the two sides increased.

The Soviets constructed a wall across Berlin in 1961, separating East from West in the city. In 1962, the Cuban missile crisis erupted when the U.S. discovered that the USSR was building missile sites on the island of Cuba in the Caribbean. The two superpowers came to the brink of war before the USSR agreed to withdraw the weapons. Although the two superpowers never became involved in direct warfare, both sides became involved in wars elsewhere in the world; the United States fought communism, and the USSR helped communist fighters.

"All free men, wherever they may live, are citizens of Berlin, and, therefore, as a free man, I take pride in the words 'Ich bin ein Berliner'.

J. F. KENNEDY, WEST BERLIN, JUNE 26, 1963

△ The discovery of Soviet-built missile sites on Cuba alarmed the United States. The missile sites were within range to launch an attack by nuclear weapons on American cities.

The 20th century saw an explosion in communications technology. The first radio broadcast was made almost at the beginning of the century, when Reginald A. Fessenden transmitted music and words in 1906.

Communications

By the end of the 20th century, people were communicating by electronic mail (e-mail) across the world at the touch of a computer key. This revolution, together with faster and improved methods of travel, has changed life for almost everyone around the globe.

Radio and television

By the 1920s, radio provided a major form of entertainment for many people around the world. Then, in 1926, a Scottish engineer named John Logie Baird developed the first successful television set. The earliest black and white TV broadcasts were made by the British Broadcasting Company (BBC) in 1936. The first major event to be broadcast internationally was the coronation of Queen Elizabeth II in 1953. Color television began in the U.S. in the same year.

Satellites

In order to send radio signals around the Earth, scientists developed communications satellites. These satellites are sent up into orbit around the Earth. Signals are beamed up to the satellite from a transmitter on the Earth's surface. The satellite then retransmits the signal back down to a receiver on the ground. The transmitter and receiver are often thousands of miles apart. The first communications

First radio broadcast by Reginald A. Fessenden.	1906
John Logie Baird develops first successful television set.	1926
British Broadcasting Company (BBC) makes first television broadcasts in UK.	1936
Color television begins in USA.	1953
First communications satellite, Echo 1, launched.	1960
First TV programs transmitted by U.S. Telstar satellite.	1962
Transatlantic phone calls transmitted by Earlybird satellite.	1965
First microprocessor is built.	1972
First personal computer developed.	1975

▷ A broadcast is transmitted from an early TV studio. At the outset, the United States moved quickly ahead of other countries in the field of TV broadcasting.

△ The CN Tower in Toronto, Canada is a communications and observation tower. When completed in 1976, it was the world's tallest free-standing structure.

Satellite broadcasts

With the use of communciations satellites, TV shows can be beamed to even the remotest parts of the world, including the Amazon jungle (right). In 1985 a Live Aid concert to raise money for famine victims was beamed to one of the largest audiences in TV history – about 1,5 billion people.

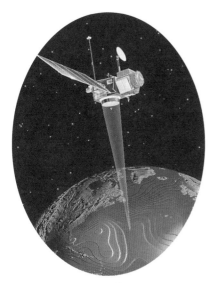

△ Today, hundreds of satellites are in orbit around the Earth, relaying radio and TV programs, and telephone calls around the world.

satellite used to relay telephone messages across the globe was called *Echo 1*, launched in 1960. The first TV programs were transmitted by the U.S. *Telstar* satellite in 1962.

Computers

The earliest computers were calculating machines, dating back to the 1600s. However, the first electronic computers were developed in the 1930s and 1940s. These machines were huge and took a long time to program. As computers became smaller and faster, more and more people began to use them. In the past 30 years, computers have revolutionized almost every aspect of modern-day life. Today, many people own a home computer, on which they use the Internet to look up information, to play games, and even to do their shopping, as well as to send and receive e-mail.

Latest technology

Some of the latest advances in technology use light instead of waves to transmit information. Glass fiberoptic cables carry information in the form of laser beams. Many TV stations now relay programs by cable, which goes directly into people's homes. These cables can also carry telephone calls as well as computer data.

△ Since the early 1990s the mobile phone has proved to be an increasingly popular means of communication.

◁ At home, people use e-mail to communicate with their family and friends. Messages can be sent to the other side of the world in a few seconds.

In the early 1960s, China and the USSR had ceased friendly relations, causing a split between the two main powers in the communist world. In the late 1960s and 1970s, divisions between the two world superpowers – the USSR and the U.S. – began to ease.

Communism Collapses

A growing dissatisfaction with communism and Soviet rule began to take hold in many Eastern European countries. Meanwhile, economic growth in the countries of Western Europe meant that the United States was not quite the dominating force it had been immediately after World War II.

Nuclear weapons

A major area of tension between the U.S. and the USSR was the arms race. This was a race to build up increasing numbers of weapons, particularly nuclear missiles. In 1969, the first of a series of meetings were held between the two sides to limit the production of nuclear weapons. These meetings, known as the Strategic Arms Limitation Talks (SALT), saw the signing of two agreements in 1972 and 1979. But the Soviet invasion of Afghanistan in 1979 caused a worsening of relations, and the U.S. continued to make defense plans in case of a Soviet attack.

In 1985, Mikhail Gorbachev became the new leader of the USSR. His program of reforms reduced the tension between the two superpowers. In 1989, Soviet troops withdrew from Afghanistan.

First Strategic Arms Limitation Talks (SALT).	1972
Second SALT agreement. Soviet invasion of Afghanistan.	1979
Ronald Reagan becomes U.S. president and launches "Starwars" defense project.	1981
Solidarity trade union banned in Poland.	1982
Mikhail Gorbachev becomes Soviet leader and starts reforms.	1985
Reagan and Gorbachev sign treaty to ban medium-range nuclear missiles.	1987
Berlin Wall is dismantled. Free elections in Poland.	1989
Collapse of communism in Eastern Europe. East and West Germany unified.	1990
Gorbachev resigns and USSR is abolished.	1991

▷ The Berlin Wall had separated communist East Berlin from non-communist West Berlin for almost 30 years. In November 1989 the people of Berlin demolished the hated wall.

△ Mikhail Gorbachev introduced a program of political, social, and economic reforms, called perestroika. His policy of glasnost (openness) gave Soviet people more freedom of expression.

△ President Ronald Reagan was a keen supporter of Mikhail Gorbachev's program of reform in the USSR. In 1987 the two leaders signed an agreement to dismantle many kinds of nuclear weapons.

Communist rule

With the end of communist rule in the USSR, many of the symbols of communism, for example statues of former leaders such as Lenin (right), were quickly dismantled.

Eastern Europe

As the policies of *perestroika* (economic reforms) and *glasnost* (openness) took effect in the USSR, governments in the Eastern European countries began to lose control. The collapse of communism in Eastern Europe took place in 1989 and 1990. Borders were opened, allowing people to travel freely for the first time since the 1940s. Free elections were held in Poland in 1989, and in 1990 in Czechoslovakia, Hungary, East Germany, Romania, and Bulgaria. East and West Germany were unified in October 1990.

The end of the USSR

Gorbachev accepted the fall of the communist regimes in Eastern Europe. However, there were many states within the USSR who also wanted freedom from Soviet central government. Inspired by the collapse of communism in Eastern Europe, the Baltic state of Lithuania declared its independence in 1990. Other states called for separation and more self-government. In 1991 there was a coup – an attempt to overthrow Gorbachev's government. The coup failed, but Gorbachev was forced to resign. His resignation on December 25, 1991 signaled both the end of the USSR and the Cold War. The former states of the USSR became 15 independent republics.

△ In Poland, the free trade union Solidarity was banned in 1982. Criticism of the communist regime was suppressed in Eastern European countries under Soviet rule.

"It is not what they built. It is what they knocked down. It is not the houses. It is the spaces between the houses. It is not the streets that exist. It is the streets that no longer exist.
A GERMAN REQUIEM, JAMES FENTON

Fenton worked as a journalist in Germany, as well as Cambodia.

As we enter the 21st century, people are becoming increasingly concerned with issues that affect the world as a whole. This is due partly to the improved speed of communication, and the ease of travel between one place and another.

Global Concerns

You can jump on a plane and be on the other side of the world within 24 hours. When you log onto the Internet, you can find out about almost any subject, or chat with people thousands of miles away. One of the major issues of the late 20th century was concern for our environment. Up until the 1960s, most people were unaware of, or unconcerned about, human impact on the Earth.

Harming the environment

In 1962, an American scientist called Rachel Carson published a book called *Silent Spring*, in which she wrote about the harmful effects of pesticides on animal life. In the 1970s, organizations such as Friends of the Earth and Greenpeace began to campaign on many environmental issues. These included the destruction of the rainforests in places such as South America and Southeast Asia, the dumping of toxic nuclear

Rachel Carson publishes Silent Spring.	1962
Environmental organization Greenpeace is founded.	1971
U.S. government bans pesticide DDT.	1972
Explosion and fire at Chernobyl nuclear reactor, Ukraine.	1986
Hole discovered in ozone layer above Antarctic.	1987
Earth Summit in Rio de Janeiro, Brazil.	1992

▷ *Violent tropical storms called hurricanes leave behind a trail of damage and destruction. Scientists are concerned that changes in the world's climate as a result of global warming may increase the number of these devastating storms.*

△ Greenpeace campaigns on many environmental issues around the world. It opposes whaling, using its boats to try and separate whaling ships from their catch.

△ The international symbol for radiation. It is used to warn people that they are close to radioactive material.

△ In tropical areas, rainforests are cut down to clear the land for farming. Trees are vital to life on Earth because they take in carbon dioxide gas and release oxygen.

waste, the effects of pollution, and protection for endangered species such as the whale and the rhinoceros.

Today, a major issue that will affect everybody on the planet in some way is global warming. When we burn fossil fuels such as oil (from which petrol and diesel are made) and coal, carbon dioxide gas is given off into the atmosphere. With the massive increase in the use of fossil fuels in our homes, factories and vehicles, the amount of carbon dioxide in the atmosphere has increased, too. Carbon dioxide is just one of the gases, known as greenhouse gases, that trap the Sun's heat around the Earth. Scientists know that more heat is being trapped inside our atmosphere and that the Earth is becoming warmer. What they cannot be sure about is the effect of global warming in the future.

Agenda 21

One thing is certain, however: global warming and other environmental issues are problems that have to be tackled by nations all over the world working together. In 1992, the representatives of countries from around the world met at the Earth Summit in Rio de Janeiro, Brazil. The result was Agenda 21 – an agenda for action in the 21st century.

Agenda 21 covers environmental issues such as pollution and wildlife protection, but it also covers human issues which are just as important for life in the 21st century. There is a huge imbalance between life in the rich countries of the developed world and the poorer nations of the developing world. Global planning to improve this imbalance is one of the main challenges facing the world in the 21st century.

Chernobyl

A serious accident happened at a nuclear power plant in Chernobyl, in the Ukraine, in 1986. It caused an enormous radioactive cloud to spread across a huge area.

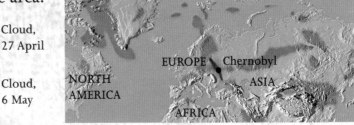

Cloud, 27 April

Cloud, 6 May

NORTH AMERICA

EUROPE   Chernobyl

ASIA

AFRICA

AD

What will life be like during the 21st century?
At the dawn of the 20th century, the airplane was still only a dream, motor cars were rare and wonderful things, and movies had only just started.

Tomorrow's World

By the end of the 20th century, all of these things were taken for granted by the vast majority of the world's population. What advances can we expect throughout the 21st century?

Medicine

Major advances in medicine in the 20th century included the discovery of penicillin in 1928, the development of a vaccine against polio in the 1950s, and the first heart transplant in 1957. Nevertheless, despite all that modern medicine can offer, new diseases can and do occur. In the early 1980s, doctors identified a previously unknown disease that attacks the body's immune system. Called AIDS (acquired immuno-deficiency syndrome), this disease is caused by the human immuno-deficiency virus (HIV) and thus far it has claimed millions of lives.

One of the most exciting areas of medicine for the 21st century is the Human Genome Project (HGP). This project, which is due to be completed in 2003, is an international project, involving 18 countries.

Doctors identify previously unknown disease called AIDS.	1980s
Start of NASA's space shuttle program.	1981
Start of Human Genome Project (HGP) – due for completion in 2003.	1990
Launch of Hubble Space Telescope.	1990
Russia, U.S., and others join together to work on International Space Station.	1993–2004
Campaign to end Third World debt gains in importance.	1999
UN estimates 11.5 million refugees in the world.	1999

▷ Nelson Mandela was one of the most respected and admired leaders of the 20th century. He led South Africa through a peaceful change after the hated system of apartheid was abolished.

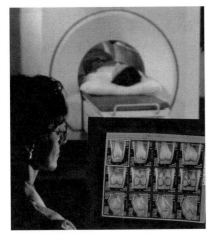

△ *A medical worker examines the pictures from an MRI (magnetic resonance imaging) scanner. It takes pictures in slices through the body.*

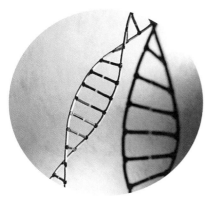

△ *A model of DNA (deoxyribonucleic acid), the genetic material that is found in the cells of living things.*

△ *UN peacekeeping soldiers in Bosnia. In the future, it is likely that troops will find themselves increasingly called upon to act as peacekeepers in places where there are conflicts and tension.*

International Space Station

The ISS should be complete in 2004. It will be used for research in medicine and other fields and is seen as a step toward future space exploration.

Its aim is to discover all of the 100,000 genes (the human genome) in the human body by studying the DNA. As a result of this, and other research, genetics will play an increasingly important role in the diagnosis, monitoring, and treatment of diseases in the 21st century.

Space technology

The Space Race started during the Cold War, when the USSR and the U.S. competed with each other to put the first person into space and onto the moon. Today, the former superpowers are working together on projects in space. The International Space Station (ISS), the largest scientific project in history, involves a total of sixteen nations.

War and peacekeeping

Everyone hopes that the 21st century will not see a repeat of the terrible slaughter of World War I and World War II. With the United Nations in place as an international organization for peace and security, nations will hopefully go to the negotiating table rather than to war. Even as the 21st century began, there was conflict in many places, for example Chechnya, in Russia. Elsewhere, peace-keeping forces maintain a fragile peace in places such as Kosovo.

Third World debt

Without doubt, a key issue in the 21st century will be the contrast between rich and poor countries. One of the main problems is "Third World debt." In the 1970s, many developing countries borrowed money from richer countries. Banks charged interest on the loan repayments. Many developing nations now struggle to repay even just the interest. There is a growing campaign to cancel Third World debt, so that developing countries can put more resources into areas such as education and health.

Timeline and Reference Section

	before 10,000 BC	10,000 to 5000 BC	5000 to 3000 BC
Events and Rulers	c. 30,000 BC Neanderthals die out. First modern humans settle North America, from Asia. 16,000 BC Last Ice Age ends.	Land bridge joining Britain and France is covered by sea. First farmers set up settled communities, with leaders who become the first kings.	Sahara region, once fertile, starts to dry up. First important settlements around the Tigris and Euphrates rivers. 4236 BC First date in the Egyptian calendar. c. 3500 BC First Chinese walled towns.
Exploration	40,000 BC Cro-Magnons move into Europe. 35,000 BC People reach America and Australia.	10,000 BC People reach tip of S. America. 6000 BC Catal Huyuk traders travel overland.	4000 BC People reach Pacific Islands by boat.
Art and Science	25,000 BC Cave people make clay figures. Cave paintings in France and Spain.	Sahara rock paintings. Pottery decorated with geometric designs. Metalwork in Near East.	c. 3600 BC Earliest known map, in Sumer. *Epic of Gilgamesh*, famous Sumerian poem.
Technology	c. 2,000,000 BC Early people use pebble tools. 500,000 BC People first learn how to make fire.	8000 BC Coracles and dugout canoes used. First clay pots. Metal tools made of copper.	c. 4000 BC Tin and copper mixed to make bronze in Near East. Invention of the wheel.
Religion and Ideas	Prehistoric people bury their dead with some kind of religious ceremony.	Sheep used in religious sacrifices in Near East. Pictures and models of bulls at Catal Huyuk.	Sumerians tell stories of a great flood. 3760 BC First date in the Jewish calendar.
Daily Life	15,000 BC People live in caves, tents or stick shelters. They make clothes of animal skins.	10,000 BC Farming starts in the Near East. 9000 BC Wheat and barley are grown.	5000 BC Towns grow into the first city-states. 3000 BC Sumerians make bread and beer.

3000 to 2000 BC | 2000 to 1000 BC | 1000 to 500 BC

3000 to 2000 BC	2000 to 1000 BC	1000 to 500 BC	
3100 BC First dynastic period. Egypt is united under one king, Menes. 2750 BC Rise of Indus Valley civilization. 2686–2160 BC Old kingdom in Egypt. Pyramids built at Giza. 2360 BC Sargon of Akkad begins conquest of Sumeria.	c. 1750 BC Indus Valley civilization collapses. c. 1500 BC Rise of Shang dynasty, China. 1361–1352 BC Reign of Tutankhamun. 1450 BC Volcano destroys Minoan Crete. 1250 BC Trojan War. 1020 BC Saul is the first king of Israel.	900 BC Kingdom of Kush is independent from Egypt. 814 BC Phoenicians found Carthage. 753 BC Traditional date for founding of Rome. 689 BC Babylon destroyed by Assyrians. 539 BC Cyrus the Great conquers Babylon.	**Events and Rulers**
Traders explore Aegean in canoe-like vessels. People from central Asia move into Europe.	About 1,500 Hebrews journey from Mesopotamia to Palestine.	700 BC Phoenicians found colony at Utica. Bantu people spread to East Africa.	**Exploration**
Harps and flutes are first made.	Babylonians invent a counting system based on the number 60. First Chinese writing.	776 BC First recorded Olympic Games. Hanging Gardens of Babylon built.	**Art and Science**
Use of bronze in China to make weapons. 2780 BC Step pyramid built at Saqqara, Egypt.	Water clocks, sand glasses and sundials used to measure time. Hittites smelt iron.	Kites invented by the Chinese. Assyrians attack city walls with siege towers.	**Technology**
Egyptians believe in an afterlife. They make mummies of people and animals.	1500 BC *Rig Vedas*, early Hindu holy songs, written in India.	500s BC Confucius teaches in China. c. 563–483 BC Life of Buddha.	**Religion and Ideas**
2600 BC Egyptians use papyrus for writing. 2000 BC Jomon people, Japan, live in pit houses.	Chinese tell fortunes with oracle bones. Phoenicians trade dye made of murex shells.	Persians begin writing on parchment. c. 700 BC Coins are first used in Lydia.	**Daily Life**

	500 to 1 BC	AD 1 to 200	AD 200 to 500
Events and Rulers	510 BC Roman Republic founded. 500 BC Achaemenid Empire in Persia. 400 BC Nok culture in West Africa. 356–323 BC Alexander the Great. 214 BC Great Wall of China built. 44 BC Julius Caesar dies.	AD 14 Death of Augustus (Octavian), first Roman emperor. AD 43 Romans invade Britain. AD 61 Boudicca leads revolt against Romans. AD 70 Romans destroy Jerusalem. AD 79 Pompeii destroyed by volcano.	AD 220 End of Han rule in China, which is split into three states. AD 320 Gupta Empire in India. Golden age of Hindu culture. AD 350 Teotihuacan begins rise to power. Rise of Mayas. AD 395 Division of Roman Empire.
Exploration	AD 470 Hanno sails by the west coast of Africa. AD 100 Silk Road links Asia and the Near East.	Romans establish trade links with China. c. AD 100 Settlers reach the Hawaiian islands.	Barbarians move into western Europe. Settlers from Germany cross the North Sea.
Art and Science	477 BC Start of Athens' Golden Age. 429 BC Birth of Greek philosopher Plato.	AD 1 First history of China completed. AD 100s Romans enjoy open-air theatre.	Classical art in the West declines. Byzantine art starts to flourish.
Technology	c. 200 BC Greeks make the Archimedean screw for raising water. Crossbow used in war.	Roman engineers use cement and concrete. AD 50 Pyramid of the Sun built in Mexico.	AD 300 Stirrup for riding in use in Asia. Chinese use rudders to steer sailing ships.
Religion and Ideas	Celts bury their dead in graves with chariots. 200s BC Buddhism spreads in India.	AD 29 Probable date of crucifixion of Jesus. AD 48 Buddhism reaches China.	AD 380 Egyptians take Christianity to Axum. AD 450 St Patrick preaches in Ireland.
Daily Life	400 BC Greeks develop democracy and public schools. Celts live in hillforts.	Chinese write on paper. They use wheelbarrows. Romans eat sugar and build public baths.	Maya build cities in Central America. China has the world's biggest cities, with restaurants.

AD **500 to 700**	AD **700 to 900**	AD **900 to 1100**	
AD 519 Kingdom of Wessex founded. AD 527–565 Justinian and Theodora rule Byzantine Empire. AD 535 End of Gupta rule in northern India. AD 540 Franks control most of Gaul and Germany. AD 618 Tang dynasty.	AD 700 Rise of Ghana Empire in Africa. AD 711 Muslims conquer Spain. AD 750 The city of Teotihuacan is destroyed. AD 750 Abbasid dynasty is founded. AD 787 First Viking attacks on Britain.	AD 900 Rise of the Toltecs in Mexico. AD 911 Vikings control Normandy. AD 960 Sung dynasty in China. AD 1000s Seljuks seize power in Baghdad. AD 1066 Battle of Hastings. The Normans conquer England.	**Events and Rulers**
Easter Island is settled by people from Polynesia, crossing the sea in canoes or rafts.	Arabs trade across Indian Ocean. AD 874 Vikings settle in Iceland.	AD 916 Arabs trade along E. African coast. AD 1003 Leif Eriksson lands in North America.	**Exploration**
AD 500 Indians devise modern numerals. Chinese invent porcelain.	AD 700s First printing in China. AD late 700s Book of Kells in Britain.	AD 1008 *The Tale of Genji* is written. First stone abbeys and cathedrals in Europe.	**Art and Science**
c. AD 600 Windmill invented in Persia and Turkey. Lateen sails on ships.	Arabs learn paper-making from Chinese. c. AD 800 Stirrups spread to the West.	Magnetic compass reaches the West. Chinese use gunpowder rockets.	**Technology**
AD 529 Monte Cassino is first abbey in Europe. AD 570 Probable date of Muhammad's birth.	AD 826 First Christian mission to Scandinavia. AD 864 Bulgars and Serbs become Christian.	AD 966 Mont St Michel monastery in France built by the Benedictines.	**Religion and Ideas**
AD 700 The Anasazi build multi-story houses, and grow corn. Chinese use canal boats.	Feudal system of strip farming in Europe. Islamic education spreads in Middle East.	AD 900s Burhs (Saxon towns) in England. after AD 1000 Normans build stone castles.	**Daily Life**

	1101 to 1150	1151 to 1200	1201 to 1250
Events and Rulers	1100 Crusaders found states in Jerusalem, Antioch and Edessa. 1115 Nomad conquerors establish Jin Empire in China. 1135 Stephen of Blois seizes English throne. 1144 King Alfonso of Portugal recaptures Lisbon from Muslims.	1152 Henry Plantagenet (later Henry II of England) marries Eleanor of Aquitaine. 1169 Saladin conquers Egypt. Normans invade Ireland from England. 1190 The Third Crusade begins.	1204 Crusaders sack Constantinople. 1206 Temujin unites Mongol tribes and becomes Genghis Khan. 1215 English King John forced to sign Magna Carta. 1241 Mongols invade Poland and Hungary
Exploration	c. 1150 Benjamin of Tudela describes travels in the Mediterranean and Levant.	1190 First recorded use of mariners' compass by Western sailors.	1245–1247 Giovanni of Carpini travels to Mongolia and back.
Art and Science	Frankish epic poem, *The Song of Roland*. c. 1120 O. Khayyam writes *Rubaiyyat*.	1168 Illuminated gospels commissioned by Henry the Lion.	1207 Epic story of the deeds of El Cid, Spain. c.1235 French poem *Roman de la Rose* written.
Technology	1147 First use of trebuchet (stone-throwing siege engine) in the West, at Lisbon.	c. 1170 Development of windmill with horizontal axle in Netherlands.	1232 Chinese first use rockets in warfare. 1235 Beauvais Cathedral started.
Religion and Ideas	c. 1130 Great age of cathedral building begins in England.	c. 1150 Angkor Wat temples completed. 1194 Founding of Chartres Cathedral.	1215 Dominican order of friars founded. 1228 Francis of Assisi made a saint.
Daily Life	Growth of major cities in Western Europe, including London, Paris, Florence and Milan.	1158 University of Bologna, Italy, founded. 1190 New city wall built around Paris.	1209 Building of London Bridge. 1249 First Oxford college founded.

1251 to 1300	1301 to 1350	1351 to 1400	
1258 Mongols capture Baghdad. 1265 Civil war ends in England with death of Simon de Montfort. 1277 Edward I of England begins conquest of Wales. 1291 Acre, last Crusader stronghold, falls to Mamelukes.	c. 1300 Ottoman clan begins to form power base in Anatolia. 1314 Robert Bruce defeats English at Bannockburn. c. 1328 Aztecs found city of Tenochtitlan. 1346 English defeat French at Crecy.	1350 Foundation of Thai kingdom of Ayutia. 1356 Ottoman troops cross from Turkey to Europe. 1365 Peter of Cyprus sacks Alexandria. 1398 Timur Lang invades India.	**Events and Rulers**
1253 William of Rubruck reaches Mongol capital in eastern Asia.	1325–1354 Ibn Battutah makes eight journeys in North Africa and Middle East.	1391 Zeno brothers from Italy explore the Frisian and Faeroe Islands.	**Exploration**
1286 Roger Bacon studies the magnifying power of lenses, in England.	1349 Construction of great East Window in Gloucester Cathedral.	c. 1350 Boccaccio writes his tales collected in the *Decameron*.	**Art and Science**
1276 Italian paper mill is first in Europe. c. 1280 First spinning wheels used in Europe.	c. 1315 First modern mechanical clocks. c. 1325 Development of first firearms.	1384 Water-powered blast furnace built in Belgium.	**Technology**
c. 1250 Matthew Paris writes *History of the English*.	1312 Pope suppresses Order of Knights Templar.	1378 Split in Catholic church results in election of two rival popes.	**Religion and Ideas**
1252 Gold florins minted in Florence. c. 1265 Great Zimbabwe built.	1346 Black Death reaches Europe. 1348 Jews in Europe persecuted.	1381 Peasants' Revolt in England. 1387 First census in China.	**Daily Life**

	1401 to 1450	1451 to 1500	1501 to 1550
Events and Rulers	1415 Henry V defeats French at Agincourt. 1434 Cosimo di Medici becomes leader of Florence. 1444 Khmer retreat from Angkor, Cambodia. 1448 Ottomans defeat Hungarians at Kosovo.	1453 Ottomans capture Constantinople. Fall of Bordeaux ends 100 Years' War between England and France. 1455 English Wars of the Roses begin. 1469 Songhai emperor conquers Timbuktu.	1516–1517 Ottomans conquer Syria and Egypt. 1526 Babur invades northern India. 1527 Forces of Holy Roman emperor sack Rome. 1547 Ivan the Terrible becomes tsar of all the Russias.
Exploration	1405–1433 Zheng Ho leads seven voyages to explore Indian Ocean.	1488 Diaz rounds Cape of Good Hope. 1492 Columbus sails to the Caribbean.	1520 Cortez conquers Aztec Empire. 1522 First round-the-world voyage.
Art and Science	1418 Brunelleschi designs dome for Florence Cathedral.	1495–1498 Leonardo da Vinci paints *Last Supper* in Milan.	1508 Michelangelo paints Sistine Chapel. 1530 Copernicus claims the Earth orbits the Sun.
Technology	c. 1420 First use of brace and bit for drilling in Flanders.	1454 Gutenberg builds first printing press with movable type.	c. 1519 First wheel-lock handguns developed in Germany.
Religion and Ideas	c. 1425 Thomas à Kempis writes *Imitation of Christ*.	1478 Ferdinand and Isabella establish the Spanish Inquisition.	1513 Machiavelli publishes *The Prince*. 1517 Luther's protest at Wittenberg.
Daily Life	1439 First standing army founded in France.	1467 Scots parliament outlaws soccer. Smallpox begins to kill people in New World.	c. 1520 Coffee reaches Europe. c. 1530 Sugar cane grown in Brazil.

1551 to 1600	1601 to 1650	1651 to 1700	
1560 Nobunaga becomes leading baron of Japan. 1588 Spanish invasion armada defeated by English fleet. 1590 Henri IV defeats Catholic League at Ivry. 1594 Moghul emperor Akbar conquers Kandahar.	1603 James VI and I unites English and Scottish thrones. 1620 Outbreak of Thirty Years' War in Europe. 1642 Civil war in England. 1644 The Manchu found the Qing dynasty in China.	1660 Monarchy restored in England. 1682 French claim Louisiana territory in America. 1683 Turkish siege of Vienna. 1696 Peter of Russia drives Turks from Azov.	**Events and Rulers**
1576 Frobisher explores Baffin Island. 1577–1580 Drake leads trip around the world.	1605 Torres sails between Australia and New Guinea.	1673 French explorers reach Arkansas. 1688 Dampier traces part of Australian coast.	**Exploration**
1572 Tycho Brahe works on star catalog. c. 1589 Shakespeare writes his earliest plays.	1628 Harvey establishes that blood is pumped by the heart.	1665 Newton experiments with gravitation.	**Art and Science**
1568 Beauvais Cathedral again becomes world's tallest building.	1608 Lippershey invents the telescope. 1650 Van Guericke builds first air pump.	1658 Invention of the pendulum clock. 1690 Papin builds first steam pump.	**Technology**
1558 Elizabeth I makes England Protestant. 1587 Japan bans Christian missionaries.	c. 1600 Islam becomes dominant religion in parts of Indonesia.	1666 Great schism (split) in Russian church. 1685 Huguenots persecuted in France.	**Religion and Ideas**
c. 1560 Tobacco introduced to Europe. c. 1584 Potatoes introduced to Europe.	1607 Tea introduced to Europe.	1658 First European banknotes introduced. 1677 Ice cream is popular in France.	**Daily Life**

	1701 to 1725	1726 to 1750	1751 to 1775
Events and Rulers	1707 Union of England and Scotland. 1702–1713 War of the Spanish succession. 1703 Peter I founds St Petersburg in Russia. 1707 Decline of Mughal Empire in India. 1715 First Jacobite rebellion in Scotland.	1725 Death of Peter the Great of Russia. 1740–1748 War of the Austrian succession. 1745–1746 Second Jacobite rebellion in Scotland ends with English victory at Culloden.	1755 Portuguese capital Lisbon destroyed by an earthquake. 1756–1763 Seven Years' War. 1757 Battle of Plassey in India. 1762 Catherine the Great comes to power. 1773 Boston Tea Party in America.
Exploration	1708 Alexander Selkirk, original Robinson Crusoe, marooned on Juan Fernandez Islands.	1728 Dutch explorer Vitus Bering sails through Bering Strait.	1770 Captain James Cook sails to New Zealand and Australia.
Art and Science	1701 Jethro Tull invents the seed drill. 1709 Bartolommeo Cristofori invents piano.	Beginning of period in European culture called the Enlightenment.	1755 Samuel Johnson publishes first English dictionary.
Technology	1709 Abraham Darby develops coke-smelting process for producing iron.	1733 John Kay invents the flying shuttle.	1759 John Harrison's marine chronometer. 1764 James Hargreaves invents spinning jenny.
Religion and Ideas	1701 Yale College founded in America.	1738 Religious reformer John Wesley founds Methodism.	1772 Denis Diderot publishes *Encyclopedia*.
Daily Life	1702 First newspaper, *Daily Courant*, published in London.	1730 Four-crop rotation system introduced in England.	1759 Start of main wave of enclosure acts in Britain.

1776 to 1800

1775 Start of
Revolutionary War.
1776 Declaration of
Independence.
1789 French
Revolution.
1792 French Republic
founded.
1799 Start of
Napoleonic Wars.

1788 First Fleet sails
to Australia and founds
settlement at Port
Jackson.

1783 Montgolfier
brothers build hot-air
balloon in France.

1779 First cast-iron
bridge built in
Coalbrookdale,
Shropshire, Britain.

1776 Adam Smith
publishes *The Wealth of
Nations*.

1796 British doctor
Edward Jenner tests
vaccine against
smallpox.

1801 to 1825

1803 President
Jefferson makes
Louisiana Purchase.
1804 Napoleon
crowns himself
emperor of France.
1805 British destroy
French and Spanish
fleets in Battle of
Trafalgar.
1815 Battle of
Waterloo.

1804 Expedition of
Lewis and Clark across
western America.

1800 Library of
Congress founded in
Washington DC.

1815 Humphrey Davy
invents safety lamp for
coal miners.

Era of Romanticism in
European literature and
art.

1802 First gas lighting
installed.
1812 Canning process
for food invented.

1826 to 1850

1825 Bolivia named
after Simon Bolívar.
1825 Decembrist
revolt against Russian
government.
1833 Slavery abolished
in British Empire.
1839–1842 First
Opium War between
China and Britain.
1848 Gold discovered
in California.

1831–1836 Voyage of
Charles Darwin on
board the *Beagle*.

1835 Hans Christian
Andersen's first fairy
tales are published.

1829 British engineer
George Stephenson
builds steam
locomotive *Rocket*.

1830 Joseph Smith
founds the Church of
Latter-Day Saints (the
Mormons).

1845–1849 Potato
famine in Ireland.
1848 First public
health law in England.

Events and Rulers

Exploration

Art and Science

Technology

Religion and
Ideas

Daily Life

	1851 to 1875	1876 to 1900	1901 to 1925
Events and Rulers	1853–1856 Crimean War. 1861 Serfs given freedom in Russia. 1861–1865 American Civil War. 1868 Meiji Restoration in Japan. 1871 Rome becomes capital of unified Italy.	1882 Germany, Austria-Hungary and Italy form Triple Alliance. 1884 Conference in Berlin divides Africa up among European countries. 1877 Queen Victoria becomes Empress of India.	1901 Commonwealth of Australia proclaimed. 1907 Russia, Britain and France form Triple Entente. 1914–1918 World War I (the Great War). 1916 Easter Rebellion in Dublin. 1917 Russian Revolution.
Exploration	1871 H. M. Stanley finds British explorer David Livingstone at Ujiji, West Africa.	1880 King Leopold II of Belgium lays claim to Congo region.	1911 Expedition led by Norwegian Roald Amundsen reaches South Pole.
Art and Science	1851 Great Exhibition in Hyde Park, London. 1873 Paris exhibition of Impressionist art.	1883 Royal College of Music founded. 1884 Mark Twain writes *Huckleberry Finn*.	1903 Wright brothers' first successful flight. 1905 Albert Einstein's theory of relativity.
Technology	1869 Completion of first railway line to cross the American continent.	1876 Alexander Graham Bell develops first telephone.	1908 Mass production of cars begins with Model T Ford.
Religion and Ideas	1859 Publication of Charles Darwin's *The Origin of Species*.	1883 Antonio Gaudi begins work on Sagrada Familia church in Barcelona, Spain.	1900 Sigmund Freud publishes *Interpretation of Dreams* and introduces psychoanalysis.
Daily Life	1851 Gold Rush begins in Australia. 1863 Antiseptics used in surgery.	1885 First skyscraper, Home Insurance Building, Chicago, completed.	1918 Women over the age of 30 given the vote in Britain.

1926 to 1950	1951 to 1975	1976 to 2000	
1925 Mussolini is dictator of Italy. 1933 Nazis come to power in Germany. 1936–1939 Spanish Civil War. 1939–1945 World War II. 1945 Atomic bombs dropped on Japan. 1948 State of Israel is founded.	1957 Treaty of Rome and founding of European Economic Community. 1961 Berlin Wall constructed. 1962 Cuban crisis. 1963 Assassination of J.F. Kennedy. 1965–1973 Vietnam War. 1966 Mao returns to power in China.	1979 Soviet invasion of Afghanistan. 1986 Chernobyl nuclear reactor explodes. 1989–1990 Collapse of communism in Europe. 1989 Chinese troops kill demonstrators in Tiananmen Square, Beijing. 1991 Apartheid ends in South Africa.	**Events and Rulers**
1929 Richard Byrd makes first flight over South Pole	1961 Soviet cosmonaut Yuri Gagarin is first person to orbit the Earth.	1981 U.S. space shuttle makes first flight. 1990 Launch of Hubble Space Telescope.	**Exploration**
1927 First sound film *The Jazz Singer* starts craze for "talkies."	1962 First TV programs transmitted by U.S. Telstar satellite.	1987 Hole in ozone layer above Antarctic. 1990 Start of Human Genome Project.	**Art and Science**
1942 U.S. government sets up Manhattan Project to research atomic power.	1960 First communications satellite, *Echo 1*, is launched.	1993 Russia, U.S. and other partners start to build International Space Station.	**Technology**
1936 Alan Turing develops ideas about computers. 1945 UN Charter signed.	1955 Warsaw Pact founded among countries of Eastern Europe	1992 Earth Summit in Rio de Janeiro, Brazil. 1994 World Wide Web (www) created.	**Religion and Ideas**
1929 Wall Street Crash and start of Great Depression. 1931 Invention of nylon.	1953 Colour TV begins in US. 1971 Invention of pocket calculator.	1994 Opening of Channel Tunnel. 1999 Euro currency in use in parts of Europe.	**Daily Life**

Kings of England

Saxons

Egbert	AD 827–839
Ethelwulf	AD 839–858
Ethelbald	AD 858–860
Ethelbert	AD 860–866
Ethelred I	AD 866–871
Alfred the Great	AD 871–899
Edward the Elder	AD 899–924
Athelstan	AD 924–939
Edmund	AD 939–946
Edred	AD 946–955
Edwy	AD 955–959
Edgar	AD 959–975
Edward the Martyr	AD 975–978
Ethelred II the Unready	
	AD 978–1016
Edmund Ironside	AD 1016

Danes

Canute	AD 1016–1035
Harold I Harefoot	AD 1035–1040
Hardicanute	AD 1040–1042

Saxons

Edward the Confessor	
	AD 1042–1066
Harold II	AD 1066

Normans

William I the Conqueror	
	AD 1066–1087
William I	AD 1087–1100

Rulers of Scotland

Malcolm II	AD 1005–1034
Duncan I	AD 1034–1040
Macbeth	AD 1040–1057
Malcolm III Canmore	
	AD 1057–1093
Donald Bane	AD 1093–1094
Duncan II	AD 1094
Donald Bane (restored)	
	AD 1094–1097
Edgar	AD 1097–1107

Notable Roman Emperors

Augustus (Octavian)	
	27 BC–AD 14
Tiberius	AD 14–37
Caligula	AD 37–41
Claudius	AD 41–54
Nero	AD 54–68
Vespasian	AD 69–79
Trajan	AD 98–117
Hadrian	AD 117–138
Marcus Aurelius	AD 161–180
Diocletian	AD 284–305
Constantine I	AD 308–337
Theodosius I the Great	
	AD 378–395

Chinese Dynasties

Hsia	before 2200 BC–1500 BC
Shang	1500–1122 BC
Zhou	1122–256 BC
Qin	221–207 BC
Han	202 BC to AD 220 (with break)
Three kingdoms and six dynasties	AD 220–581
Sui	AD 581–618
Tang	AD 618–907
Five dynasties and ten kingdoms	AD 907–960
Sung (ruled part of China only)	AD 960–1279

Famous Battles of Ancient Times

Marathon Greeks beat Persians	490 BC
Salamis (sea) Greeks beat Persians	480 BC
Gaugamela (Arbela) Greeks beat Persians	331 BC
Cannae Hannibal beat Romans	216 BC
Actium (sea) Octavian beat Antony	31 BC
Teutoberg Forest Germans beat Romans	9 BC
Tours (Poitiers) Franks beat Muslims	AD 732
Lechfeld Emperor Otto beat Magyars	AD 955
Hastings Normans beat English	AD 1066
Manzikert Turks beat Byzantines	AD 1071

The Seven Wonders of the Ancient World

The Pyramids of Egypt
Built in the 2000s BC, and the only Wonder to survive. The largest is the Great Pyramid of Cheops, 482 ft high.

Hanging Gardens of Babylon
Terraced gardens built about 600 BC by King Nebuchadnezzar for his wife.

Statue of Zeus at Olympia
Carved by Phidias in the 400s BC. Made of ivory and gold, it stood on the site of the first Olympic Games.

Temple of Artemis at Ephesus
Marble temple with over 100 columns, which took about 120 years to build. Destroyed in AD 262.

Mausoleum at Halicarnassus
Huge tomb in memory of King Mausolus of Caria in Asia Minor, who died in 353 BC.

Colossus of Rhodes
Statue of the sun god Apollo, about 118 ft high, at the harbour entrance. Destroyed by earthquake in 224 BC.

Pharos of Alexandria.
Lighthouse built about 270 BC in harbor of Alexandria, Egypt. Destroyed by earthquake in AD 1375.

Kings and Queens of England, 1100 to 2000

Henry I	1100–1135
Stephen	1135–1154
Henry II	1154–1189
Richard I	1189–1199
John	1199–1216
Henry III	1216–1272
Edward I	1272–1307
Edward II	1307–1327
Edward III	1327–1377
Richard II	1377–1399
Henry IV	1399–1413
Henry V	1413–1422
Henry VI	1422–1461
Edward IV	1461–1483
Henry VI (restored)	1470–1471
Edward V	1483
Richard III	1483–1485
Henry VII	1485–1509
Henry VIII	1509–1547
Edward VI	1547–1553
Mary	1553–1558
Elizabeth I	1558–1603
James I	1603–1625
Charles I	1625–1649
Commonwealth and Cromwell's Protectorate	1649–1660
Charles II	1660–1685
James II	1685–1688
William III and Mary	1689–1702
Anne	1702–1714
George I	1714–1727
George II	1727–1760
George III	1760–1820
George IV	1820–1830
William IV	1830–1837
Victoria	1837–1901
Edward VII	1901–1910
George V	1910–1936
Edward VIII (abdicated)	1936
George VI	1936–1952
Elizabeth II	1952–today

Presidents of the USA

George Washington	1789–1797
John Adams	1797–1801
Thomas Jefferson	1801–1809
James Madison	1809–1817
James Monroe	1817–1825
John Quincy Adams	1825–1829
Andrew Jackson	1829–1837
Martin Van Buren	1837–1841
William Henry Harrison	1841
John Tyler	1841–1845
James Polk	1845–1849
Zachary Taylor	1849–1850
Millard Fillmore	1850–1853
Franklin Pierce	1853–1857
James Buchanan	1857–1861
Abraham Lincoln	1861–1865
Andrew Johnson	1865–1869
Ulysses S. Grant	1869–1877
Rutherford B. Hayes	1877–1881
James Abram Garfield	1881
Chester A. Arthur	1881–1885
Grover Cleveland	1885–1889
Benjamin Harrison	1889–1893
Grover Cleveland	1893–1897
William McKinley	1897–1901
Theodore Roosevelt	1901–1909
William H. Taft	1909–1913
Woodrow Wilson	1913–1921
Warren G. Harding	1921–1923
Calvin Coolidge	1923–1929
Herbert C. Hoover	1929–1933
Franklin D. Roosevelt	1933–1945
Harry S. Truman	1945–1953
Dwight D. Eisenhower	1953–1961
John F. Kennedy	1961–1963
Lyndon B. Johnson	1963–1969
Richard Nixon	1969–1974
Gerald Ford	1974–1977
Jimmy Carter	1977–1981
Ronald Reagan	1981–1989
George Bush	1989–1993
Bill Clinton	1993–2000
George W. Bush	2001–present

Dynasties of China 1279 to present

Yuan (Mongol)	1279–1368
Ming	1368–1644
Qing (Manchu)	1644–1912
Establishment of the Republic of China	1912
China united under Nationalist Government	1928
Establishment of People's Republic of China	1949

Battles of World War I

August 25–30, 1914
Battle of Tannenberg
September 6–9, 1914
First Battle of the Marne
February 1915
Battle of the Masurian Lakes
April–December 1915
Gallipoli campaign
February–July 1916 Battle of Verdun
May 31 – June 1, 1916
Battle of Jutland (naval battle)
July 1 –November 1916
Battle of the Somme
April 9 – May 17, 1917
Battle of Vimy Ridge
April 16 – May 1917
Nivelle Offensive
July 31 – November 10, 1917 Battle of Passchendaele
July 15 – August 6, 1918
Second Battle of the Marne

Battles of World War II

July 1940–May 1941
Battle of Britain and Blitz
June 1941 Operation Barbarossa
German invasion of Russia
September 1941–January 1944
Siege of Leningrad
December 7, 1941
Japanese attack on U.S. Pacific Fleet at Pearl Harbor
May 1942 Battle of the Coral Sea
June 1942 Battle of Midway
August 1942–February 1943 Battle of Stalingrad
October 1942 Battle of El Alamein
July 1943 Battle of Kursk
June 6, 1944 D–Day landings
October 23–6, 1944 Battle of Leyte Gulf
December 1944 Battle of the Bulge

Index